Wireless LANs En

Installing a Wireless Network

Key Considerations

A wired network solution may not be the best solution for every network. In many cases, adding a new segment or converting an existing one to wireless media typically provides users with increased flexibility and convenience.

You should consider the following factors before purchasing wireless components: the size of your budget, bandwidth requirements, and the compatibility and capability of the equipment you install.

Decision-Making Factors

Ask yourself these questions when deciding to install or convert all or part of an existing network: Do you really need mobile network connections? Are the costs justified? And can you live with what could be reduced bandwidth? The answers are often the deciding factors in whether or not a wireless network solution is feasible.

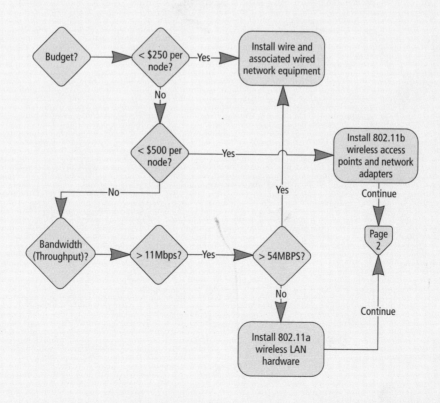

Wireless LANs End to End™

Installing a Wireless Network *continued*

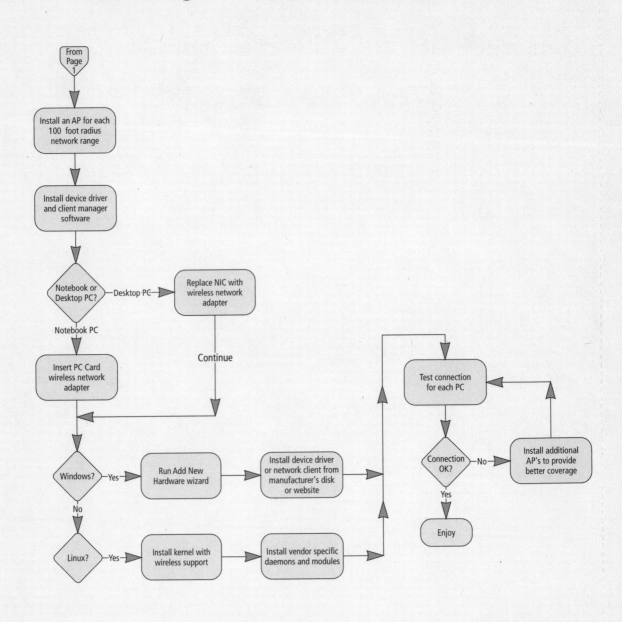

Wireless LANs
End to End™

1st Edition

Wireless LANs End to End™

1st Edition

Walter R. Bruce, III

Ron Gilster, Series Editor

**Best-Selling Books • Digital Downloads • e-Books • Answer Networks
e-Newsletters • Branded Web Sites • e-Learning**

New York, NY ✦ Cleveland, OH ✦ Indianapolis, IN

Wireless LANs End to End™

Published by
Hungry Minds, Inc.
909 Third Avenue
New York, NY 10022
www.hungryminds.com

Copyright © 2002 Hungry Minds, Inc. All rights reserved.
No part of this book, including interior design, cover
design, and icons, may be reproduced or transmitted in
any form, by any means (electronic, photocopying,
recording, or otherwise) without the prior written
permission of the publisher.

Library of Congress Control Number: 2001118282

ISBN: 0-7645-4888-3 ✓

Printed in the United States of America

10 9 8 7 6 5 4 3 2 1

1O/SQ/QT/QS/IN

Distributed in the United States by Hungry Minds, Inc.

Distributed by CDG Books Canada Inc. for Canada; by
Transworld Publishers Limited in the United Kingdom; by
IDG Norge Books for Norway; by IDG Sweden Books for
Sweden; by IDG Books Australia Publishing Corporation
Pty. Ltd. for Australia and New Zealand; by TransQuest
Publishers Pte Ltd. for Singapore, Malaysia, Thailand,
Indonesia, and Hong Kong; by Gotop Information Inc. for
Taiwan; by ICG Muse, Inc. for Japan; by Intersoft for
South Africa; by Eyrolles for France; by International
Thomson Publishing for Germany, Austria, and
Switzerland; by Distribuidora Cuspide for Argentina; by
LR International for Brazil; by Galileo Libros for Chile;
by Ediciones ZETA S.C.R. Ltda. for Peru; by WS

Computer Publishing Corporation, Inc., for the
Philippines; by Contemporanea de Ediciones for
Venezuela; by Express Computer Distributors for the
Caribbean and West Indies; by Micronesia Media
Distributor, Inc. for Micronesia; by Chips Computadoras
S.A. de C.V. for Mexico; by Editorial Norma de Panama
S.A. for Panama; by American Bookshops for Finland.

For general information on Hungry Minds' products and
services please contact our Customer Care department
within the U.S. at 800-762-2974, outside the U.S. at 317-
572-3993 or fax 317-572-4002.

For sales inquiries and reseller information, including
discounts, premium and bulk quantity sales, and foreign-
language translations, please contact our Customer Care
department at 800-434-3422, fax 317-572-4002 or write to
Hungry Minds, Inc., Attn: Customer Care Department,
10475 Crosspoint Boulevard, Indianapolis, IN 46256.

For information on licensing foreign or domestic rights,
please contact our Sub-Rights Customer Care department
at 212-884-5000.

For information on using Hungry Minds' products and
services in the classroom or for ordering examination
copies, please contact our Educational Sales department at
800-434-2086 or fax 317-572-4005.

For press review copies, author interviews, or other
publicity information, please contact our Public Relations
department at 317-572-3168 or fax 317-572-4168.

For authorization to photocopy items for corporate,
personal, or educational use, please contact Copyright
Clearance Center, 222 Rosewood Drive, Danvers, MA
01923, or fax 978-750-4470.

Hungry Minds is a trademark of Hungry Minds, Inc.

About the Authors

Walter R. Bruce, III, a writer and consultant, has spent over a dozen years training computer users, writing, and publishing books about computer technology. He has written many internationally published books on a variety of operating system, database, telecommunication, and networking topics, and has directed the publication of hundreds of computer-related books for three successful publishing companies. Walter holds an undergraduate degree in mathematics as well as a law degree. He was practicing law as a JAG in the United States Air Force (USAF) when he discovered his affinity for teaching people how to use computers. Walter installed his first network in the Pentagon while working for the Judge Advocate General of the USAF. For the last several years, he has directed Novell Press, the official publisher of books about Novell networking technology. Walter currently resides with his family in the Silicon Valley area of Northern California.

Ron Gilster, *End to End* Series Editor, is a best-selling author on the subjects of networking, PC hardware, and career certification. He has over 35 years of experience in computing, networking, and data communications, serving as a technician, consultant, trainer, and executive—most recently as the general manager of the Internet and backbone operations of a large regional wireless communications company.

Acknowledgments

Having worked for three different publishing companies over the last eleven years, I am aware of the incredible hours of work that go into the publication of every book. Many people play an essential role in each book's publication, but their work seems to go unnoticed and without thanks. So let me say thank you to Katie Feltman for having confidence in me and signing me to do this book, to Marcia Ellett for her strong project editing and encouragement, to Gabrielle Chosney for her crisp copyediting, to Harshal S. Chhaya for his invaluable technical review, to Mary Bednarek for permitting me to write this book and for being my friend; and thank you to all the unnamed people at Hungry Minds and John Wiley who buy the paper, hire the printer, design and produce the cover, hire and manage the proofreader and indexer, design and implement marketing plans and promotions, sell the book to the retailer, pay the bills (especially the royalties), and perform all the other unnamed tasks that keep a major publisher in business.

Special thanks to Jack Putterflam of the Pepperdine Information Technology department, to Robert Griffin, Assistant Director for Distance Learning with the Center of Excellence for Remote and Medically Underserved (CERMUSA) project, and to Mike Shanafelt, Information Technology Specialist, also with CERMUSA. All three of these gentlemen were kind enough to share their considerable wireless LAN experience and insights with me.

I also want to express appreciation to Ronnie Holland of WildPackets, Inc. for providing an evaluation copy of AiroPeek, WildPacket's excellent software-based wireless protocol analyzer utility.

Finally, I want to thank my family, Terry, Rich, Rob, Heather, Heidi, Monty, and Tahj (yes, I have a big family), for putting up with me for all these years. You're all the wind beneath my wings.

Credits

Acquisitions Editor
Katie Feltman

Project Editor
Marcia Ellett

Technical Editor
Harshal S. Chhaya

Copy Editor
Gabrielle Chosney

Editorial Manager
Ami Frank Sullivan

Vice President and Executive Group Publisher
Richard Swadley

Vice President and Executive Publisher
Bob Ipsen

Vice President and Publisher
Joseph B. Wikert

Editorial Director
Mary Bednarek

Project Coordinator
Maridee Ennis

Proofreader
Mary Lagu

Indexer
Johnna VanHoose Dinse

To Nana. We miss you.

Preface

Welcome to *Wireless LANs End to End*. If you are in the market for a wireless *local area network (LAN)* for your home, office, or campus, or if your job requires that you install, set up, or maintain a wireless LAN, then this is the book for you.

Why I Wrote This Book

My interest in local area networks goes back about fifteen years, to the time when I was still a young Air Force JAG officer working in the Pentagon in the office of the United States Air Force Judge Advocate General. As a sometimes computer nerd, one of my duties was to provide advice to the USAF military legal department on office automation issues. In that capacity, I suggested that we install the department's first local area network to connect our various offices spread around the Pentagon. I then helped to install the network, including running cable down the fifth-floor E-ring ceiling. Several years later, while working as an editor for Macmillan Computer Publishing, I once again helped install the company's first local area network. Since that time, I have generally harassed the IS department of every company for whom I have worked to get the most out of each corporate LAN. And, of course, my home is fully wired, with a network jack in every bedroom and two in my office.

About a year ago, I was helping one of my sons, Robert—a high school senior—research prospective universities. His first choice was Pepperdine University, which we learned had recently installed wireless access to the campus-wide computer network. I was intrigued. Since that time, I have done a great deal more research about wireless LANs, including interviewing several technicians and LAN administrators who have recently set up large wireless networks. More importantly, I set up my son's computer, at Pepperdine, to wirelessly access the campus network. Whether he is in the library, cafeteria, or student lounge, he can always access his homework assignments, e-mail, and, of course, the Internet. I also added wireless access to my existing home office network. In short, I have become a certified "wireless geek." Whether I'm at home, at the office, in an airport or hotel, or sipping a cappuccino at Starbucks, wireless LAN technology enables me to stay current with my e-mail, keep my editors happy by continuing to write, and browse the Net. Now it's your turn to get "un-wired."

Who Should Read This Book

Wireless networking is not a new idea, having been available from several vendors for at least five years. The emergence of an industry standard, however, has caused the use of wireless LAN technology to explode. This book is intended for anyone installing a wireless LAN, or considering doing so.

If you are responsible for planning, acquiring, installing, or maintaining your company's local area networks, you should definitely get acquainted with wireless LAN technology. Sooner or later, the end users in your company will demand the flexibility of wireless networking. This book will help you plan, install, configure, and maintain a wireless network of any size.

Information Services departments on many college and university campuses have already discovered the improved usability and cost savings associated with wireless LANs. If you are responsible for a campus network and are in the process of planning or installing a wireless network, you too need this book.

One of the most appealing aspects of the current crop of industry standard wireless networking equipment is the ease with which you can set up a local area network. For home and home office users, however, the reasonable price of wireless networking technology may be the most appealing aspect of all. Setting up a home or small office wireless network is both inexpensive and easy. In some cases, it's almost as simple as opening the box and plugging the equipment in. In most cases, however, you can avoid little "gotchas" by doing a little reading beforehand. Therefore, this book is also intended for anyone who is considering installing a home or small office wireless network.

How This Book is Organized

The book is presented in twenty chapters, which are grouped into five parts:

I.   Planning a Wireless Network

II. Installing a Wireless Network

III. Managing a Wireless Network

IV. Using Wi-Fi

V.   Connecting Sites with Wireless Technology

Following is a summary of the subjects covered in each part of the book.

Part I: Planning a Wireless Network

The first part of the book helps you plan for installing a *wireless local area network (WLAN)*. Even if you have experience with local area networks (LANs), you need to take a step back and survey the technology, the facility where the network will be installed, and the equipment that is available before you jump in and start building a WLAN.

Chapter 1 gives you a high-level look at wireless networking technology, introducing you to terminology and concepts that you need to understand to plan and implement a wireless LAN. Chapter 2 examines in some detail the industry standard on which the most widely available WLAN hardware and software is based, IEEE 802, including the wireless section 802.11. Chapter 3 contains an overview of other similar technology—Bluetooth, HomeRF, and other wireless standards—so you will make an informed decision if you continue with your plan to install an IEEE 802.11–based network. Chapter 4 explains how to conduct a site survey in order to quantify in detail the wireless networking requirements in a particular facility. Chapter 5 then examines wireless networking equipment to help you prepare for making buying recommendations or decisions. Finally, Chapter 6 covers planning for a WLAN to be installed in your home.

Part II: Installing a Wireless Network

After you have a plan mapped out for your wireless local area network, you will be ready to get down to business. Part II of this book helps you install a WLAN based on the planning described in Part I of the book. Chapter 7 gives you a few practical pointers on installing and configuring wireless access points in your facility—the core of your wireless local area network. Chapter 8 helps you set up the wireless client stations that will connect to the wireless LAN. Chapter 9 introduces you to several types of tests that are useful in installing, configuring, and troubleshooting a WLAN. Chapter 10 covers the unique issues that may arise when installing a WLAN in a home. Chapter 11 then examines WLAN installation issues that are of particular interest when installing a wireless network on a college campus.

Part III: Managing a Wireless Network

Planning and installing a WLAN is by no means the end of your job as the network engineer in charge of keeping the WLAN running. Part III of this book helps you put measures into place that will ensure that the network is both secure and up-to-date. Chapter 12 gives you a few practical pointers on setting up basic security for the wireless network, including how to correctly set up *Wireless Equivalent Privacy*

(WEP), the standard encryption system that is supported by all Wi-Fi wireless equipment. Chapter 13 discusses several ways that you can achieve an enhanced level of security for your WLAN, including the use of *virtual private networks (VPNs).* Chapter 14 digresses somewhat by providing an overview of the *Public Key Infrastructure,* the best way to secure any electronic communication. Finally, Chapter 15 covers the best strategies for keeping your WLAN running most efficiently through timely upgrades.

Part IV: Using Wi-Fi

One aspect of successfully rolling out a local area network is providing adequate guidance and training for the people who will use the network. Consequently, the fourth part of the book is written for those individuals who will be using Wi-Fi wireless networks at work, at home, and on the road. You can suggest that a user read the appropriate chapter, or you can design a training program around the information you find there. The content of each chapter does not assume that the reader has read the rest of the book.

Chapter 16 provides an introduction to wireless networking terminology to a user who will encounter a WLAN in the workplace. The chapter also explains how to connect to the WLAN using a Windows- or Mac OS-based computer. Chapter 17 provides equivalent guidance for the home user, including instructions on connecting to the Internet and on using AOL over a wireless local area network. Chapter 18 discusses how to connect to public wireless networks that can be found in hotels, airports, and even Starbucks coffee shops.

Part V: Connecting Sites with Wireless Technology

Most wireless local area network equipment is used to enable communication between computers that are all situated in the same building. If your company is spread out over several buildings that are not physically connected, communicating between the buildings via a network is problematic. This problem can be solved in many ways, but wireless site-to-site networking technology can provide a solution that is both elegant and economical. Part V of the book explores how to plan for and set up such a multisite network using wireless networking equipment. Chapter 19 explains how to plan the use of wireless network equipment to *bridge* (connect) two or more sites. Chapter 20 provides additional information and guidance on selecting and installing the wireless network equipment.

How to Use This Book

You can use this book as a reference to help you with wireless networking issues as they arise, or you can use it as a "how-to" guide to planning, installing, configuring, and using a wireless local area network. Because of the number of wireless local area network equipment manufacturers, the book does not assume that you are using any particular brand or model of equipment or related software. Discussions in the book of specific brands or models of equipment or software are not intended as endorsements or recommendations, but merely as illustrative examples.

Always keep in mind that personal computer technology is continually changing, and usually for the better—becoming cheaper, faster, and more useable. The hot new technology of today may seem tired and outdated two years from now, if not sooner. As you read this book, use the information found here as a starting point for your research. Review Chapter15 in particular for a discussion of the wireless networking advancements that you are likely to see hit the market first.

Icons Used in This Book

Throughout the book, I have used special notation to alert you to points of particular significance. Rather than using icons in the margin, a clean design places a box around each special section.

TIP

A tip box indicates a shortcut or easier way to accomplish a task, or provides some information that may not seem obvious at first.

NOTE

A note box contains a short discussion of information that is in contrast to the information presented in the surrounding text, is of particular interest, or is of fundamental importance, and therefore deserves your attention.

CAUTION

A caution box alerts you to the possibility that the covered topic can cause problems for you if you aren't especially careful.

CROSS REFERENCE

A cross-reference box points you to another section in the book that contains relevant information.

SIDEBAR

A sidebar box contains interesting information that is related to the surrounding content, but that you don't have to read if you are in a hurry or just aren't interested.

Contents

Part I

Planning a Wireless Network

Chapter 1: How Wi-Fi Wireless Networks Work

Chapter 2: A Short Course in IEEE 802.11b

Chapter 3: Bluetooth, Home RF, and other Wireless Systems

Chapter 4: Performing a Site Survey

Chapter 5: Selecting the Right Hardware

Chapter 6: Planning a Home Wireless Network

How Wireless Networks Work

In This Chapter

This chapter discusses how local area networks work, with particular emphasis on wireless networks. It covers the following topics:

- ♦ The components of local area networks
- ♦ The components of wireless networks
- ♦ Wireless networking technology

This book is primarily about wireless networks, but before you can understand how they operate, you need to understand the fundamentals regarding any computer network. This chapter introduces you first to local area networking concepts and then to wireless networking terminology and concepts that will be useful to you throughout the remainder of the book.

LANs and WLANs

A computer *network* consists of computers connected together in a way that enables them to transfer data. Computers have been commonplace in offices for nearly twenty years, but over the last ten years, computer networks have become almost as essential to office efficiency as telephones and file cabinets. Even my technophobic brother-in-law sees the benefit of installing a network in his law office, although he refuses to use a computer himself.

Typically, networks are used in offices and some homes (including mine, of course) for the following reasons:

- ♦ To share files
- ♦ To share printers
- ♦ To share schedules
- ♦ To share an Internet connection
- ♦ To make interoffice e-mail possible

You will notice that "sharing" is a bit of a theme here. Computer networks help people share *information* (for example: files, e-mail, and schedules) and potentially expensive *resources* (for example: printers and Internet connections) more efficiently.

Much of a worker's time at the office is spent communicating something to someone else, and electronic communication is often the most efficient way to do this, especially if he is sharing information with more than one person at a time.

Many people today communicate almost exclusively by phone and by e-mail. However, to use e-mail, you usually need an Internet connection. The best way to connect everyone in your office to the Internet is to install a network and hook this network to the Internet. Clearly, the Internet and networks share a reciprocal relationship, the growth of each spurring growth in the other.

A network among computers that are found in the same physical location is called a *local area network* (LAN). Most business and personal networks are LANs.

Many businesses, agencies, and organizations install computers in branch offices or buildings that may or may not be located in the same city, state, or country. A network that connects computers throughout an organization, regardless of physical location, is called a *wide area network* (WAN).

From the inception of computer networks, signals have traveled between workstations over wires—dedicated connections strung computer to computer, or telephone systems provided ad hoc connections as needed. Just as many people now find wireless telephones indispensable, they are also rapidly taking to wireless computer networking as it grows in availability and popularity. A local area network that uses wireless technology to connect computers in the network is called a *wireless local area network* (WLAN).

Network Components

A network consists of many components working together to enable the smooth flow of electronic data. The most common network components are *workstations* and *servers*. The next few sections discuss workstations and servers, as well as other categories of network components.

Workstations

A *workstation*, also called a *client,* is a computer that is connected to the network and intended for use by one person at a time.

Peer is another term sometimes used to refer to a computer that an individual uses for work or play. The controversial (and nearly defunct) Napster software popularized so-called *peer-to-peer software*. This type of software allows individuals to download software over a network directly from someone else's computer.

Servers

A network *server* is usually a computer that provides one or more services to other computers on a network. The following types of servers can be found on a network:

♦ **File server.** A computer that contains or controls one or more storage devices, such as hard disks, optical disks, tape drives, and so on, is called a *file server*. A file server makes storage space available to workstations on the network. The storage space can be used as an extension of a workstation's local storage, and in some cases, may be the only mass storage available to a workstation. Very often, several users will store electronic files on a file server so that they can have mutual access to the files.

♦ **Print server.** A computer or other device that controls one or more printers is called a *print server*. Many high-end printers have built-in print-server features that enable multiple network workstations to send output to these printers without the need to connect directly to any computer on the network. Most corporations have print servers located throughout the workplace, providing all users convenient access to a printer without the need to place a printer in every cubicle.

♦ **Mail server.** A computer that provides a system for sending electronic messages (e-mail) to users on a network is called a *mail server*. Mail servers can provide an electronic messaging service among the users of the network, between the network's users and Internet users, or both. Mail servers and electronic messaging services have been around longer than the Internet. Many businesses are coming to rely more and more heavily on e-mail as their primary way to communicate with employees and customers.

♦ **Application server**. A computer that runs centralized application software (such as mission-critical database software or enterprise resource planning software) that provides service to workstations on the network is called an *application server*, or simply *appserver*. When computation-intensive applications are run on an application server, no individual workstation's resources are taxed. Perhaps more importantly, the IS department can ensure redundancy, regular backups, peak-load capacity, and optimal performance in a central computer rather than at every workstation.

♦ **DHCP server**. A *dynamic host configuration protocol* (DHCP) server automatically assigns an IP address to every computer on a network, instead of requiring the system administrator to assign them manually.

Other servers often found on networks include the following:

♦ Audio/video servers

♦ Chat servers

♦ Fax servers

♦ FTP servers

♦ Groupware servers

♦ IRC servers

♦ (E-mail) List servers

♦ News servers

♦ Proxy servers

♦ Telnet/WAIS

♦ Web servers

Network Infrastructure

In order to communicate, two workstations must be electronically connected. The equipment over which the electronic signals travel between computers on the network is called the *network infrastructure*.

Just as drivers take the state and federal highway systems for granted, users often don't notice network infrastructure. They only notice it if something goes wrong. For the most part, this book is about how to design and build a wireless highway system between the workstations and servers in your LAN or WAN.

When you think of the network infrastructure, you may think of connective wiring that runs through the ceilings and walls of a building between all the network computers. The reality is a little different. In a typical LAN, a strand of wiring similar to phone cable is run from each modular jack installed in the wall to a central location such as a phone closet. All these cables are then connected to a box called a *patch panel*. The patch panel acts as a *network hub* that is similar conceptually to the hub of a wheel. The network hub receives signals transmitted by each computer on the network and sends the signals out to all other computers on the network.

Figure 1-1 depicts a network with a star-shaped topology. (The physical design of a network—in other words, the way computers in a network are physically connected—is referred to as the network's *topology*. Types of topologies include *star*, *ring*, and *bus*.)

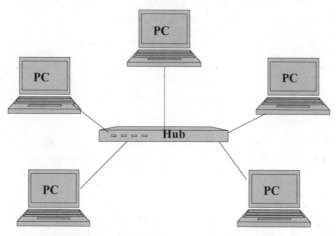

Figure 1-1: A typical LAN topology

Besides wiring and network hubs, other equipment is needed to connect a large number of computers. The next three sections discuss bridges, routers, and switches, and their roles in the network infrastructure.

Bridges

A network *bridge* provides a pathway for electronic packets of data when they cross between networks or segments of networks. Network bridges are sometimes used to connect networks on different floors in the same building, or in different buildings; sometimes, they connect networks of different types.

A bridge is "simple-minded" in its approach to passing network traffic. It gives the signal a boost and sends it on its way—no analysis and no discrimination. All packets are treated the same. By contrast, routers and switches are more selective.

Switches

Switches play a similar role to that of bridges, but do more than simply forward data without considering the source or destination. Data is transmitted over networks in bundles called *packets*. Each packet not only contains the raw information, it also contains information about the computer to which it is addressed and the computer that sent it—analogous to the address and return address on a postal envelope. A switch reads the addressee information in each packet and sends the packet directly to the network segment to which the addressee is connected. Packets that are not addressed to a particular network segment are never transmitted over that segment, and the switch acts as a filter to eliminate unnecessary network traffic.

When a network is small, it is sufficient to connect all the computers to the same network hub. Larger networks should employ one or more bridges to connect network segments. However, as you add each segment using a bridge, the network traffic on all segments increases because all computers on all segments broadcast their messages to all segments.

To keep network traffic from increasing unnecessarily, network architects can use switches to connect networks in lieu of bridges. Only traffic that is addressed to a computer on a particular network segment is sent to that segment.

Similarly, run-of-the-mill network hubs send packets indiscriminately to all ports of all computers connected to the hub. A special type of hub called a *switched hub* examines each packet, determines the addressee and port, and forwards the packet only to the computer and port to which it is addressed.

Networks that use switches and switched hubs make more efficient use of the available transmission bandwidth than simple bridges and standard hubs.

Routers

Routers are also more discriminating than bridges, but in a different way than switches. A router reads the addressee information in each packet and

communicates with other routers using the Internet Control Message Protocol (ICMP) to determine the best *route* for each packet to take.

Routers are, however, packet-type-specific. They only understand how to deal with Internet Protocol (IP) packets. When other types of network packets are transmitted over a network, along with IP packets, a device called a *brouter* can be used. A brouter combines the function of a bridge with that of a router. It routes IP packets, but simply passes on all other types of packets.

Cutting the Wires—WLAN Components

If you have never helped pull network cables through office dropped ceilings, or crawled around in the mud in the incredibly tight space under your house while dragging network cable, you can't fully appreciate the convenience of wireless networks. However, I have, and I do. Wireless networking offers convenience and flexibility that just isn't possible with standard wired networks.

A wireless LAN is considered a network, but it has a different cast of characters than a wired LAN. The next few sections introduce you to the following wireless network components and terminology:

- ♦ Wireless stations
- ♦ Access points
- ♦ Ad hoc mode
- ♦ Infrastructure mode
- ♦ Wireless bridges and routers
- ♦ Roaming

WLAN Stations—It Takes Two

Wireless networking requires at least two radios. Each computer or device containing a radio that transmits and/or receives data over the wireless network is called a *station*. As in wired networks, a station can be a *client* or a *server*. Most often, however, WLAN stations are personal computers containing a wireless network adapter that enables them to communicate wirelessly with the LAN.

The best selling feature of most wireless technology is portability. Many early adopters of wireless networking were end users who had notebook computers. If your computer is portable, a portable network connection is an intuitive next step.

Apple notebook computers were the first to boast a wireless connection called an AirPort. Now, every vendor of wireless network adapters offers a PC card (also called PCMCIA) version of the adapter (see Figure 1-2).

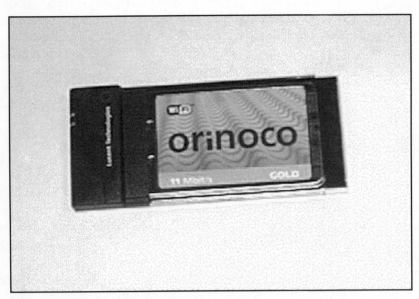

Figure 1-2: A PC card wireless network adapter

Even an adapter designed for installation in a desktop computer is, in most instances, a hardware adapter that enables the use of the PC card adapter in the desktop (see Figure 1-3).

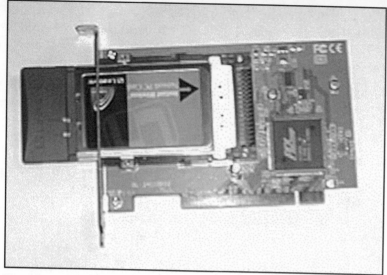

Figure 1-3: A PCI wireless network adapter

Access Points

Somewhat similar in function to a network hub, an *access point* (AP) in a wireless network is a special type of wireless station. An access point can be a computer that contains a wireless network adapter as well as access-point management software. More often, an access point is a dedicated standalone device whose purpose is to receive radio transmissions from other stations on the WLAN and forward them to the rest of the (wired) network.

An access point, whether a dedicated device or access-point software running on a PC, enables the network administrator to manage the following parameters:

♦ **SSID.** The name of the wireless network. Although a unique name is not required, most system administrators change the SSID from the default name that comes installed in the AP. To ensure communication between an AP and a station, both station and AP must have specified matching SSIDs. This parameter is not, however, a security feature, because most APs broadcast the network name and only some APs permit the administrator to disable this broadcast.

- **Channel.** The channel on which the AP is broadcasting. Multiple radio channels are available for use by wireless networks. The exact number of channels varies according to the type of wireless network you are using and the country in which you install the WLAN.

- **Encryption key.** Unless the WLAN is intended for use by the general public, every wireless LAN should be protected by encryption. The most popular wireless network technology uses a protocol called Wired Equivalent Privacy (WEP), which uses the RC4 encryption alogorithm to ensure privacy. This type of encryption requires the network administrator to enter the same alphanumeric string in the AP and all the stations. Any station without this *key* cannot get on the network.

Some vendors sell two lines of access points, one line for use in enterprise/business environments and the other for home use. The enterprise/business variety typically enables more configuration options and comes with more powerful and feature-rich software. For example, when Microsoft launched Windows XP, it spotlighted the new operating system's enhanced support for wireless networking, including support for a more robust user authentication security system. At the XP launch, Agere, Lucent's wireless networking company, announced that a new version of its top-of-the-line access points was shipping with built-in support for the same authentication scheme. By contrast, Agere's home APs, its *residential gateways,* do not come with support for this enhanced security system.

Access point functionality is commonly "bundled" into the same device as several separate but related functions. For instance, in addition to its normal function, the access point shown in Figure 1-4 performs the functions of the following:

- a router
- a switched hub
- a DHCP server
- a *network address translation* (NAT) box (see sidebar)

Similar devices may even throw in a print server. This Swiss-Army-knife-like approach is often a real bargain for use in a home WLAN.

Figure 1-4: A multifunction device that functions as a wireless access point, router, switched hub, NAT, and DHCP server

---

NETWORK ADDRESS TRANSLATION IN CABLE/DSL MODEMS

The most common protocol for transmitting data around a network is called *TCP/IP*. Evey individual computer on a TCP/IP network must have its own *IP address*, a 32-bit numeric address. Each IP address is written as four numbers separated by periods (for example, 192.168.1.100). Each number can have a value from zero to 255.

A *network address translation* box is a device that enables a LAN to use a set of IP addresses for the computers on the network and a different set, often a single IP address, for traffic outside the network. A NAT also acts as a *firewall* because it hides the real IP addresses of networked computers from computers outside the network. A NAT also enables networks to conserve Internet IP addresses by allowing many users on the internal network to share the same external IP address.

Several networking device manufacturers offer routers with NAT capabilities that are designed and marketed for use in a home or small business to connect all the computers in a small network to the Internet. These devices are commonly called *cable modem/DSL routers* because they connect a small network to the Internet through either a cable modem or a DSL modem. In addition to implementing NAT services, a cable/DSL router usually acts as a DHCP server.

For example, the access point in Figure 1-4 is also a cable/DSL router, DHCP server, switched hub, and NAT. All computers that use this device as a router or AP are automatically assigned an IP address (the DHCP function) and can share the same IP address to connect to the Internet (the NAT function) through the DSL or cable modem.

In an office environment, you should implement each of these functions separately. It is unlikely, for example, that in an office you will want to have a network hub co-located with an AP or even with a printer. The location of each network hub is determined by your building design. Try to install all the hubs (patch panels) in the same room on each floor of your office building. However, APs and printers need to be distributed throughout the enterprise to be close to the computers they serve. Figure 1-5 depicts a typical WLAN configuration with client stations, access point, file servers, print server, DHCP server, and router.

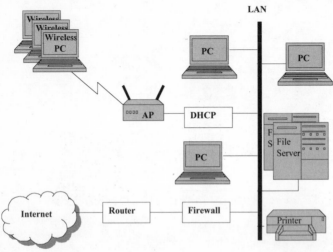

Figure 1-5: A typical WLAN

Station-to-Station: Ad Hoc Networks

In the majority of business applications, wireless stations are used as part of a wireless network with servers, routers, printers, and so on, as depicted in Figure 1-2 in the preceding section. However, you can create a much simpler network using wireless technology.

Whenever two wireless stations are close enough to communicate with each other, they are capable of establishing a form of peer-to-peer network called an *ad hoc network*. In small offices or in a home, you can use an ad hoc wireless network as the only network, without the use of an access point. However, in most cases, ad hoc networks are temporary in nature. Ad hoc wireless networks occur spontaneously and dynamically.

> **NOTE**
>
> A computer-to-computer network is also possible over a network cable between two computers, but not among three computers unless at least one of the computers has more than one network adapter card.

The area in which computers in an ad hoc network can communicate with each other (sometimes referred to metaphorically as "seeing" each other) is called a *basic service set* (BSS). Figure 1-6 depicts three computers in two basic service sets. Notice that computer A can "see" computer B, and computer B can "see" computer C, but A and C can't "see" each other. A and B can communicate in one BSS, and B and C can communicate in a different BSS. Because these three computers cannot all communicate at the same time, they are not all in one BSS.

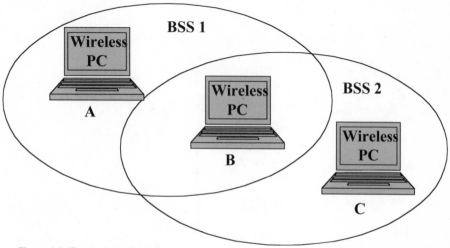

Figure 1-6: Two basic service sets

Station-to-AP: Infrastructure Mode

An AP is capable of integrating multiple BSSs by creating a *distribution system* (DS). By adding an AP to the two ad hoc networks shown in Figure 1-6, you can create a distribution system that enables all three computers to communicate.

When a BSS forms a self-contained network, not connected to a distribution system, it is called an *independent BSS* (IBSS).

An AP is also capable of integrating LANs into the distribution system through a feature called a *portal*. A portal is the logical point at which data enters the wireless system from the wired LAN. The WLAN depicted in

Figure 1-7 demonstrates the use of an AP to link several basic service sets and a wired LAN together into a network. In wireless networking terminology, this linking process is called a *distribution system service* (DSS). This example also depicts a type of BSS called an *infrastructure BSS*.

When you use an AP to combine a DS, one or more BSSs, and potentially one or more LANs, the resulting network is called an *extended service set* (ESS), as shown in Figure 1-7. As noted in the section on access points, you can assign a name to each wireless network—the *service set identifier* (SSID), also known as the *extended service set identifier* (ESSID). The remainder of this book will help you plan and implement an ESS in your home, office, or enterprise.

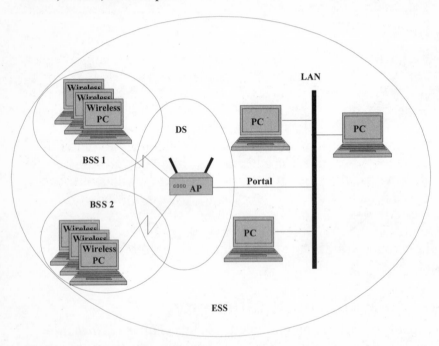

Figure 1-7: An extended service set (ESS)

How Wireless LANs Work

This section briefly explores how wireless networks do what they do, particularly wireless networks that comply with the IEEE 802.11 standard.

The IEEE 802.11 wireless networking standard defines five ways that data can be transmitted between two wireless devices. In network-technology-speak, these transmission methods are called *physical layers*. (Chapter 2 goes into more detail about the multilayer network reference model.) Each physical layer is independent of other physical layers. Each pair of 802.11-compliant radios uses one of these physical layers to communicate. In a wired network, the physical layer most often used is called Ethernet (a standard defined by IEEE 802.3).

NOTE

One of the five physical layers available in IEEE 802.11 is the *infrared layer*. Because there are no wireless networking products currently available that implement this physical layer, I have chosen not to discuss it in this chapter.

The ISM Band

Wireless networks use radio waves as their transmission medium. The most widely used wireless network technology is commercially called Wi-Fi (a trademark short for *wireless fidelity* that is licensed for use by the Wireless Ethernet Compatibility Alliance trade group based on equipment passing compliance testing). Wi-Fi is based on the Institute for Electrical and Electronics Engineers (IEEE) 802.11b standard. An online newsletter columnist recently published an article that criticized 802.11b designers for selecting the same radio frequency band used by some wireless telephones, microwave ovens, and another wireless standard called Bluetooth. He apparently wasn't aware that in 1985 the Federal Communication Commission (FCC) made changes to the radio spectrum regulation and assigned three bands designated as the industrial, scientific, and medical (ISM) bands. These frequency bands are

♦ 902 MHz—928 MHz, a 26 MHz bandwidth

♦ 2.4 GHz—2.4835 GHz, a 83.5 MHz bandwidth

♦ 5.725 GHz—5.850 GHz, a 125 MHz bandwidth

The purpose of the FCC change is to encourage the development and use of wireless networking technology. The new regulation permits a user to operate radio equipment that transmits a signal within one of the three ISM bands without obtaining an FCC license, within certain guidelines.

One of the IEEE 802.11 physical layers, IEEE 802.11a, uses the third ISM band, usually called the 5 GHz frequency band, whereas IEEE 802.11b uses the 2.4 GHz band. Because the 5 GHz band is broader (it covers more frequencies), it has the potential to send data at a faster rate. IEEE 802.11a specifies a maximum data rate of 54 Mbps, whereas IEEE 802.11b transmission rates top out at 11 Mbps.

CAUTION

Even though the FCC doesn't mandate a federal license, you still need to be sensitized to the potential for frequency interference, both inward and outward. If you intend to use a wireless network in a company that already uses radio equipment, and perhaps already has a person or department designated as a frequency manager, check with the appropriate parties in your company before implementing the network. Similarly, most hospitals and other medical care facilities, as well as military and law enforcement agencies, need to maintain tight control over radio transmissions within their facilities. If you plan to operate a wireless network in facilities of that sort, make sure to obtain appropriate clearance first.

As the online newsletter columnist pointed out, quite a few devices compete for the same radio airwaves within the frequency band that wireless networking devices use. However, this should not be surprising because the FCC has limited nonlicensed devices to a small number of frequency bands. Technologists have, consequently, developed ways to minimize actual interference.

Frequency Hopping Spread Spectrum

The Frequency Hopping Spread Spectrum physical layer is one of five available physical layers in IEEE 802.11. This physical layer uses a technique initially conceived for military applications called *frequency-hopping spread-spectrum* (FHSS) to reduce the likelihood that two radio devices will be operating at the same frequency at the same moment in time.

FHSS does not broadcast at a specific frequency, but adds a carrier signal to the data signal that hops many times per second to a different frequency in a predetermined pseudorandom pattern. FCC regulations require that this type of frequency modulation use at least 75 different discrete frequencies per channel. The FCC also specifies that the signal cannot remain at any single frequency longer than 400 milliseconds (ms). The chance of encountering interference is reduced by the frequent hopping; however, if a radio detects interference on a particular frequency, it transmits the same data again on the next hop at a different frequency.

Each pair of radios using this technique agrees on the hopping pattern it will use. By using *orthogonal* hopping patterns (patterns that never overlap on a given frequency at precisely the same moment), many pairs of radios can communicate over the same frequency band.

Because the signal transmitted by a radio using FHSS is never broadcast on a specific frequency for more than a split second at a time, unintended radio receivers will see the signal as momentary impulse noise.

NOTE

The Bluetooth wireless networking standard also uses an FHSS technique and broadcasts within the same band as 802.11 networks, but Bluetooth devices use a technique that hops 600 times faster than the 802.11 technique. Consequently, it is very unlikely that an IEEE 802.11 device would interfere with a Bluetooth device—although a Bluetooth device might interfere with a nearby 802.11 device. The standards bodies that develop and approve both standards are working together to come up with a way to reduce the potential for interference in either direction.

The IEEE 802.11 physical layer that uses the FHSS technique is capable of transmitting data at either one or two Mbps, depending on which of two different signal modulation techniques it employs. To transmit at one Mbps, the radios transmitting over the FHSS use a modulation technique called two-level *Gaussian frequency shift key* (GFSK) modulation. If the signal is strong enough, however, the radios use a four-level GFSK modulation technique to double the speed to two Mbps.

MODULATION TECHNIQUES

Computer data is digital (a series of 1s and 0s) whereas a radio signal is analog (a series of waves). The process of converting a digital signal into an analog signal is called *modulation*. Converting the analog signal back to a digital signal is *demodulation*. From these two terms comes the term *modem* (short for modulation-demodulation), used to describe a device that modulates and demodulates signals sent over phone lines or coaxial cable. The radios used in wireless networks are analogous to phone and cable modems, but they send data using radio waves rather than electrical impulses.

Radio waves vary in amplitude (size), frequency (waves per second), and phase (timing of when a wave starts). Interference tends to affect the amplitude of a radio signal, but not its frequency or phase. In order to pack lots of data into an analog signal, technologists have devised clever ways to use changes in frequency and phase to store information.

Because the FCC regulates the frequency at which a radio can transmit its signal, there is a natural upper limit to the speed at which information can be easily encoded in a radio signal. The higher the frequency, the higher the potential data rate, but you can't just increase the frequency of the radio waves in order to send information faster without violating FCC regulations. Instead, to send data at faster and faster speeds, you have to use increasingly more complicated modulation techniques.

Many types of modulation techniques exist. After considering the alternatives, the IEEE has chosen particular modulation techniques for each of the 802.11 physical layers so that manufacturers can build interoperable products.

Direct Sequence Spread Spectrum

Direct-sequence spread-spectrum (DSSS) is another technique included in the IEEE 802.11 specification. The IEEE 802.11 physical layer that uses DSSS can also transmit data at up to two Mbps. DSSS was first used by the military. Radios that use DSSS spread their signals across the entire available ISM band at very low power. By spreading the signal, interference by narrow-band signals is less likely to result in data errors. In addition, unintended radios see this signal as background noise and ignore it. When listening to a cheap radio placed too close to an 802.11 device, you may hear a low hum in the background.

Before transmitting the signal, the DSSS radio converts the data stream into a longer sequence by adding a string of bits called a *chip* or a *pseudo-noise (PN) code*. The IEEE 802.11 standard specifies a chip of at least 11 bits in length. This technique seems counterintuitive because the radio now has to send more bits than it did before adding the chips. However, this chipping process increases the likelihood that the receiver can recover the original data on the first try. If some portion of any chip is lost, the receiver can use statistical techniques to determine what the original chip was, without having to retransmit the chip. The signal is effectively "louder" than if the data were transmitted raw.

All IEEE 802.11-compliant, wireless networking radios that use DSSS use the same chip code. To ensure multiple transmissions at the same time within the same ISM band, IEEE 802.11 split the 2.4 GHz band into 14 channels, one every five MHz in the band. Not all 14 channels are available in any given country, although 11 are accessible in the United States and Canada. In general, availability depends on local radio frequency regulations. Because DSSS spreads the signal, channels that are within 30 MHz of each other may potentially interfere. Consequently, only three wireless networks can operate at the same time in the same vicinity without interference. However, most implementations of IEEE 802.11 permit *roaming* from one access point to another. When the signal to one access point gets weak, the client radio searches for a stronger signal from another access point. The weaker access point then passes off the client to the stronger. If both access points are using the same channel, the process still works; but the network traffic on both access points will be higher than if they were each using an exclusive channel.

The IEEE 802.11 physical layer that uses the DSSS technique is capable of transmitting data at either one Mbps or two Mbps, depending on which of two different signal modulation techniques it uses. To transmit at one Mbps, the radios use a modulation technique called *differential binary phase shift keying* (DBPSK). If the signal is strong enough, the radios can use another modulation technique, called *differential quadrature phase shift keying* (DQPSK), to double the speed to two Mbps.

High Rate Direct Sequence Spread Spectrum

The High Rate Direct Sequence Spread Spectrum physical layer is the most widely used IEEE 802.11 physical layer, even though it is the layer that was most recently added (in 1999) to the standard. This layer, specified by the IEEE 802.11b supplement to the initial standard, uses an extension of the IEEE 802.11 DSSS standard. It uses the same 2.4 GHz ISM band and channels as the DSSS physical layer, and in fact, the two are backward-compatible.

HR/DSSS employs a frequency modulation technique called *complementary code keying* (CCK). The CCK technique enables data transmission at either a 5.5 Mbps or 11 Mbps rate. Because this transmission rate is as fast as standard Ethernet (10 Mbps), and several times faster than most Internet connections, it is adequate for use in most LANs. However, 11 Mbps is still a bit slow for transmission of voice and images.

Coded Orthogonal Frequency Division Multiplexing

Another new 802.11 physical layer added at the same time as the HR/DSSS layer is called the *coded orthogonal frequency division multiplexing (COFDM) layer*. This layer, specified in the 802.11a supplement to the 802.11 standard, operates in the 5 MHz ISM band. Because it operates at a higher frequency, it is capable of higher transmission rates. As designed, this physical layer is capable of transmission speeds up to 54 Mbps.

Rather than using a frequency-hopping or direct spread-spectrum technique, the COFDM layer transforms digital data into multiple analog signals that it transmits simultaneously in parallel. The 802.11a physical layer uses the following three 100 Mhz-wide *unlicensed national information infrastructure (U-NII) bands*:

♦ 5.15–5.25 GHz

♦ 5.25–5.35 GHz

♦ 5.725–5.825 GHz

Each of these three bands is split into four channels, totaling 12 20 MHz-wide channels. Each channel is then split into 52 (roughly) 300 KHz-wide subchannels.

The *orthogonal* part of this layer's name comes from the fact that the subchannels are permitted to overlap because the signal transmissions are timed not to interfere. The result is more efficient use of the radio spectrum.

The major benefit of using the 802.11a physical layer is increased transmission speed, but this speed comes with a cost. At the higher frequency, the FCC puts additional limits on the transmission power. In addition, higher frequency radio waves don't radiate as far at the same power output as lower frequency signals. Radios must be closer together to use this physical layer than to use the HR/DSSS physical layer.

As with FHSS and DSSS, COFDM can achieve multiple transmission rates by using different modulation techniques:

♦ Using *binary phase shift keying* (BPSK) modulation, the COFDM physical layer can achieve data transmission rates at 6 and 9 Mbps.

♦ Using *quadrature phase shift keying* (QPSK) modulation, the transmission rate can be 12 or 18 Mbps.

♦ Using *quadrature amplitude modulation* (QAM), the rate can be either 24 or 36 Mbps.

♦ Using 16-QAM modulation, the rate can be either 24 or 36 Mbps.

♦ Using 64-QAM modulation, the rate can be either 48 or 54 Mbps.

In addition to higher transmission speeds, COFDM has the following advantages over the other 802.11 physical layers:

♦ About four times as many available channels

♦ Less competition with other types of devices using the same ISM band (portable phones, Bluetooth, microwave ovens, and so on)

Because of COFDM's complexity, vendors of wireless networking equipment have been slower in releasing products that can transmit over this physical layer. However, the allure of higher transmission rates will soon change that situation. Several vendors are already shipping 802.11a-compliant products.

New Physical Layers

The IEEE 802.11 group is defining a new physical layer that uses OFDM in the 2.4 GHz band. This will allow 802.11a data rates (up to 54 Mbps) in the band used by 802.11b. This work is being done by the 802.11g Task Group and is expected to be complete by the end of 2002. The new standard will be called 802.11g and will be backward-compatible with 802.11b.

Newer physical layers with even higher data rates may be defined in the coming years.

802.11b, WECA, and the Wi-Fi Standard

Currently, IEEE 802.11b is the reigning de facto standard for wireless networking. According to IDC, in the year 2000, worldwide WLAN equipment revenue increased 80 percent, passing the one-billion-dollar mark in total sales. A significant factor in this growth is the assurance that competing products are interoperable. Prior to the adoption of the IEEE 802.11b supplement to 802.11, interoperability was spotty and sales were slow. The IEEE 802.11b working group that developed the supplement did so with the explicit desire to encourage competing manufacturers to create products that would work together reliably.

In 1999, understanding the potential benefits of standardization, several leading companies who were developing wireless networking technology formed the Wireless Ethernet Compatibility Alliance (WECA), a nonprofit organization. WECA's primary purpose is to certify interoperability of IEEE 802.11b and IEEE 802.11a products.

To ensure interoperability, WECA established a test suite that defines how member products are tested by an independent test lab. Products that pass the tests are entitled to display either the Wi-Fi (IEEE 802.11b-compliant) or Wi-Fi5 (IEEE 802.11a-compliant) trademark, a seal of interoperability.

Although there is no technical requirement stating a product must pass these tests before its manufacturer can claim IEEE 802.11b-, or IEEE 802.11a-compliance, the steady growth in sales of Wi-Fi-certified products seems to confirm that certification greatly increases consumer confidence.

Summary

This chapter discusses the fundamentals of local area networks, with particular emphasis on wireless networks. It covers the components of local area networks, components of wireless networks, and wireless networking technology.

Armed now with a familiarity with networking and wireless networking terminology, you are better equipped to use the remainder of the book to plan and implement a wireless network in your office, enterprise, or home.

Chapter 2

A Short Course in IEEE 802

In This Chapter

This chapter discusses the wireless networking industry standard IEEE 802.11 and the conceptual model that underlies it. Topics covered in the chapter include the following:

- ♦ The ISO/OSI 7-layer reference model
- ♦ IEEE 802 and its reference model
- ♦ IEEE 802.3—Ethernet
- ♦ IEEE 802.11—Wireless LAN
- ♦ IEEE 802.11b—2.4-GHz higher-speed wireless LAN
- ♦ IEEE 802.11a—5-GHz high-speed wireless LAN

When asked on the eve of the Windows XP launch to name the most significant recent technological advances, Bill Gates answered that years from now, people will look back and say that, at least, we got 802.11 right. This chapter gives you some fodder for conversation should you have the opportunity to speak with Bill any time soon.

The ISO/OSI Reference Model

If you think about the steps a letter has to go through to get from your mailbox to its intended recipient, you should be amazed at the reliability of our mail system. The fact that networking technology works so well, most of the time, is equally amazing. One of the factors that has helped facilitate the continued growth of networking is the general agreement on a model for conceptualizing and discussing how networks function—ISO's *Open System Interconnection* (OSI) *reference model*.

As its name implies, the International Organization for Standardization is an international organization that was founded in 1946 for creating all types of standards for business, government, and society. It goes by the name ISO, which derives from the Greek word *iso*, meaning *equal*. ISO is made up of national standards institutes from 140 countries, including the American National Standards Institute (ANSI—the U.S. standards body). ANSI, which was founded in 1918, is a voluntary organization made up of more than 1,300 companies. It has established such standards as the ANSI C programming language standard and the *fiber distributed data interface* (FDDI) standard for sending data over fiber-optic cable, among others.

ISO's Open System Interconnection (OSI) networking architecture is not widely supported in commercial products; rather, the *Transmission Control Protocol* (TCP) and *Internet Protocol* (IP) architecture—collectively known as *TCP/IP*—is the de facto standard. Nevertheless, the OSI 7-layer model is widely used to teach and explain how networks, including TCP/IP networks, do what they do. Studying this model is useful because it is the basis of the IEEE 802.11 reference model for wireless networking. The next section explains OSI 7-layer model in detail.

TIP

If you need to memorize the OSI 7-layer model to pass a certification exam, for example, try the following mnemonic device:

All People Seem To Need Data Processing

This mnemonic device helps you list the layers from top (highest layer) to bottom (lowest layer): *Application, Presentation, Session, Transport, Network, Data Link,* and *Physical.*

The OSI 7-Layer Reference Model

The OSI 7-layer model (ISO/IEC 7498-1:1994) has been around, more or less in the same form, since 1984 when ISO and *International Telegraph and Telephone Consultative Committee* (CCITT, from the French spelling—but now known as the *International Telecommunications Union-Telecommunications Standardization Sector*, abbreviated *ITU-T*) agreed to work together to establish a single suite of compatible networking protocols. Although the current de facto suite of networking protocols, TCP/IP, wasn't that developed by OSI and CCITT, the OSI 7-layer model does an adequate job of helping to conceptualize how networking protocols should work. It has been universally adopted as a teaching or *reference* model. Think of it as a framework that will help you understand how LANs and WLANs work.

Figure 2-1 depicts the seven layers of the OSI model. The layers toward the bottom of the model are, naturally, called the *lower layers,* and the layers toward the top of the model are called the *higher layers*.

To better understand the OSI model, picture one of those Russian multilayered wooden dolls that hides a tiny solid doll within many layers of hollow outer dolls. The hollow dolls on the outside are analogous to the lower layers of the OSI model, and the tiny doll in the middle is analogous to the top layer of the model.

In a network, each layer of the model performs a set of services that is independent of the other layers. In a sense, all the layers beneath a given layer are "transparent" (or at least taken for granted), assuming each layer follows a certain set of rules. Any time two computers are communicating over the network, each layer in the OSI model on either end of the line operates as if it were dealing directly with the same layer at the other end.

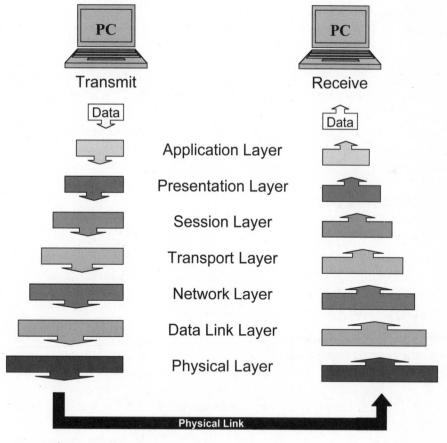

Figure 2-1: The OSI 7-layer reference model

By building networking protocols in this fashion, it is possible to work on each layer independently and simultaneously, and even to continue to innovate within each layer without the risk of "breaking" the entire system. In other words, you can paint one of the hollow Russian dolls a different color or make it out of different material without affecting the other dolls in the stack.

Networks transmit information in *network data frames,* or simply *frames*. Each frame starts with a string of bits called a *header* and ends with another string of bits called a *tail*. Because the Russian dolls are hollow, the lower-level layers leave a "hole" in the frame between the header and the tail. This hole is progressively filled by the higher-level layers.

The OSI model describes how the various layers interact with each other. Each layer of the networking model must provide a defined set of *services* to the higher layers in the model. However, the model does not specify particular methods or protocols that a layer should use to provide these services. The details of what happens within each layer are "transparent" to the other layers in the model. As long as each layer provides the services defined in the model for that layer, many different protocols can be used to provide those services. This concept is analogous to many situations in daily life. If you ask someone to "overnight" a package to you, for example, you may not care which carrier the other party uses—FedEx, UPS, or Airborne—to provide this overnight *service*.

The Physical Layer

The *Physical layer* is the lowest, or outermost, layer of the OSI reference model. It sends the bit stream around the network on an electrical and mechanical level. This bit stream can take the form of electrical impulses, light, or radio signals. The majority of this chapter and this book deals with the Physical layer. Chapter 1, for example, discusses the five available types of Physical layers that are specified in 802.11.

The type of cable used in a wired network is an obvious Physical-layer issue. Similarly, the type of signal used in a wireless LAN is a Physical-layer issue. In general, "nonintelligent" hardware, such as cable, antennas, and simple network hubs, are all part of the Physical layer in the OSI reference model. Decisions at this level are largely practical—taking into consideration ease and cost of installation, relative speed of transmission, signal strength, and so on. In the Russian doll analogy, the type of material that is used to construct the doll (wood) is a "physical-layer" issue.

Data Link Layer

The *Data Link layer*, which is the second layer of the OSI model, is responsible for the physical connection between two systems communicating over a given network. At this layer, the frame begins to take form—in other words, the Russian doll begins to take shape. The largest frame that the Data Link layer can send is called the *maximum transmission unit* (MTU). The network data frame at the Data Link level consists of the following:

♦ Logical source and destination addresses of the addressor and addressee

♦ A *checksum*—a number that is computed from the packet contents to be used by the receiving computer to confirm that the packet has no errors

The Data Link layer provides the following services:

♦ It handles the connection, physically and logically, between the sending computer and the receiving computer. In other words, when a computer receives information, the Data Link layer turns the signals it receives from the Physical layer into frames. When a computer sends information, this layer converts frames into the appropriate signals to send over the Physical layer to the destination computer. Two aspects of this function are as follows:

  • Defining the way that a computer on the network is able to access, transmit, and receive data over the Physical layer

  • Controlling the transferring of frames (over the Physical layer) from source to destination, including flow control, frame synchronization, and error checking

Network components that reside primarily in the Data Link layer include the following:

♦ Network interface cards (NICs) including wireless network adapters

♦ Switches

♦ Bridges

♦ Intelligent hubs (hubs that control network traffic flow and that provide controls for adding or removing stations from the network)

The IEEE 802.11 standard operates entirely within the Physical and Data Link layers.

Network Layer

The *Network layer* is the next layer in the OSI reference model. Its primary functions are switching, routing, and addressing—taking a logical network address that is provided by the Data Link layer and translating it into a "physical" address.

Chapter 1 describes the function of switches and routers, but the addressing concept is straightforward. For example, every Ethernet device has a unique address called a *MAC address* (MAC stands for *medium access control*; more about that later in this chapter) that is assigned by the manufacturer. This is the device's *physical,* or *hardware, address*. Each device (or *host*) on a TCP/IP network is assigned a 32-bit IP address. A computer's IP address is its *logical address*. The Network layer for an IP network translates the logical address into the physical address, and vice versa, as data is sent and received by the computer. In a TCP/IP network, the Network layer maintains a table called the *Address Resolution Protocol (ARP) cache* (a small table kept in RAM) that maps the IP address to the physical (MAC) address.

ARP Cache Poisoning

A hacker can gain long-term access to a network by using an attack called *ARP cache poisoning.* If the hacker can access the network, he broadcasts a forged ARP response associating the hacker's MAC address with the IP address of an authorized computer on the network. ARP then places the hacker's MAC address in the ARP cache in place of the real MAC address of the authorized system. From then on, network traffic intended for the authorized system will go to the hacker instead. After a period of time, the hacker can reverse the process, and no one will be the wiser.

Reasonable perimeter security `(firewalls, and so on) protects against this type of attack, but the addition of wireless stations on your LAN may cause the old problem to resurface.

The OSI Network layer is responsible for the following:

♦ Translating between logical network addresses and physical addresses

♦ Determining a route by which the frames can travel to their destination, a task generally handled by a router

♦ Taking care of directing network traffic and dealing with network congestion

♦ Breaking the packets into smaller units if the source computer provides packets larger than the MTU, the largest packet that the Data Link layer can send

Network components that reside in the Network layer include routers and brouters.

Transport Layer

The fourth layer of the OSI model is the *Transport layer*. This layer is primarily responsible for data transfer between hosts, including end-to-end error recovery (ensuring that all data is transferred) and flow control (ensuring that a host is not overloaded with data). Its services include the following:

♦ Packaging the data into small packets for transmission on the source end and reassembling the packets into the original message on the receiving end

♦ Sending acknowledgment that packets are received

♦ Managing the flow of packets across the network

♦ Providing error checking to ensure against loss or duplication of data

Network devices that provide Transport-layer services include gateways and brouters.

Session Layer

The fifth layer in the OSI reference model, the *Session layer*, is responsible for establishing, maintaining, and ending network sessions between hosts. The Session layer's services include the following:

♦ Name recognition to ensure that the correct parties participate in the session

♦ Synchronization of the data stream

♦ Management of timing and duration of data transmission during each session

Gateways provide Session-layer services, among others.

Presentation Layer

The Presentation layer is the sixth layer of the OSI reference model. Although some network protocols don't implement the Presentation layer, its main function is to provide a translation service between applications and the network protocols. Services typically performed by this layer include the following:

- ◆ Security services, such as encryption and decryption
- ◆ Data compression
- ◆ Character conversion

Gateways sometimes perform Presentation-layer services.

Application Layer

The *Application layer* is the layer at which applications gain access to network services. This final layer is intended for use by application software that is written to operate across a network, such as e-mail software, FTP, DNS, SNMP, and TELNET software. It provides the following services:

- ◆ Access to network services, such as network file transfer and database access that directly support the applications
- ◆ Network services that support user applications
- ◆ Network access, flow control, and error recovery

Network server software and gateways provide these services.

Introducing IEEE 802

The IEEE 802-1990 document, titled "IEEE Standards for Local and Metropolitan Area Networks," provides an overview of the family of standards called the *IEEE 802 Standards*. This document was approved by the IEEE Standards Board in May 1990 and by the American National Standards Institute (ANSI) in November 1990. As the title of the document states, this family of standards purports to define standards for local area networks and metropolitan area networks.

Now, more than ten years later, the IEEE 802 family of standards has met with almost universal approval and support from hardware and software manufacturers, as well as from consumers. The great majority of local area networks, wide area networks, metropolitan area networks, and even wireless networks use one or more of the standards included in 802, the most widely adopted being 802.3, Ethernet.

Although most of this book covers IEEE 802.11, a standard often called *wireless Ethernet*, it is helpful to understand how IEEE 802.11 fits into the overall IEEE 802 family.

The sections that follow examine the IEEE 802 family in the context of the OSI model, and provide a short summary of many of the 802 standards.

> **NOTE**
> In addition to the standards described in this chapter, several others are under development or may have recently been adopted by the time you read this. Refer to the IEEE Web site at
> `http://standards.ieee.org/catalog/olis/lanman.html` for current information.

The IEEE 802 Reference Model

Studied one at a time, the group of IEEE 802 standards seems like a confusing maze of barely-related protocols. However, if you compare them to each other, you begin to see the family resemblance. The diagram in Figure 2-2 shows how the members of the IEEE 802 family relate in the context of the IEEE 802 reference model that is an extension of the OSI reference model.

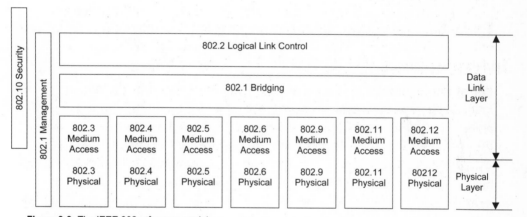

Figure 2-2: The IEEE 802 reference model

The Physical (PHY) Layer

In Figure 2-2, the Physical layer protocols—802.3, 802.4, 802.5, 802.6, 802.9, 802.11, and 802.12—are depicted as parallel rectangular blocks. There is a physical (PHY)-layer component to each of these protocols. This part of the model is the same as the OSI model.

The MAC Sublayer

In the OSI model, every layer is supposed to be independent of the next; however, in practice, the physical medium—type of cable, for example—has some bearing on the way multiple devices share access to the network. These means of sharing access to the network are called the *medium access protocols*. In the OSI model, medium access is a function of the Data Link layer, whereas the physical medium resides in the Physical layer.

There are two broad methods (with a number of variations) of accessing network media:

♦ **Contention.** Each network device attempts to communicate as the need arises and then makes adjustments if the network is busy. Ethernet uses a version of contention access.

♦ **Tokens.** Each device is permitted to communicate only when it holds a *token*. Token Ring and Token Bus are examples of medium access protocols that use this type of media access method.

In order to conceptually distinguish between medium access functionality and other data link issues, the IEEE 802 reference model has defined a sublayer called the *Media Access Control (MAC) layer*, which is closely tied to the Physical layer. Each IEEE 802 Physical layer standard (Ethernet, Token Ring, Token Bus, and so on) specifies both the Physical layer aspects of the protocol as well as how medium access is to take place (denoted by the rectangular boxes in the IEEE 802 reference model).

For example, the IEEE 802.3 standard (Ethernet) specifies the media types that can be used—a Physical layer issue—and specifies use of the *Carrier Sense Multiple Access/Collision Detection* (CSMA/CD) medium access protocol—a Data Link layer and Media Access Control sublayer issue.

You may recall that each device needed to access the network is assigned a unique identification number by its manufacturer. This number is called a *MAC address,* because the MAC sublayer keeps track of the physical address of each device that requests access to the network.

> **CAUTION:** The MAC address serves as a unique identifier for each network device, but it should not be viewed as a security device because the MAC address is easily discovered by a hacker and just as easily cloned.

The Logical Link Control Sublayer

At the top of the IEEE 802 reference model is another sublayer that is not in the OSI model—the *Logical Link Control (LLC) sublayer*, defined in IEEE 802.2. The primary function of the Logical Link Control sublayer is to provide a common interface to the Network layer while allowing for multiple physical-layer topologies.

♦ It handles the connection between the sending computer and the receiving computer.

♦ It is responsible for transferring the frames (over the Physical layer) from source to destination without errors.

IEEE 802.1—Glossary, Network Management, and Internetworking

Standards and documents in the IEEE 802.1 series include a glossary of relevant terminology, standards that involve network management and internetworking issues, as well as the IEEE 802 Overview and Architecture document. The IEEE 802.1 series includes the following standards:

♦ **IEEE 802.1B, 1995 Edition**—Defines a protocol that provides a means of remotely managing *local area networks* and *metropolitan area networks* (LANs and MANs).

♦ **IEEE 802.1D, 1998 Edition, IEEE 802.1t-2001, and IEEE 802.1w-2001**—Define the operation of media access control (MAC) bridges.

♦ **IEEE 802.1E, 1994 Edition**—Defines services and protocols that permit downloading of memory images to multiple destination systems, including the capability to remotely manage this process.

♦ **IEEE 802.1F-1993 Edition**—Specifies management information and procedures that apply across the IEEE 802 family of standards, such as attributes to represent MAC addresses.

♦ **IEEE 802.1G, 1998 Edition**—Sets out extensions to the IEEE 802.1D MAC bridges standards, including remote operation of these bridges.

♦ **IEEE 802.1H, 1997 Edition**—Provides a technical report and guidelines on further extension of IEEE 802.1D related to MAC bridging of Ethernet in local area networks.

♦ **IEEE 802.1Q-1998, IEEE 802.1u, and IEEE 802.1v, 2001**—Define an architecture for *virtual bridged local area networks,* as well as the protocols and algorithms needed to provide those services.

♦ **IEEE 802.1X-2001**—Specifies a port-based network access control scheme.

CROSS-REFERENCE: For further discussion of port-based network access control, refer to Chapter 13.

IEEE 802.2—Logical Link Control

As discussed in the "The Logical Link Control Sublayer" section, earlier in this chapter, the IEEE 802.2 1998 Edition standard defines a *Logical Link Control (LLC) sublayer* of the Data Link layer in the OSI model.

IEEE 802.3—Ethernet

Ethernet, developed in 1976 by Xerox, with help from DEC and Intel, is the most widely adopted local area network Physical-layer protocol. IEEE 802.3, 2000 Edition, *CSMA/CD Access Method and Physical Layer Specification*, specifies a baseband Physical-layer protocol that is very similar to the original Ethernet. The original Ethernet transmitted data at 10 Mbps. IEEE 802.3 provides for data transmission at various rates up to 1000 Mbps—so-called Gigabit Ethernet. IEEE 802.3 also specifies a protocol for 10-Mbps broadband transmission (see the sidebar "Baseband versus Broadband").

Different MAC layer protocols can be distinguished by the way two devices on the network contend for the data channel when both attempt to send data simultaneously over the network. Both the original Ethernet and 802.3 (also called Ethernet) use a method called *Carrier Sense Multiple Access/Collision Detection*. If two devices try to send data at precisely the same moment, a "collision" occurs. When using this protocol, a device that detects a collision waits a random amount of time before sending the data again. If the device detects another collision, it waits again, but this time for twice as long. Because each device presumably waits for a different random amount of time, the second or subsequent collision is with a packet from a different device than the first collision. Heavy traffic on the network will result in a larger number of collisions and slower overall throughput. This process repeats until data transmission is successful.

BASEBAND VERSUS BROADBAND

In a *baseband* transmission electrical impulses are sent out without the need to change the frequency of the signal. By contrast, a *broadband* transmission requires that the signal be *modulated* to change its frequency so that it can be transmitted within a particular frequency range or *channel*. By using a *frequency division multiplexing* (FDM) technique, many different channels can be transmitted simultaneously over some types of media, including coaxial cable. Thus, the same wide bandwidth cable can be used to transmit both data and television without interference from a broadband signal.

The terms *broadband* and *wide bandwidth* are frequently used in discussions about networks and the Internet when what is really meant is that the speed of the connection is relatively fast. The fact that a signal has been modulated to be transmitted over a broadband medium doesn't make it faster per se. However, when a signal is modulated by adding a very high frequency, the result may be faster transmission than before. In the case of a local area network, however, broadband transmission is not necessarily faster than baseband. The key advantage of broadband cable in a LAN would be the availability of the wide bandwidth medium to send other types of wide bandwidth signals, such as television and digital video, over the same cable plant.

IEEE 802.4—Token Bus

IEEE 802.4-1990, Token-Passing Bus Access Method and Physical Layer Specifications, specifies the Physical-layer protocol that uses a token-passing bus access method. In a *bus topology*, all devices are connected to a backbone cable. This Physical-layer protocol can be used to transmit data at speeds up to 20 Mbps.

IEEE 802.5—Token Ring

IEEE 802.5-1998E, Token Passing Ring Access Method and Physical Layer Specifications, specifies the Physical-layer protocol that uses a token-passing ring access method. In a *ring topology*, all devices are connected in a closed loop. This Physical-layer protocol can be used to transmit data at speeds up to 16 Mbps.

IEEE 802.6—Metropolitan Area Network

IEEE 802.6 1994 Edition, *Distributed Queue Dual Bus (DQDB) Access Method and Physical Layer Specifications*, lays the foundation for a set of Physical-layer standards to allow *Distributed Queue Dual Bus (DQDB)* subnetworks to provide a number of different telecommunications services—including high-speed data, voice, and some video services—throughout a metropolitan area. This standard lays out only general principles. IEEE 802.6j-1995 provides more details about implementation.

IEEE 802.7—Broadband LANs

IEEE 802.7-1989, *Recommended Practices for Broadband Local Area Networks*. As its name implies, this document is a set of recommendations concerning the physical, electrical, and mechanical characteristics of a properly designed *broadband* cable medium that provides the physical transmission medium for either the Ethernet (IEEE 802.3) or Token Bus (IEEE 802.4) 10-Mbps broadband protocols.

The recommendations in IEEE 802.7 are different from the CableLabs Certified Cable Modem project and the associated Data Over Cable Standard Interface Specifications (DOCSIS). DOCSIS establishes an industry standard for cable modems that connect consumers to the Internet over cable TV infrastructure.

IEEE 802.7 is not explicitly intended to create a cable modem standard; rather, it is intended to make recommendations for a Physical layer that is a suitable medium for LAN use within the context of the entire IEEE 802 family of standards. Cable modems are compatible with IEEE 802 networks and can be used to connect a LAN to the Internet, although most cable Internet service providers provide service only to home users.

IEEE 802.9—Integrated Services LAN

IEEE 802.9-1995, *Integrated Services (IS) LAN Interface at the Medium Access Control (MAC) and Physical Layers*, defines a unified access method offering integrated (voice and data) services over the network to the desktop for a number of publicly and privately administered networks. The standard also specifies the interface for the MAC and Physical layers.

IEEE 802.10—Security

IEEE 802.10-1998, *Standard for Interoperable LAN/MAN Security (SILS),* sets out specifications for a Data Link layer security protocol—the *Secure Data Exchange protocol*. This protocol is supported by the Application layer *Key Management protocol*. The Secure Data Exchange protocol and the Key Management Protocol together typically provide a method for secure bridging of data across a network connection, especially across large enterprise-wide networks, to form virtual LANs (VLANs).

IEEE 802.11—Wireless

IEEE 802.11, *Wireless LAN Medium Access Control (MAC) and Physical Layer (PHY) Specifications*, specifies the standards for wireless networking. Chapter 1 described five different ways of transmitting data over a WLAN. These five alternatives can be depicted as five Physical layers in an IEEE 802.11 model (see Figure 2-3):

♦ Frequency Hopping Spread Spectrum (FHSS)

♦ Direct Sequence Spread Spectrum (DSSS)

♦ High Rate Direct Sequence Spread Spectrum (HR/DSSS)

♦ Coded Orthogonal Frequency Division Multiplexing (COFDM)

♦ Infrared light

The first edition of the IEEE 802.11 standard, adopted in 1997, specified the FHSS and DSSS protocols that can transmit at either one or two Mbps using the 2.4-GHz ISM frequency band. An updated edition of IEEE 802.11,

Edition 1999, includes speeds up to 54 Mbps using COFDM transmitted over the 5-GHz ISM band.

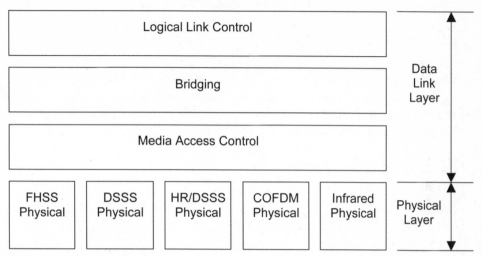

Figure 2-3: A model of IEEE 802.11

802.11b—Higher-Speed Wireless

IEEE 802.11b-1999, *Higher-Speed Physical Layer Extension in the 2.4-GHz Band*, is the supplement to 802.11 that establishes the specifications for High Rate Direct Sequence Spread Spectrum (HR/DSSS), the protocol used by Wi-Fi-certified wireless networking devices. Although 802.11b was adopted in a separate document, it is not a separate standard from 802.11; rather, it adds subsections to 802.11 that specify the HR/DSSS protocol.

This HR/DSSS Physical layer is backward-compatible with the DSSS Physical layer, using the same 2.4-GHz ISM band and channels as the slower protocol. The primary difference between HR/DSSS and DSSS is HR/DSSS's frequency modulation technique, a technique that enables data transmission at either 5.5 Mbps or 11 Mbps. Because 11 Mbps is as fast as standard Ethernet (10 Mbps) and is several times faster than most Internet connections, it is quite adequate for use in most LANs. However, 11 Mbps is still a bit slow for transmission of voice and images.

802.11a—High-Speed Wireless

IEEE adopted 802.11a-1999, *High-speed Physical Layer in the 5-GHz Band*, at the same time as it adopted 802.11b. Like 802.11b, this document supplements 802.11; it sets out specifications for the *Coded Orthogonal Frequency Division Multiplexing* (COFDM) protocol.

By operating at higher frequencies than HR/DSSS and by using a variety of modulation techniques, this COFDM layer is able to provide data transmission rates of 6, 9, 12, 18, 24, 36, 48, and 54 Mbps. The closer the two communicating radios are and the stronger the signal, the faster they will communicate. Put another way, the radios will attempt to communicate at the highest speed. If they encounter too many errors (dropped bits), the radios will step down to the next fastest speed, repeating the process until a strong connection is achieved.

An increasing number of vendors are announcing wireless networking equipment that complies with 802.11a. Several vendors have announced AP products that support both 802.11b and 802.11a by providing slots for two radio cards. The network administrator can choose to install one wireless networking PC Card, two cards of the same type, or one of each type. This two-card AP solution doesn't require you to upgrade all clients to the faster standard before you can provide a faster connection to clients who need it.

It is only a matter of time before vendors start to offer one wireless networking PC Card that supports both HR/DSSS and COFDM Physical layers. It seems unlikely that such a card would support both standards at the same time (because the standards work in different ISM frequency bands). Several vendors, however, have announced their intentions to provide cards that do just that. Such a dual-protocol card would enable a portable client station to roam between 802.11b WLANs, 802.11a WLANs, or heterogeneous WLANs that support both standards.

In addition to the higher transmission speeds, COFDM has the following advantages over the other HR/DSSS Physical layers:

♦ About four times as many available channels, resulting in about eight times the system capacity

♦ Less competition with other types of devices using the same ISM band (portable phones, Bluetooth, microwave ovens, and so on)

♦ As much as four to five times the data link rate and throughput of 802.11b in a typical office environment

Because of these advantages, WLANs that deploy 802.11a-compliant equipment can either provide the same throughput as 802.11b at lower AP deployment costs or provide increased throughput for similar AP deployment costs.

802.11g

IEEE 802.11g, a supplement to 802.11, is in the works and may have been ratified by the time you read this book. This addition to the WLAN standard sets specifications for protocols that can transmit data up to 54 Mbps—so-called "turbo" speed—over the 2.4-GHz frequency band. The draft proposal combines technologies from the 802.11a and 802.11b Physical layers as well as technology from Intersil (CCK-OFDM) and Texas Instruments (Packet Binary Convolutional Coding).

Only time and the marketplace will determine whether 802.11a or 802.11g becomes the dominant high-speed standard. 802.11g-based products are backward-compatible with 802.11b-based products, but 802.11a-based products will have the advantage of first-to-market status.

802.11e

IEEE 802.11e is also an unratified extension to 802.11, intended to add support for multimedia and Quality of Service (QoS) to wireless LANs. *QoS* is a networking term that means "guaranteed throughput level," a feature needed to support transmission of streaming video and high-quality voice. Because 802.11e is an enhancement to the MAC sublayer, it will work with all the Physical layers—802.11a, 802.11b, and 802.11g. For data transmission, you don't really notice momentary delays—except perhaps when you are watching a complex Web page download. However, when you are watching a movie over a WLAN connection, even the slightest interruption of service is an irritation. IEEE 802.11e is intended to address this QoS issue.

Although 802.11e is still in draft form, a protocol called Whitecap2, from ShareWave (owned by CirrusLogic at the time of this writing), incorporates QoS support in a proprietary extension to IEEE 802.11b. Products using Whitecap2 may be commercially available by the middle of 2002.

IEEE 802.12—Demand-Priority Access

IEEE 802.12, 1998 Edition, *Demand-Priority Access Method, Physical Layer and Repeater Specifications*, defines a Physical-layer protocol that combines the simplicity and fast access of the Ethernet protocol with the stronger control, better collision avoidance, and deterministic delay features of the Token Ring protocol and transmits at 100 Mbps.

In the demand-priority network, the repeater devices maintain control. The repeaters grant access to the requesting stations in a cyclic sequence, using a round-robin protocol according to assigned priority levels. Requesting stations are deemed either normal priority or high priority. Within each of these two priority levels, a second level of priority is assigned based on the sequential location of the station in the network.

Each repeater in a demand-priority network has at least two local ports and an optional cascade port for connecting to another repeater. Up to five levels of cascade are permitted, to support networks of up to four km in diameter and backbones up to two km in length.

A gigabit version of the Demand Priority protocol has been proposed and is under development.

Summary

This chapter explores the wireless networking industry standard IEEE 802 and its underlying conceptual model. It introduces you to the ISO/OSI 7-layer reference model, the IEEE 802 reference model, and each member of the 802 family of standards. To complete your orientation in wireless personal computer networking technology, turn to Chapter 3 for an overview of the leading wireless technology that is not based on the 802 standards.

Chapter 3

Bluetooth, HomeRF, and HiperLAN/2

In This Chapter
This chapter discusses the following:

- ◆ Bluetooth
- ◆ HomeRF
- ◆ HiperLAN/2

Wireless communication technology is not a new development. Over 100 years have passed since the Italian inventor, Guglielmo Marconi, performed his first experiments with wireless telegraphy. However, the use of radio signals to transmit computer data is new enough to mean that the technology is still evolving. If you are about to install a wireless network using the IEEE 802.11b standard, how can you be sure that you are choosing the best technology? This chapter helps you answer that question.

When deciding how to spend your money or that of your company on computer technology, it is often smart to follow the crowd—buy the technology most people are buying to avoid investing heavily in a technology that will be quickly orphaned. The stronger the demand for a technology, the lower the probability that the manufacturers of that technology will abandon it. The demand for wireless networks is increasing rapidly, and IEEE 802.11b-based WLANs are garnering the largest market share. Nonetheless, this chapter briefly explores three similar but different standards that are also attracting a great deal of attention: Bluetooth, HomeRF, and HiperLAN/2.

The Bluetooth Standard

In 1994 the *Bluetooth* wireless technology, named for the tenth-century Danish King Harald Blaatand "Bluetooth" II, was invented by the L.M. Ericsson Company of Sweden. In February 1998 Ericsson, IBM, Intel, Nokia, and Toshiba founded the Bluetooth Special Interest Group (SIG) Inc. to develop an open specification for always-on, short-range, wireless connectivity based on Ericsson's Bluetooth technology. Their specification was released publicly on July 26, 1999. The Bluetooth SIG now includes 3COM, Microsoft, Lucent, Motorola, and nearly 2,000 other companies.

Bluetooth is intended as an international standard that facilitates the use of Bluetooth-enabled devices anywhere in the world. Although similarities exist between Wi-Fi and Bluetooth, think of the two standards as complements of one another rather than competitors. Nonetheless, as a part of your planning for a wireless network, you should become familiar with what Bluetooth has to offer. According to the November 2001 report from Frost & Sullivan, the global market for Bluetooth-enabled devices is expected to grow over the next few years, with shipments exceeding one billion by 2007 and expected revenues of $318 billion.

IEEE 802.15 and Bluetooth 3.0

Bluetooth devices usually communicate with other devices in relatively close proximity, rather than with an entire LAN. In contrast to a traditional local area network (LAN), a *personal area network* (PAN) consists of several computing devices communicating in close proximity.

Although not yet fully adopted by IEEE, IEEE 802.15.1, a standard for wireless PANs (WPANs) will likely soon become a part of the IEEE 802 family of standards. The IEEE 802.15.1 proposed standard is derived largely from the Bluetooth 1.0 standard. It may already be adopted by the time you read this book. Although a few differences may exist between the adopted IEEE 802.15.1 standard and the original Bluetooth 1.0 standard, Bluetooth 1.0-compliant devices should be easily upgradable to work with IEEE 802.15.1-compliant devices.

Three working groups within IEEE are currently moving towards WLAN standards:

- ♦ The IEEE 802.15 Task Group 1 (or 802.15.1) is focused on deriving a WPAN standard based on the Bluetooth 1.0 specification that will enable the transfer of data between a WPAN device and an 802.11 device.

- ♦ The IEEE 802.15 Task Group 2 (or 802.15.2) is focused on reducing interference between all devices that comply with the IEEE 802standards.

- ♦ The IEEE 802.15 Task Group 3 (or 802.15.3) is tasked to boost the peak data transfer rate to 20 Mbps or higher, probably by using the 5 GHz ISM frequency band.

The first two working groups have nearly concluded their work with the adoption of 802.15 and are on track for a full IEEE vote by the end of 2001. Work towards a faster WPAN transmission speed is well underway.

As IEEE works toward the 802.15 standard, the Bluetooth SIG is simultaneously working on Bluetooth Version 3.0. Any new Bluetooth standard will likely also become an updated IEEE 802.15 standard.

Wireless Cables and More

The Bluetooth technology was originally intended as a wireless replacement for cable — USB without the wires. However, in practice it is being applied more broadly to enable a wide range of devices to communicate with each other. The standard defines a way for a variety of electronic devices to communicate wirelessly with minimal user intervention. To the end user, this communication is effortless, yet robust. The technology is designed to be low-cost and low-power to preserve the pocketbook and conserve battery life. Prices for Bluetooth devices are still higher than optimum for widespread adoption, but power consumption is reasonable. As more and more electronic devices are mass produced, causing prices to sink, Bluetooth sales should take off.

In offering a wireless alternative to cables, Bluetooth improves upon existing wireless cable-replacement technology. The Bluetooth RF technology actually builds on the Infrared Data Association (IrDA) Object Exchange Protocol (OBEX) framework. Most laptop computers, PDAs, and printers already have IrDA-based wireless connectivity, but its functionality is hindered by infrared's requirement for line-of-sight proximity of devices. Just as your TV's remote control must be pointed directly at your TV to work, the infrared ports on two PDAs must be lined up to trade data, and your laptop has to be "pointing" at the printer to print over the infrared connection. Because Bluetooth uses radio waves rather than light waves, line-of-sight proximity is not required.

Like IEEE 802.11b, Bluetooth offers wireless access to LANs, including Internet access. Unlike 802.11b devices, Bluetooth devices can potentially access the Public Switched Telephone Network (PSTN — the phone system) and mobile telephone networks. In fact, the capability to handle both voice and data simultaneously may enable Bluetooth to thrive alongside Wi-Fi by making possible such innovative solutions as a hands-free mobile phone headset, print-to-fax, and automatic PDA, laptop, and cell phone—address book synchronization.

Piconets, Masters, and Slaves

The way Bluetooth devices communicate is similar in concept to the IEEE 802.11b ad hoc mode. A Bluetooth device automatically and spontaneously forms informal PANs, called *piconets,* with other Bluetooth devices. The connection and disconnection of these devices is almost without any user command or interaction—a capability called *unconscious connectivity*. A particular Bluetooth device can be a member of any number of piconets at any moment in time (see Figure 3-1). Each piconet has one *master*, usually the device that first initiates the connection. Other participants in a piconet are called *slaves*.

Bluetooth connections can be data-only, voice-only, or data and voice:

◆ **Data-only.** When communicating data, a master can manage connections with up to seven slaves. Many additional slaves can be "parked" in a low-power state, waiting to be added to the piconet. This type of connection can be *asynchronous*.

♦ **Voice-only.** When the Bluetooth piconet is used for voice communication (for example, a wireless phone connection), the master can handle no more than three slaves. In order to support conversations between real people, voice-only piconets must be over *synchronous* connections.

♦ **Data and voice.** A piconet transmitting both data and voice can exist between only two Bluetooth devices at a time. This type of connection is called *isochronous*, meaning the data must be delivered within certain time contraints, but not as rigidly as in synchronous connections. The voice portion must be synchronous, but the data portion can be asynchronous.

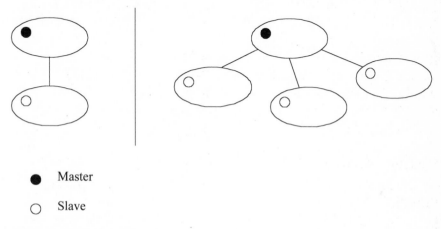

● Master

○ Slave

Figure 3-1: Bluetooth piconets

The Bluetooth standard permits each device to join more than one piconet at a time. A group of different piconets with one or more devices in common is called a *scatternet*. Figure 3-2 depicts a scatternet made up of several piconets.

When used for voice, the *Synchronous Connection Oriented* (SCO) link provides 64 Kbps voice transmission in each direction. The master establishes a point-to-point link with a single slave in the piconet, but can support up to three simultaneous SCO links. SCO packets are never retransmitted.

Bluetooth *Asynchronous Connectionless* (ACL) links, used to transmit data, have a raw data rate of 1 Mbps; however, the maximum available asymmetric data rate is 723.2 Kbps in either direction, with 57.6 Kbps in the return direction. Alternatively, an asynchronous channel can support a symmetric link at 433.9 Kbps.

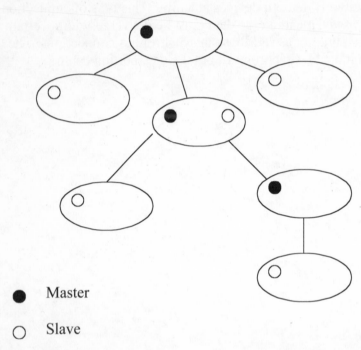

●   Master

○   Slave

Figure 3-2: A scatternet made up of several piconets

Bluetooth devices can send data over a piconet using sixteen different types of packets. The actual data rate delivered by a Bluetooth connection is determined by the amount of information sent in each packet and the type of error correction used. Sending more information in each packet (that is, sending longer packets) causes a faster data rate. Conversely, more robust error correction causes a slower data rate. The application using a Bluetooth connection will determine the type of packet used and, therefore, the data rate.

The Bluetooth Reference Model

Bluetooth has a different reference model (architecture) than IEEE 802.11b. It is comprised of the following layers (see Figure 3-3):

- Radio Frequency (RF)
- Baseband
- Link Manager Protocol (LMP)
- Host Control Interface (Optional)
- Logical Link Control and Adaptation Protocol (L2CAP)
- Data
- TCP/IP; HID; RFCOMM
- Applications

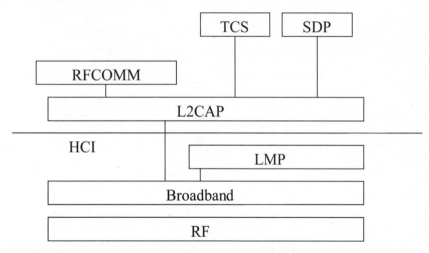

Figure 3.3: The Bluetooth reference model

The first three layers (RF, Baseband, and LMP) are typically implemented in hardware and firmware, and the top four layers in software.

Radio Frequency Layer

IEEE 802.11b and Bluetooth both use the 2.4 GHz ISM band. Bluetooth radios transmit a signal with a nominal antenna power of 0dBM (1mW), with extensions for operating at up to 20dBm (100mW). Because the Bluetooth standard is intended for worldwide adoption, this signal strength complies with transmission regulations in most countries. Bluetooth is designed to connect devices at distances from 10 centimeters to 10 meters; however, at the optional 20dBm transmission power, the range can exceed 100 meters. Assume that most Bluetooth devices are being designed for use within 10 meters of other compatible devices.

Bluetooth uses a form of the *Frequency Hopping Spread Spectrum* (FHSS) protocol to make full use of the 2.4 GHz ISM band and to reduce the likelihood of interference. It hops 1,600 times per second between 79 discrete 1 MHz-wide channels from 2.402 GHz to 2.480 GHz. The radio transmits at a specific frequency for no more than 625 microseconds before hopping to the next frequency. The protocol uses the modulation scheme called *Gaussian Prefiltered Binary Frequency Shift Keying* (GPBFSK).

So that many piconets can exist in the same vicinity without mutual interference, each piconet establishes its own random hopping pattern. If interference does occur, each piconet switches to a different channel and tries again. When transmitting voice, *Continuously Variable Slope Delta Modulator* (CVSD) modulation is used because it is designed to compensate for high bit error rates.

Even though Bluetooth and IEEE 802.11b devices use the same ISM frequency band, their use of different modulation schemes means you should be able to use Bluetooth devices and Wi-Fi (802.11b) devices in the same vicinity with no noticeable interference.

Baseband Layer

The *Baseband layer* of the Bluetooth architecture controls each device's radio by performing the following services:

- RF channels management
- Error correction
- Hop pattern selection

- Security, including authentication of devices to be linked and link keys management

- Management of *Synchronous Connection Oriented* (SCO) links for voice, and *Asynchronous Connectionless* (ACL) links for data

- Handling paging and inquiry of other Bluetooth devices in close proximity

- Handling packets

- Application of a time-division duplex (TDD) scheme

Bluetooth uses five logical channels to send different types of data. The *Link Control* (LC) channel and *Link Manager* (LM) channel are used in the link layer, whereas the UA, UI, and US channels carry user information about *asynchronous, isochronous,* and *synchronous* links.

Link Manager Protocol Layer

The *Link Manager Protocol (LMP) layer* performs the following services:

- Establishment of the connection

- Security functions—authentication and encryption management

- Mode mangement

- Information exchange and requests

- Link setup, configuration, and control of the SCO or ACL link, including Quality of Service (QoS) and power control

- Piconet management, including managing link keys and attaching and detaching slaves

The master and slave in a piconet negotiate link settings in the LMP layer, including the clock offset, slot offset, timing accuracy, link manager version, and supported features such as authentication and SCO packets.

Because each participant in a piconet is either a master or a slave, part of the negotiation and link management process is determining the role of each party to the link and handling any switching between master and slave. The LMP layer also handles parking and unparking slaves on a piconet. The devices on each piconet communicate with each other over SCO or ACL links. The LMP on the master manages the channel sharing with the help of the LMP on each device.

Logical Link Control and Adaptation Protocol

Most application software interacts with the *Logical Link Control and Adaptation Protocol* (L2CAP) layer. Essentially, the L2CAP provides the network layer functions to applications and higher layers. The L2CAP layer performs the following services:

♦ Providing applications simultaneous use of a link between two devices

♦ Reducing the size of packets sent by applications—up to 64K—to the size of packets accepted by the Baseband layer—at most, 2,745 bits

♦ Enabling applications to demand QoS on parameters such as peak bandwidth, and latency and delay variation, and then determining whether the link is capable of providing it

Host Controller Interface

In many instances, Bluetooth can be implemented as an add-on adapter in the form of a PCI card, a PC card, or a USB adapter. In these implementations, the lowest three layers of the Bluetooth architecture—RF, Baseband, and LMP—are handled in hardware and/or firmware. The top layers of the architecture, starting with L2CAP, are implemented in the *host's* software (in the PC). In a device that implements all layers in hardware/firmware, the HCI layer isn't needed.

When Bluetooth is implemented in a PC adapter, a *Host Controller Interface* (HCI) driver on the *host* (the PC) accepts the data from L2CAP (implemented in software), formats the data, and sends it over the PC's physical bus (PCI, card bus, or USB) to the HCI in the Bluetooth hardware. The HCI then passes the data to the Baseband layer.

Application Layer

As in the OSI model, the Bluetooth *Application layer* is the top layer of the reference model, and the layer at which applications gain access to L2CAP services such as *Object Exchange Protocol* (OBEX), *Transmission Control Protocol* (TCP), *RFCOMM* (wireless emulation of RS-232), and *Service Discovery Protocol* (SDP). The Application layer is intended for use by application software written to operate across a piconet connection and perhaps across a network such as e-mail, TCP/IP, Point-to-Point Protocol (PPP), or File Transfer Protocol (FTP), as well as telephony applications.

Because many types of devices will be able to add Bluetooth functionality, the Bluetooth SIG Inc. has published a collection of *profiles* that specify the minimum set of capabilities that both sides of a Bluetooth connection should support in order to accomplish the connection described in each profile. Examples of profiles published by Bluetooth SIG Inc. include the following:

♦ **Service Discovery Application Profile.** Specifies the features and procedures required for an application in a Bluetooth device to discover the services that are registered in other Bluetooth devices.

♦ **Cordless Telephony Profile.** Defines the requirements for a single three-in-one, chameleon-like phone handset that can operate as an intercom, a PSTN phone, or a mobile phone, depending on whether the Bluetooth technology senses that the handset is at the office, at home, or on the road.

♦ **Intercom Profile.** Specifies the requirements for the intercom portion of the three-in-one handset in the preceding profile.

♦ **Serial Port Profile.** Lists the requirements necessary for Bluetooth devices to emulate a serial (RS-232) connecting two Bluetooth devices.

♦ **Headset Profile**. Defines the requirements for wireless telephone headsets that permit the user to keep the mobile phone in his pocket while talking over a live PSTN or mobile telephone connection.

♦ **Dial-Up Networking Profile.** Specifies the requirements for supporting a Bluetooth dial-up to an Internet access provider over a modem or cellular phone.

♦ **Fax Profile.** Defines the protocol and procedure requirements necessary to use a Bluetooth device as a wireless fax.

♦ **LAN Access Profile.** Defines LAN access using PPP over RFCOMM, as well as PC-to-PC access using PPP over serial cable emulation.

♦ **File Transfer Profile.** Specifies the requirements for Bluetooth devices to support electronic file transfers.

♦ **Synchronization Profile.** Defines the requirements for Bluetooth devices to support automatic synchronization of schedules and address lists between PDS, laptops, and cell phones.

Bluetooth Examples

The products that will first take advantage of Bluetooth technology include the following:

♦ Mobile phones

♦ Personal Digital Assistants (PDAs)

♦ Bluetooth adapters for PCs

♦ Consumer electronic products

The Microsoft Pocket PC 2002 operating system, launched in October 2001, supports both Bluetooth and IEEE 802.11b, but only through add-on adapters. Around the same time, however, Microsoft launched Windows XP with native driver support for 801.11b, but without support for Bluetooth. Microsoft cited the lack of commercially available Bluetooth devices as the main reason for not including the necessary HCI device drivers out of the box. Bluetooth device vendors will need to supply the drivers with each product to enable operation with a Windows XP PC.

PDAs

Perhaps the first Bluetooth device for the Palm handheld is a clip-on device from TDK Systems Europe. This device, called the BlueM, has a thin sled design and slides onto the back of the Palm m500, m505, and m125 handhelds, as well as IBM C500 devices, connecting via the docking port on the bottom of the PDA. The one-ounce BlueM enables the Palm handheld to communicate with other Bluetooth-enabled devices, including PCs, notebooks, printers, and other handhelds that are within range.

PC Adapters

Toshiba is currently shipping the first Bluetooth PC Card that adds the Bluetooth wireless technology to any PC with a PC Card slot. It supports PCs with Pentium 133MHz, 64MB RAM, and either Windows 98SE or Windows 98ME. The Toshiba adapter card supports Bluetooth profiles for file transfer, dial-up networking, LAN access, and fax. It also includes a SPANworksTM application for presentation sharing, chat, business card exchange, and synchronization with Bluetooth-enabled notebook PCs, handheld PCs, and other products that began to reach the market in 2001. This card has a range of up to 100 feet in a typical office environment, built-in 128-bit encryption, and advanced authentication features for robust, enterprise-level security.

Consumer Products

On average, Bluetooth SIG Inc. qualified a new Bluetooth wireless product each day during the third calendar quarter of 2001. Several of these products are already commercially available in Europe, Asia, and the United States.

In response to interest by the automotive industry, the Bluetooth SIG formed the Car Working Group in December 1999. This working group has defined how Bluetooth wireless technology will enable hands-free use of mobile phones in automobiles. The Bluetooth SIG membership was expected to vote by the end of 2001 on a new Hands-Free Profile that will incorporate the Car Working Group's recommendations.

WLANs

Wireless developer Patria Ailon recently announced the arrival of Ailonet, an intelligent, wireless base station based on IEEE 802.11b/802.11a and Bluetooth, GPRS, and Linux technologies. Ailonet is a multipurpose wireless application platform for corporate and public WLANs that supports sharing of Internet connections, files, printers, and other peripherals in the home network. It can also function as an intelligent component of a sophisticated home or business video-surveillance security system.

Zoos

The Denver Zoo is the first zoo in the world with a Bluetooth network. This network gives visitors an interactive zoo tour via a pocket PC as well as access to other information about the zoo. Zoo staffers also use the Bluetooth-based network to collate and record information on the zoo's animals and plant life and to wirelessly access their corporate network facilities from anywhere in the zoo (*BluetoothWorld*, Issue 4, May 2001, Telecoms.com).

HomeRF

The HomeRF standard is a direct competitor of the IEEE 802.11 wireless networking standard. HomeRF is sponsored by the Home Radio Frequency Working Group (HomeRF WG), which was launched in March 1998. The group now has six promoter companies: Compaq, Intel, Motorola, National Semiconductor, Proxim, and Siemens, as well as more than 70 member companies.

IEEE 802.11b is primarily used in the corporate environment, but HomeRF was developed from the beginning as an affordable wireless technology for home users. Whether HomeRF is truly more affordable has yet to be proven.

HomeRF networks have a maximum range of 150 feet, large enough to cover the typical home, garage, and yard. A revised version of the standard, HomeRF 2.0, increased data rates for HomeRF networks to a maximum of 10 Mbps. The initial version of HomeRF was capable of transmitting data at up to 1.6 Mbps. For home use, even broadband Internet access over cable modem or DSL seldom exceeds 1.5 Mbps download speeds; so even HomeRF 1.0 is fast enough to keep up with the Internet.

HomeRF 2.0 enables the introduction of new types of devices, applications, and services, including bandwidth-intensive applications such as CD-quality audio distribution to wireless speakers and streaming video. HomeRF's integration of data and telephony services is intended to promote the development of the following enhanced services:

♦ Wireless home networks that share voice and data between PCs, peripherals, enhanced cordless phones, and other devices such as portable, remote displays or "Web" pads

♦ Internet access from around the home via portable display devices

♦ Sharing of a single ISP connection between PCs and other devices

♦ Forwarding of incoming telephone calls to multiple cordless handsets, FAX machines, and voice mailboxes

♦ Review of incoming voice and other calls, as well as e-mail messages from the same PC or PC-enhanced cordless telephone handset

♦ Control of home electronic systems with speech commands into a PC-enhanced cordless handset

♦ Support for MP3 and other audio files that use audio streaming from anywhere in the home

If manufacturers continue to support HomeRF and HomeRF 2.0, new information appliances and other devices will be developed to take full advantage of the integrated voice and data capabilities.

The HomeRF Physical Layer

From the inception of Home RF, efforts have been made to keep its development and implementation costs down, with the goal of controlling and managing costs to consumers. To that end, rather than designing the protocol from scratch, parts of many existing protocols were used. For example, HomeRF uses a variation of the Frequency Hopping Spread Spectrum (FHSS) radio frequency technology that was specified in the original IEEE 802.11, 1997 standard. The HomeRF Working Group has, however, modified FHSS to facilitate single-chip implementation. This, too, should result in cost savings to the consumer.

HomeRF MAC Layer

The HomeRF 2.0 specification incorporates a subset of the Digital Enhanced Cordless Telephony (DECT) standard, which supports all typical consumer telephony features plus enhanced features that would be useful in both home and small-business applications. Using DECT, HomeRF 2.0 can support up to four simultaneous conversations over as many as eight handsets. HomeRF 2.0 also includes support for QoS to ensure adequate bandwidth for synchronous operations, such as voice and continuous video.

HomeRF 2.0 uses a Time Division Multiple Access (TDMA) modulation scheme (similar to that used in GSM digital cellular) to provide isochronous voice and streaming video support. In addition, the standard uses a Carrier Sense Multiple Access/Collision Avoidance (CSMA/CA) contention scheme to support asynchronous data transmission.

Comparison of HomeRF and IEEE 802.11b

As you have probably gathered by now, the major distinction between HomeRF and 802.11b is that HomeRF 2.0 was designed to handle voice as well as data, whereas 802.11b handles only data. HomeRF is also designed to interoperate with PSTN (the phone system). Another less significant difference is that HomeRF offers speeds up to 10 Mbps, whereas 802.11b supports speeds up to 11 Mbps.

Various trade magazines and analysts cite other advantages of HomeRF—such as price differentials and security differences—but these distinctions are debatable. Prices for Wi-Fi systems are falling dramatically, and a number of ways to improve the security of your WLAN are not dependent on the wireless networking protocol.

Unless you or your company has a strong immediate need for integrated voice and data over your wireless LAN, you should probably stick with 802.11b wireless networks—at least until you decide you need a faster alternative, such as 802.11a.

ETSI HIPERLAN/2

Another competitor to the IEEE 802.11 standard originated in Europe. Products using the HiperLAN/2 technology developed by the European Telecommunications Standards Institute (ETSI) are expected to show up in the U.S. marketplace in the near future.

What distinguishes HiperLAN/2 from IEEE 802.11b is speed—up to 54 Mbps—coupled with the capability to combine data with voice and video using spectrum in the 5 GHz band. A joint project of European telecom equipment giants Nokia and Ericsson, the technology was almost assured a future in Europe, until in December 2001, Ericsson announced that it was switching its focus to IEEE 802.11a.

In competing against 802.11a, HiperLAN2's real advantage lies in its capability to offer voice and video support along with high-speed data support. 802.11a is primarily a data strategy. However, the ratification of the 802.11e standard (which provides MAC enhancements for QoS) may lessen the advantage.

Summary

This chapter discusses three wireless technologies that may be viable alternatives to 802.11b: Bluetooth, HomeRF, and HiperLAN/2. You should survey the networking landscape before investing a lot of time and money into an emerging technology such as wireless networking. After considering the alternatives, however, you will probably find that either Wi-Fi (802.11b) or Wi-Fi5 (802.11a) is the best choice, unless you have a special need for enhanced wireless voice or video networking capabilities.

If you have stayed with me this far, you are probably eager to roll up your sleeves and start installing your first wireless network. Turn now to Chapter 4 to discover how to perform a critical first step in installing a functional WLAN—the *site survey*.

Chapter 4

Performing a Site Survey

In This Chapter
This chapter discusses the following:

- ♦ Site survey focus
- ♦ Site survey documentation
- ♦ Drafting a WLAN site design
- ♦ Testing the design

Sometimes you can start a project in so many different places that you don't know where to begin. When installing a wireless network, however, the place to begin is certain: with a *site survey*. If you are installing a network in your home, the survey may be quick and easy. On the other hand, if you are installing a wireless network across a college or corporate campus or a multisite enterprise, the survey may take days or even weeks to complete.

Whether you perform site surveys in-house or hire them out will depend on the size and scope of the project, as well as the staffing of your IS team. In either case, this chapter provides a broad overview of the questions a wireless networking site survey should answer and the information it should gather.

This chapter focuses primarily on site surveys performed in a single building. Site surveys for multiple buildings—even multiple geographic locations—raise additional considerations and are covered in Chapter 20.

Why Do a Site Survey?

Installing a computer network, wired or wireless, is an engineering project. Although it may not be a complicated project, it always involves implementing a technological solution in the real world. Any good engineer makes a plan before starting a new project. Otherwise, he ends up painting himself into the proverbial corner and then performing extra work to paint over his footprints.

Probably the most important reason to perform a site survey is to ensure that your WLAN doesn't leave dead spots in coverage. If you have ever experienced a dead spot, you know how frustrating it feels to place your laptop PC on a conference room table in an important meeting only to find that your wireless network card cannot find the signal to the access point (AP).

Survey Focus

To ensure the best coverage, the site survey should focus on four general areas:

1. Signal coverage
2. Network capacity
3. RF interference
4. Power requirements

The next few sections explain the significance of each area.

Signal Coverage

The area covered by a wired network is determined largely by where you can run wires. Wired LAN connection points are tangible, finite, and easily identifiable physical locations. Determining connectivity is usually a matter of locating the nearest RJ45 wall jack. WLANs, on the other hand, are spherical in shape with "fuzzy" edges. There are an infinite number of connection points not necessarily bound by the physical confines of the structure from which the WLAN broadcasts its signal; yet not every point within the sphere receives a useable signal.

The survey should gather enough information for you to design a wireless network that provides at least the same amount of connectivity as a wired LAN. In fact, you really want to provide significantly better coverage by enabling connectivity anywhere in the building that it will be needed, without forcing users to search for a wall jack. However, even if you provide a net improvement in coverage, you may still experience problems; for example, if you miss a spot where a single user needs coverage, the user who can't connect to the network will not be a happy camper.

Many variables affect whether you get an adequate signal at any given point in the building. A few factors that determine signal strength follow:

- **Linear distance from the transmitter (AP).** The further away from the AP, the weaker the signal. Wi-Fi standards promise a maximum operating range of 100 feet at 11 Mbps to 300 feet at one Mbps. Indoors, a realistic range at 11 Mbps is about 60 feet. As Wi-Fi5 networks become more prevalent, the maximum range may vary. Range may differ from vendor to vendor, as well.

- **The power of the transmitter.** Wi-Fi access points transmit at less than one watt. The maximum power allowed is regulated by government agencies around the world.

- **The directivity or gain of the antennas attached to the AP and to the workstation's wireless network card.** Antenna specifications vary depending on vendor, type, and materials. Adding a higher gain antenna at either end of the connection can increase the effective range. Whether the antenna is omnidirectional or directional will also affect signal strength at a particular spot in the building.

CROSS-REFERENCE
See Chapter 20 for a discussion of the difference between omidirectional and directional antennas.

- **The construction materials used in the walls, floors, and ceilings.** Some construction materials are relatively transparent to radio signals, whereas other materials, such as marble, brick, water, paper, bulletproof glass, concrete, and especially metal, tend to reflect some of the signal, reducing coverage.

- **The position of the receiver relative to the shape of each access point's coverage area.**

- **The shape of the building.**

- **The location of rooms where users will most likely need WLAN access.**

- **Physical objects permanantly installed in the building, such as metal doors, heating ductwork, and elevator shafts.**

- **Physical objects that have been added by building occupants, such as furniture, appliances, plants, and people.**

If you install a WLAN in a residence, one access point may be sufficient; but in most office environments, you will need many access points. Most manufacturers recommend approximately 30-percent overlap of AP cells to facilitate roaming from cell to cell without losing the signal. Because the shape of the AP's coverage is spherical, reaching up and down as well as out, the coverage may reach several floors of the building—unless it is blocked by the materials used to construct the building.

Ultimately, the only way to ensure adequate coverage in a specific location is to test the site in many locations using a pair of radios—usually an AP and a laptop with a wireless network adapter. Most wireless networking hardware vendors include utility software with their products that can be used to test signal strength and throughput (the amount of data that is transmitted without errors); however, several software products designed specifically for wireless site surveys are also available. Intel Pro/Wireless 2011 LAN Site Survey Utility and Cisco Aironet Wireless Site Survey are two excellent proprietary site survey utilities that will help you design and test a wireless network site plan. Other multivendor testing software is available to help you test and fine-tune your plan. One of these is AiroPeek (WildPackets, Inc.), the industry's first comprehensive 802.11b wireless LAN analyzer.

Network Capacity

Wireless LANs use a contention-type transmission protocol through which only one wireless station transmits at a time. Consequently, the more stations trying to use the same WLAN, the slower it will become—the same way traffic on a freeway will slow to a crawl at rush hour. One of the primary goals of the site survey is to determine the number of stations that will access the WLAN.

When setting up a wired network, it is good practice to segment the network into workgroups of computers most likely to communicate with one another. This rule is true for WLANs as well. The goal of segmenting a LAN is to keep traffic down on the network by establishing a *collision domain* that handles only messages intended for the computers in the workgroup. (A *collision domain* is a group of network devices connected so that they receive all messages sent by any member of the group.) In a wired network, you can use bridges and routers to accomplish this goal. However, because a wireless AP broadcasts to all stations that are on the same channel, you should assign at least one AP and a unique channel to each workgroup to accomplish the desired segmentation. Each AP then acts as a bridge to the rest of the network.

802.11b WLANs have 14 DSSS channels from which to choose. However, due to frequency overlap (see Table 4-1), no more than three channels can be used within range of each other without risking interference. Consequently, you can divide the WLAN in any given broadcast area into as many as three segments.

Table 14-1: The 802.11b DSSS Channels

DSSS Channel	Frequency (GHz)	U.S. and Canada	Europe	France	Spain	Japan
1	2.412	X	X			X
2	2.417	X	X			X
3	2.422	X	X			X
4	2.427	X	X			X
5	2.432	X	X			X
6	2.437	X	X			X
7	2.442	X	X			X
8	2.447	X	X			X
9	2.452	X	X			X
10	2.457	X	X	X	X	X
11	2.462	X	X	X	X	X
12	2.467		X	X		X
13	2.472		X	X		X
14	2.484					X

One of the goals of the site survey, therefore, is to determine how to segment the WLAN to balance network capacity. You should gather the following information:

♦ **The number of users.** AP manufacturers will normally specify the number of devices that can be handled by a single AP. As a general rule, allocate no more than 30 workstations per AP.

♦ **Organizational structure.** Determine which users work together and should be on the same network segment.

- **The sort of application software used.** Applications that make heavy use of network printers, file servers, or the Internet put a heavier load on the network than software that stores and retrieves information from the local storage medium.

- **The type of network services needed, such as file servers, printers, HTTP, FTP, and so on.** Using network services means network traffic.

- **The equipment that will be connected to the network, now and within the next three years.** The more devices on the network, the greater the traffic.

- **Security requirements.** Adding a layer of security uses processing resources and may increase network traffic. Security considerations also may determine whether you will be permitted to use wireless network equipment at all.

- **Expected company growth.** Plan for the capability to grow the WLAN as the company grows without having to create a new design.

RF Interference Immunity

An increasing number of devices around the home and office use radio frequency (RF) electromagnetic waves to transmit information wirelessly. With this obvious convenience comes potential "contention" in the form of interference. Before you go to the trouble and expense of installing a wireless LAN, attempt to determine how *immune* the WLAN will be to radio frequency interference.

The potential sources of RF interference will depend on the frequency band in which your WLAN operates. 802.11b WLANs operate in the 2.4-GHz ISM frequency band, which is potentially very busy. Bluetooth devices, HomeRF WLANs, some portable phones, and all microwave ovens operate in this range.

802.11b WLANs can also be an internal source of interference. As noted in the preceding section, 802.11b WLANs can choose from 14 channels. Each channel is only five MHz from the next, but if used, it occupies 22 MHz of bandwidth. If two or more 802.11b WLAN segments are broadcasting on channels that are separated by less than 30 MHz, they may potentially interfere with each other.

WLANs that comply with 802.11a, on the other hand, operate in the five-GHz ISM frequency band. This band is much less crowded, with a reduced likelihood of interference.

Other potential sources of RF interference include hospital equipment and military communications equipment. This interference can occur in both directions, so you should always consult your organization's frequency manager to determine whether your enterprise already uses equipment that transmits on the same frequency bandwidth as your WLAN.

If your site survey identifies potential sources of RF interference, you should perform additional testing with actual radios near the interference to determine whether reception will be adequate. One of the possible advantages of the HomeRF-type wireless network over Wi-Fi networks is the use of FHSS signal transmission technology. Because of FHSS's frequent hops from frequency to frequency, actual interference is significantly less than interference experienced by DSSS-type networks in the same environment.

In practice, microwave ovens are the most likely culprits when it comes to interference with IEEE 802.11b networks. By keeping workstations and APs 30 feet or more away from microwave ovens, the interference can be effectively neutralized.

If and when Bluetooth devices become widely adopted, they will also have the potential to create significant interference; however, these devices generate short bursts of data at short range. Interference can be managed by keeping Bluetooth devices away from Wi-Fi devices whenever possible.

The most common sources of interference are furniture, cubicle partitions, and people who populate the office environment. You can mitigate this type of interference by mounting access points above furniture, partitions, office equipment, and people, suspending the APs high on a wall or from the ceiling.

Power Requirements

Each wireless device that accesses the network also needs access to electrical power. Workstations should be supplied with enough power because modern building and electrical codes usually require an adequate number of electrical outlets. However, if your installation requires access points to be suspended from the ceiling or high on a wall, you need to evaluate the best way to get electrical power to these high-mounted access points.

Although each AP and workstation doesn't need its own dedicated power supply, it is desirable to isolate the power to each wireless device AP as much as possible. The following provisions for power are listed in descending order of desirability:

- An isolated ground circuit with an *uninterruptable power supply* (UPS) that is also a surge suppressor and signal filter
- An isolated ground circuit with a surge suppressor
- A dedicated circuit with a surge suppressor
- A nondedicated circuit with a UPS
- A nondedicated circuit with a surge suppressor

If it isn't possible to dedicate a circuit to each access point, avoid using circuits attached to the following:

- Hardwired devices
- Devices that may cause power surges
- Heat-producing devices, such as space heaters, laser printers, or photocopiers
- A device that draws more than 20 percent of the rated circuit value
- Devices that, when combined, draw greater than 60 percent of the rated circuit value

When considering where to run fixed network cable to connect APs to the wired backbone, note the location of any existing electrical conduit as well as any conduit that may need to be added to run power to the APs. Avoid running network cable next to this electrical conduit because of potential interference and attenuation of RF signal.

Gathering Requirements

Before installing both wired and wireless networks, you need to *gather requirements*—in other words, you need to obtain the answers to some questions that will help you define the scope of the task.

Planning the installation of a wireless network is very similar to planning the installation of a wired network. In fact, you may never install a purely wireless network. Most wireless networks have one or more APs that interface with a wired network. In most corporate environments, a wireless network serves as an add-on to an existing wired network. Even if you plan to install a wireless network in a home or small business as an alternative to a wired network, you will need to run at least one wire to each AP.

To ensure complete signal coverage, ask yourself the following questions before installing a wireless LAN:

1. Will workstations be mobile?
2. Will workstations *roam* throughout the area covered by the WLAN?
3. How many workstations will be served initially by the WLAN?
4. Is the number of wireless workstations expected to grow and, if so, how quickly?
5. Where is each network server located?
6. What services does the network need to supply to the wireless workstations—file service, print service, Internet service, and so on?
7. Is there an existing cable plant?
8. Are there existing bridges, routers, switches, and so on?
9. Is there an existing phone system?
10. Is there an existing wireless system?
11. Are there sources of RF interference in the building—for example, microwaves, portable phones, and so on?
12. How difficult will it be to pull cable, if that becomes necessary?
13. What are the building codes that apply to installation of cable in this locality?
14. What is the distance between each workstation?

To answer these questions, you may need to obtain blueprints, talk to the facility's manager or even the architect, interview end users, and study zoning regulations. Most important, walk around the site and look at it yourself—in other words, *survey* the site, including testing RF reception thoroughly throughout the facility, especially in places where stations will be located.

Site Survey Documentation

No one likes to fill out forms, but they do have their benefits. If you create a set of forms to use for your site survey, you will not only reduce the likelihood that you will forget to ask a crucial question, you may also be able to spread out the work of collecting information because you can hand the forms to someone else to fill out.

There are several categories of useful site survey forms:

♦ **Site maps** enable you to visualize the placement of APs in relation to workstations and any wired network infrastructure.

♦ **Pre site survey forms** help you gather information that enables you to determine threshold feasibility and use your time most efficiently when you perform the actual survey.

♦ **Interview forms** structure the process of gathering needed information from the people who will be using the WLAN.

♦ **Resource-list forms** assist in collecting information about network resources.

♦ **Network diagrams** provide a visualization of any existing network infrastructure.

Pre Site Survey Form

Before you begin the site survey, you can collect data by sending out pre site survey forms (see Figure 4-1) to network administrators and/or users. This form (which could easily be implemented electronically) will help you determine up front the number of wireless workstations you will need to set up, as well as the portions of the building that will need to be covered by the wireless network.

The following information should be requested on your form:

1. Location of each workstation

2. Computer type—for example, laptop, desktop, Palm, Pocket PC, and so on

3. Operating system—for example, Windows 9x, Me, XP, NT, 2000, Linux, Mac OS 9.x, X, Palm, Windows CE, and so on

4. If mobile, the on-site locations where the wireless station will be used

5. A checklist of network-centric services to which the computer will need access

Figure 4-2 shows an example of a pre site survey form intended for a network administrator. A network administrator should fill out one of these forms (which could also be implemented electronically) for each logical workgroup. This form helps determine the number of required APs as a function of the number of workstations that need to communicate, as well as the amount of potential traffic on the WLAN. The following information should be requested:

1. Workgroup name and location
2. Number of workstations in the group
3. Maximum distance between two workstations in the group
4. LAN services needed, such as file service, print service, DHCP, HTTP, FTP, and so on.
5. Do routers exist on the LAN? What type?
6. Does a firewall exist on the LAN? What type?
7. Is this workgroup on a separate LAN segment?
8. Will all users need Internet access?
9. What is the highest level of security needed within the workgroup?
10. Do some computers in the workgroup need higher security-level access than others?
11. Does the network currently have a *virtual private network* (VPN) server? What type?
12. Does the network use an authentication server for dial-up access? What type?
13. Are there other RF generating devices operating within the vicinity of this workgroup? What type?

The pre site survey forms help you identify workgroups that can be assigned to the same AP or group of APs. You should also begin to get a picture of the traffic that the WLAN must handle.

After you collect the completed pre-survey forms, take time to analyze them. The information they contain will enable you to come up with your first estimate of the WLAN's overall cost. You should be able to determine the approximate number of wireless stations the WLAN needs to support, as well as the number of APs required. Depending on your budget, you may even determine that the estimated costs outweigh the benefits and decide to scale back the WLAN, or postpone it altogether.

1. Name: _____   Date: _____

2. Office/Cube Number: _____

3. Phone number: _____   Email address: _____ ____

4. My computer is a: ☐ Laptop   5. My computer operating system is:
                       ☐ Desktop   ☐ Windows 95   ☐ Mac OS 9.1
                       ☐ Palm   ☐ Windows 98   ☐ Mac OS X
                       ☐ Pocket PC   ☐ Windows Me   ☐ Linux 7.2
            Other: ☐ _____   ☐ Windows XP   ☐ Palm OS
                                          ☐ Windows NT   ☐ Windows CE
                                          ☐ Windows 2000   Other: ☐ _____
                                                                  ☐ I don't know

6. In addition to my office/cube, I regularly use my computer in the following location(s):
   ☐ Board room   ☐ Cafeteria
   ☐ Library   ☐ Break room
   ☐ Conference room #_____   ☐ Lab #_____
   ☐ Conference room #_____   ☐ Lab #_____
   ☐ Conference room #_____   ☐ Lab #_____
   ☐ Conference room #_____   ☐ Lab #_____
   ☐ Conference room #_____   ☐ Lab #_____
   ☐ Reception area   ☐ Atrium
   ☐ Other _____   ☐ Other _____

7. When I use my computer I regularly need network access to use:
   ☐ Printing   ☐ AOL
   ☐ Email   ☐ Instant Messenger
   ☐ Hotmail   ☐ FTP
   ☐ Internet   ☐ Newsgroups
   ☐ File server   ☐ Calendar/Scheduler
   ☐ NetMeeting   ☐ Other _____

8. Interviewer's Notes:

   _____

   _____

   _____ __ _____

   _____

   Interview completed by: _____   Date: _____

Figure 4-1: An example of a pre site survey form for users to fill out

Workgroup name: _____ _____

1. Number of workstations: _____

2. Floor: _____   Quadrant: _____

3. Approximate furthest distance between workstations in the workgroup. _____ _____

4. LAN services needed:
    - ☐ ____ File server(s)
    - ☐ ____ Print server(s)
    - ☐ DHCP
    - ☐ HTTP
    - ☐ FTP
    - ☐ NNTP
    - ☐ SMTP
    - ☐ Database server
    - ☐ Groupware

5. The network has:
    - ☐ ____ router(s) of type _____
    - ☐ ____ firewall(s) of type _____
    - ☐ VPN of type _____ IPSEC? _____
    - ☐ Dial-up access
    - ☐ Authentication server of type _____

6. The following RF producing devices are found within 30 feet of computers in this workgroup :
    - ☐ Microwave oven   ☐ ___ 802.11b (Wi -Fi) WLAN(s)
    - ☐ ___ Portable phone (s) 2.4 GHz   ☐ ___ 802.11a (Wi -Fi5) WLAN(s)
    - ☐ ___ Bluetooth devices   ☐ _____(other)

7. The highest level of security needed for any computer in the workgroup is __ _____

8. The following workstations need higher -level security than the others in the workgroup:
    _____
    _____
    _____
    _____
    _____

9. Interviewer's Notes:
    _____
    _____
    _____
    _____

Interview completed by: _____   Date: _____

Figure 4-2: An example of a pre site survey form for a network administrator

Interview Forms

If you obtained pre-survey forms from each user and network administrator, then the on-site interviews with these individuals should be quick and easy. You will only need to confirm the information gathered on the pre-survey forms and ask for updates. Note that the sample forms shown earlier (refer to Figures 4-1 and 4-2) provide a space for interviewer notes.

As an alternative to distributing pre-survey forms, you may choose to gather all your information during the survey interview. The pre-survey form then becomes your interview form.

Although you may be able to obtain enough information from the network administrators and IS staff to complete the survey, end users are the best source for information relating to usage of the WLAN. In addition, if you involve users before the WLAN is installed, they may be more forgiving if problems arise later.

Site Maps

An up-to-date set of blueprints or other documents, such as floor plans and interior design plans, that show the building's dimensions in detail are perhaps the most crucial documents to obtain before you perform the site survey. The plans documents need to show the location of walls and large metal objects—such as elevators, steel pillars, and support beams—that could attenuate radio signals. If the building has a sprinkler system, try to obtain a blueprint that shows the location of the sprinkler heads.

Ideally, you should already have a detailed schematic diagram that shows where network cable runs through your building. Even though you intend to install wireless stations, you need to connect the WLAN to the wired LAN at various points; therefore, you need to know where the wire runs and where it can be accessed.

Using the existing blueprints or floor plans and network wiring schematic, create a working *site map*—a set of blueprints or floor plans that show precise dimensions and include all potential signal attenuators. Superimpose on this site map the wiring diagram of any existing network cabling. These drawings will be the basis for your new WLAN design. Also, mark the locations of all fixed devices, such as servers, printers, and desktop computers, which were identified in the presite survey documents as potential wireless stations.

Be sure to note the following devices and locations on your site plan:

♦ Desktop PCs, Macs, and Linux workstations

♦ Networkable printers

♦ Servers

♦ Server rooms/closets

♦ Phone wiring closets

♦ Hubs, routers, switches, bridges, and brouters

♦ Hard-wired electrical devices

♦ Microwave ovens

♦ Copy machines

♦ Fax machines

♦ Heavy-duty electric motors

♦ Refrigerators

♦ Electric staplers

♦ Air conditioners

♦ Stationary power tools (table saws, electric drill presses, and so on)

♦ Space heaters

♦ Fluorescent lights

♦ Devices drawing more than 20 percent of the circuit rating

♦ Any other RF-generating equipment

If the WLAN is going into a warehouse environment, the site plan should note stock locations, including the maximum height that stock is stacked.

Conducting a Walk-Through

The next step in the site survey process is to physically tour the site—a process I call a *walk-through*. Armed with the pre-survey documents and the site map, physically inspect the areas where you will install the wireless network. Confirm the information that you have already gathered and update the site plan, if necessary, to include any additional objects that may block or reduce the RF signal.

At this point, you should start to formulate the best locations for the access points. Although the technology that enables wireless local area networks is highly scientific, the process of determining the optimum WLAN site design ultimately involves a good deal of trial and error. As you think about the best locations for access points, you can also begin to test these trial locations while you do the walk-through.

The following tools are useful during the walk-through:

- A digital camera, to record the physical space layout at the time of the site survey
- A distance measuring wheel, to confirm or update physical dimensions on the site map
- An access point
- A directional and omnidirectional antennna
- A laptop computer with a wireless NIC installed
- Representative examples of other wireless NIC-equipped mobile units, such as PDAs or inventory scanners, that you expect will become WLAN stations
- A battery, from which you can run the access point in an area that doesn't yet have a conveniently located power source

Take careful notes as you inspect the site. Paper and ink, and even your time, are cheap compared to the costs you and your company may incur if you have to fix problems resulting from a hasty site survey.

After you have completed the walk-through, you must draft a site design—a relatively easy task if you have been continually updating the site map.

Drafting the Design

As you may recall from the first portion of this chapter, the following four issues should be addressed by the site design:

1. Signal coverage
2. Network capacity
3. RF interference
4. Power requirements

Now that you have gathered the pre-survey data, created a site map, conducted interviews, and performed a walk-through, you are well-equipped to draft a plan for the wireless network that will address all four key issues.

The result of the survey should be a report that clearly sets out the instructions for installing the WLAN infrastructure—AP by AP, wireless station by wireless station. Several of the site survey software packages automatically generate a site survey at the end of the process.

Although you could draft the entire plan on paper before testing it, in practice it is usually more efficient to work on one AP coverage area—often called a *cell*—at a time. As you establish the location and boundaries of each AP cell, mark it on your site plan and move to the next area.

As you draft the design, keep the following guidelines in mind for AP placement:

- ◆ The indoor range of DSSS radios is approximately 60 feet at the 11 Mbps speed, and about twice as far at half the speed (5.5 Mbps).

- ◆ The outdoor range of DSSS is about 500 feet (at 11 Mbps) to about 1000 feet (at 5.5 Mbps).

- ◆ Avoid placing APs against solid objects such as walls, especially corners.

- ◆ Avoid placing APs inside plenums (the air space above dropped ceilings)—although I did hear of a case where antennas were installed in the elevator shaft in the middle of a building, resulting in strong reception throughout the building.

- ◆ Whenever possible, place each AP near the center of the area to be covered.

- ◆ Avoid overlapping AP cells if they are using the same channel.

- ◆ Select channels with at least 30 MHz separation for adjacent overlapping cells.

- ◆ When the entire area to be covered is relatively small—such as a home or small business that can be covered by one or two access points—establish the center and boundaries by testing the largest area first and then filling in with an additional access point(s).

- ◆ When you estimate that the overall area to be covered requires more than two APs, start with a cell on one side of the overall area and establish its boundaries through testing before moving to the next cell.

- ◆ Consider using directional antennas to cover irregularly shaped areas, and long narrow areas; otherwise, use omnidirectional antennas.

- ◆ For indoor installation, it is often most advantageous to suspend APs from the ceiling, with each antenna pointing down. Alternatively, you can run a feed line to an external antenna that is suspended from the ceiling.

♦ Place directional antennas and omnidirectional antennnas in a vertical orientation.

♦ When installing a WLAN on multiple floors of a building, start with the top or bottom floor, moving down or up one floor at a time. Consider the spherical shape of the signal, as well as attentuation by building materials in floors and ceilings, when you are computing overlap between cells on adjacent floors.

Whenever you need to use more than one access point, consider how best to connect the extended service sets (ESSs) managed by the various APs. You will need to use at least one hub, but you may want to consider using a switched hub to control the traffic across the various ESSs. If you are installing more than a dozen APs, you probably need to use multiple hubs with a bridge between them.

Testing

To determine the soundness of your site plan, test the placement of each AP by evaluating both the signal strength and data throughput that can be achieved at all locations within each cell in which a user is likely to place a wireless station. Moving the AP just a few feet one way or the other can sometimes make a world of difference.

Most wireless networking hardware vendors include software with the APs and with each wireless NIC that provides most of the information you need to test signal strength and throughput. Figure 4-3 shows the Orinoco (Agere) Client Manager software and its Link Test dialog box. In this example, the dialog depicts the test of a mobile station communicating in infrastructure mode with an access point; the signal strength is excellent.

Figure 4-4 shows the same pair of wireless devices when the signal strength between them is poor. Using a mobile device, such as a laptop or PDA, and this Client Manager utility or a similar software utility, you can slowly walk around any given workspace and determine where the signal is weak and where it is strong. In this manner, you can determine the actual range of the AP and find *RF shadows* that are cast by large objects blocking the APs' broadcasts.

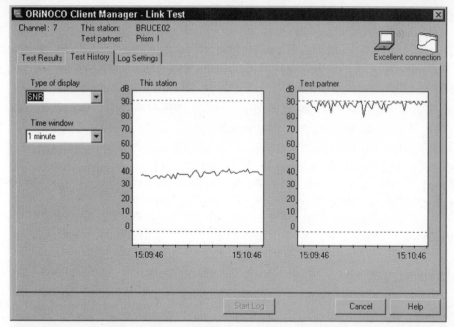

Figure 4-3: The Orinoco Client Manager Link Test dialog showing excellent signals from workstation and AP

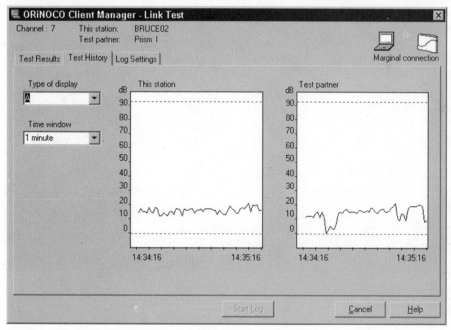

Figure 4-4: The Orinoco Client Manager Link Test dialog box showing poor signals from workstation and AP

In addition to testing for signal strength, you should test the amount of data throughput. Generally, signal strength and throughput vary together, but interference may sometimes cause enough intermittent loss of signal to result in a high number of lost messages. When this occurs, you may be able to move the AP a short distance and correct the problem.

Figure 4-5 shows the Test Results dialog box of the Orinoco Client Manager. In addition to a bar graph depicting signal strength, this dialog denotes the total number of messages *sent* from the workstation, the total number of messages *received* by the access point, and the total number of messages lost over a given period of time. If the signal is weak enough that some messages have been sent at slower speeds, this dialog also indicates the number and percentage of messages that have been transmitted at each of the four available speeds.

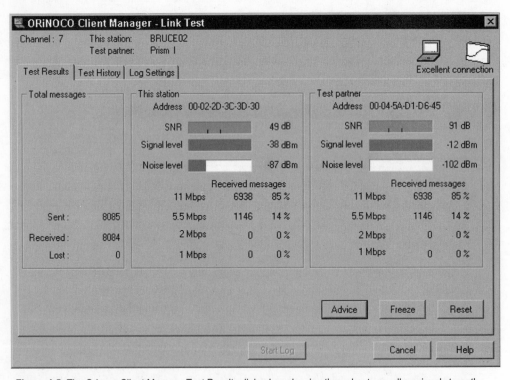

Figure 4-5: The Orinoco Client Manager Test Results dialog box showing throughput as well as signal strength

A few wireless networking vendors have produced software that not only enables you to test signal coverage and throughput, but also generates a comprehensive written report of the site survey results. For example, Intel PRO/Wireless 2011 LAN Site Survey Utility is a free utility software package available for download from Intel's Web technical support site (`http://support.intel.com`). It can perform an impressive array of tests and enables you to easily document the tests that you perform during the site survey. When you have completed the survey, you can use this Site Survey Utility to print a report that includes detailed instructions on where and how to install each AP.

Site Survey Training

Determining the proper placement of an access point is more an art than a science. If you plan to install a very large WLAN, with a potentially substantial price tag, it may be worth the price of admission to get some formal training in site surveying. Several courses are available from high-tech trainers. Cisco, for example, offers a two-and-a-half day course on wireless LAN site surveys.

Contracting for the Site Survey

You always have the option to contract the site survey. You may be able to find a number of wireless networking consultants and/or value-added-resellers in your area who are more than willing to perform the site survey—for a "small" fee.

Summary

This chapter introduces you to the concept of site surveys. It describes the four most important goals of wireless networking site surveys and provides a broad overview of the questions a wireless networking site survey should answer.

When you finish your site survey, you may be anxious to see the WLAN in action. However, first spend a few minutes reviewing the available hardware in order to decide exactly what to purchase and install. Chapter 5 will help you make these important decisions.

Chapter 5

Selecting the Wireless Network Equipment

In This Chapter

This chapter discusses the following:

- Wi-Fi certification
- Access point hardware
- Network interface adapters
- Upcoming standards, including upcoming IEEE 802.11a products and IEEE 802.11g

Perhaps the most frightening part of an IS professional's job is making buying recommendations to a CIO. In the good old days, "No one ever lost his job for recommending IBM." But in today's business climate, nothing is simple. This chapter guides you through the hair-raising process of selecting equipment for a wireless network, including access points and wireless network adapters.

Wi-Fi-Certified Hardware

One aspect of selecting wireless networking hardware is easier than it used to be—ensuring equipment interoperability. As discussed in Chapter 3, IEEE 802.11b is not the only wireless networking standard, but it is currently the most widely adopted standard and is supported by a growing number of vendors. Because IEEE 802.11b leaves some room for vendor customization, an industry group called Wireless Ethernet Compatibility Alliance (WECA) has established a suite of interoperability tests.

WECA is a voluntary organization of over 100 companies that make or support wireless networking products. These companies recognize the value of building a high level of consumer confidence in the interoperability of 802.11b-based products. At the time of this writing, members of WECA include (but are not limited to) the following:

♦ 3Com

♦ Agere Systems

♦ Apple

♦ Cisco

♦ Compaq

♦ Dell

♦ Epson

♦ Gateway

♦ HP

♦ IBM

♦ Intel

♦ Microsoft

♦ NEC

♦ Nokia

♦ Sony

♦ Toshiba

If you decide to build a wireless network around the IEEE 802.11b standard, look for the Wi-Fi logo on the products you buy. Each product that displays this logo has successfully passed the Wi-Fi interoperability tests conducted at Agilent's Interoperability Certification Lab (ICL). As of this writing, 200 products from 58 WECA member companies have received Wi-Fi certification since March 2000.

TIP

You can access an up-to-date list of certified products on WECA's Web site, www.weca.net (see Figure 5-1), or www.wirelessethernet.org. These sites are also good places to find links to the various manufacturers' Web sites, where you can usually find links to online documentation and downloadable software.

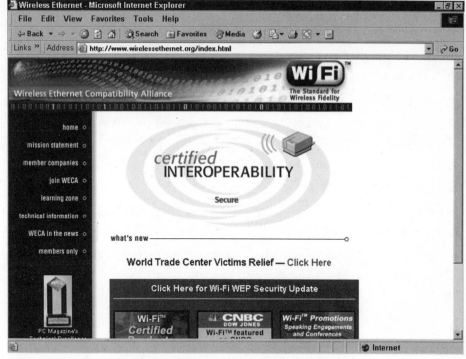

Figure 5-1: The Wireless Ethernet Compatibility Alliance (WECA) Web site

The Wi-Fi Interoperability Test Plan

The Wi-Fi interoperability tests are designed to ensure that hardware from different vendors can successfully establish a communication session with an acceptable level of functionality. The test plan includes a list of necessary features. The features themselves are defined in detail in the 802.11b standard, but the test plan specifies an explicit expected implementation.

For example, the Wi-Fi test plan states that the product being tested must, at least, permit all printable ASCII characters to be used in specifying a service set identifier (SSID) element. In addition, an access point must respond to SSID probe requests. These two requirements help ensure that 802.11b station hardware and access points can determine whether they have matching SSIDs in order to establish an extended service set (ESS). The following features are also tested:

- Beacon interval
- Traffic indication map (TIM) element
- Support for encrypted and unencrypted data payload
- Power save mode
- Support for the Wired Equivalent Privacy (WEP) encryption protocol
- Correct support for receiving a request to send (RTS) signal and for generating a clear-to-send (CTS) signal
- Handling of fragmented packets
- Packet response times
- Data rates
- Error handling
- AP notification of bridges when a station roams from one AP to another

If you want to know exactly what aspects of interoperability are examined by the Wi-Fi test suite, you can download the Wi-Fi interoperability test plan from the WECA site.

Although the Wi-Fi logo ensures a generally acceptable level of interoperability, it still leaves some features that can be implemented differently among product manufacturers. One notable example is the way APs handle roaming wireless stations. Section 2.17 of The Wi-Fi test plan states that, "When a station roams from an old AP to a new AP, the new AP is responsible for ensuring that any bridges between the two APs are properly notified of the station's new location." However, the test plan then notes that the manner of implementing this handoff between APs is left up to the AP manufacturer. Consequently, if you plan to install multiple APs in the same vicinity, they need to be from the same manufacturer to ensure that stations can successfully roam throughout the WLAN.

It's All in the Chips

A significant factor driving the rapid expansion of Wi-Fi-certified products is the existence of high-quality radio chip sets that implement the 802.11b standard. These chip sets typically consist of a *digital signal processor chip* (also called a *baseband processor*) and a *medium access controller chip*. You can find a chip set from either Intersil or Lucent in the majority of purchasable 802.11b access point and wireless NICs.

The reference design for Intersil's PRISM II chip set has Wi-Fi certification and is the most widely used by wireless networking hardware manufacturers. Intersil also has a newer PRISM 2.5 chip set that integrates the signal process and medium access control functions onto a single chip. Manufacturers who use one of the PRISM chip sets include the following:

◆ 3Com	◆ GemTek	◆ Siemens
◆ Addtron	◆ Intel	◆ SMC
◆ Bromax	◆ LeArtery Solutions	◆ Symbol
◆ Cisco Aironet	◆ Linksys	◆ Z-Com
◆ Compaq (WL100)	◆ Nokia	◆ Zoom Telephonics
◆ D-Link	◆ Nortel	
◆ Farallon	◆ Samsung	

The Lucent technology chip set consists of a digital signal processor chip called the *Theseus chip* and a medium access controller chip called the *Hermes chip*. Lucent's chip set is used by another large group of manufacturers, including the following:

◆ 1stWave	◆ Compaq (WL110)	◆ IBM
◆ Agere ORiNOCO	◆ Dell (1150)	◆ Sony
◆ ARtem	◆ ELSA	◆ Toshiba
◆ Avaya	◆ Enterasys Roamabout	
◆ Buffalo	◆ Hewlett Packard	

> **NOTE**
>
> Manufacturers may sometimes switch from one original equipment manufacturer to another. The preceding lists were accurate at the time of this writing. Check with the manufacturer's specifications or a company representative to determine the chip set used in any product line you are researching.

In some cases, the hardware from different companies is actually manufactured by the same *original equipment manufacturer* (OEM), resulting in virtually identical products with different names. This is particularly true for PCMCIA cards. Most, if not all, of the Hermes-based cards are manufactured by Lucent, for example (see Figure 5-2). Cisco purchased the Aironet company, which manufactures virtually identical cards sold under the Cisco, Dell, and Xircom labels.

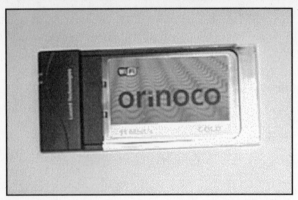

Figure 5-2: A Hermes-based PC card manufactured by Lucent and sold under the ORiNOCO brand name

In other cases, equipment that uses the same technology may have been manufactured by different OEMs. Most of the PRISM-based products fall into this category. The two PC cards shown in Figure 5-3 both use PRISM chip sets, but are produced by different OEMs.

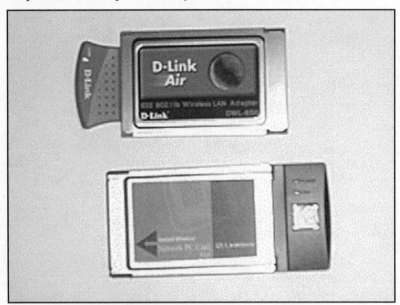

Figure 5-3: Two wireless LAN PC cards based on the PRISM chip set

The fact that so many available Wi-Fi products are based on only two chip set families increases the chance that products from different companies will be interoperable, even beyond the requirements of Wi-Fi certification.

Access Points

The access point (AP) is the heart of each segment of a wireless LAN. Not coincidentally, APs are likely to be the most expensive components in a WLAN. Depending on the manufacturer and included features, the price of an AP ranges from about $150 to $1,500.

Although it is certainly true that with APs "you get what you pay for," the lowest-priced units are surprisingly capable, probably because all access point designs must comply with 802.11b and undergo the same Wi-Fi-certification testing. Plus, nearly all start with one of two chip set families. The Intersil PRISM 2 AP chip set used by many manufacturers, for example, includes all of the following:

♦ A wireless LAN AP controller chip

♦ Baseband processor chip

♦ An I/Q modulator/demodulator and synthesizer

♦ A 2.4 GHz RF/IF converter and synthesizer

♦ A 2.4 GHz power amplifier and detector

Differences exist, however, between the bargain-priced units and the fully loaded models. The features you will find useful, or even mandatory, depend on the intended use for your wireless network.

Industrial-Strength

For most business uses requiring more than a couple of APs, the most important requirements for a wireless access point are as follows:

♦ Ease of installation, setup, and maintenance

♦ Availability of reliable technical support

♦ Adequate network capacity to support existing users and projected growth

♦ Range and coverage

♦ Security

♦ Total cost of ownership

The last requirement—total cost of ownership (TCO)—can be a slippery marketing buzzword, but it is a real issue for all IS departments that need to keep budgets under control (especially during lean economic times). However, TCO is a complex function of all the other requirements listed above combined. The following sections explore the selection of access point products in terms of the first five requirements.

Ease of Installation, Setup, and Maintenance

To achieve the best range and coverage, you often want to install APs toward the center of large rooms, suspended from the ceiling or hanging from a wall. All the 802.11b access points currently available are roughly the size of a small hardback book (see Figure 5-4). They don't take up much space and are not very heavy; however, make sure that each AP comes with its own mounting bracket or that such a bracket is readily available.

Figure 5-4: APs are generally about the size of a small hardback book.

All APs are powered by electricity, so consider whether electrical outlets are conveniently located. Hiring an electrician to pull a new electrical circuit for each AP could be a significant expense. Fortunately, a few of the high-end APs (models from Cisco and ORiNOCO, for example) can be powered over the Ethernet cable that already runs to the AP. A device called a *power injector* provides DC power over the Ethernet cable to the AP. In some cases, this feature alone may convince you to select a particular vendor's AP solution.

APs from all vendors ship with several utility programs that help you perform the site survey and then set up and configure the device. An important selling feature of any AP is that, ideally, the setup process can be accomplished quickly and efficiently, especially if your project requires many boxes. The ease of setup and configuration will depend partly on the available utilities and partly on whether all APs can be configured remotely—that is over the network, rather than by connecting a computer directly to each AP.

Most available APs can be configured either through the RJ45 Ethernet port or through an RS232 port. The best varieties enable you to configure the device by connecting through the Ethernet port and accessing an embedded set of Web pages. In certain cases, it may be more convenient to configure all APs in the lab rather than waiting until you are in the field with APs hanging from the ceiling. However, the best APs come with centralized management software that enables you to manage all the APs after the APs are in place from a single SNMP (*Simple Network Management Protocol*) utility program or through a Web interface using a Web browser. The best utilities automatically locate and catalog all the APs in the WLAN and enable you to configure them from a single management screen.

As a colleague recently reminded me, selecting computer technology is like shooting at a moving target. By the time you make a purchase and install it, something better is announced or on the shelf. Luckily, many features of 802.11b access points are implemented in updateable firmware. Before you decide which AP to buy, determine whether you will be able to get feature upgrades and fixes from the vendor and whether you can perform the updates by flashing the firmware.

CAUTION

If you add or replace an external antenna to an AP, keep in mind that the FCC has limited the power output permissible from an AP operating in an unlicensed frequency band. Each AP manufacturer submits each AP to the FCC for licensing as an entire system, including antenna. Several manufacturers sell add-on antennas that have also received FCC approval. If you purchase and install an antenna from a company other than the manufacturer of the AP, you run the risk of building a system that would exceed the FCC imposed power limits. The same caution applies to after-market amplifiers.

Most of the time, APs are installed without changing the original equipment antennas. However, you may have situations where the range and coverage of a particular AP could be significantly improved by replacing a stock antenna with a higher gain upgraded version, or perhaps by installing an antenna in a better location and then running a lead cable from the antenna to the AP. Some APs have only internal antennas, whereas others provide the option of adding external antennas. External antennas, as a rule, produce a stronger signal than internal antennas; so you probably want to choose only APs with upgradeable external antennas.

Availability of Technical Support

For large installations, a significant factor related to ease of maintenance and TCO is the availability and quality of technical support from the product manufacturer or system integrator. The least expensive APs on the market cost less than 20 percent of the initial cost of the most expensive units; however, if necessary technical support is available less than 20 percent of the time, you may regret the decision to save money up front.

Only real-world experience tells you whether technical support is adequate; so whenever possible, stick with manufacturers and/or system integrators with whom you have had good experiences.

Don't be shy about changing your mind later if your initial choice proves to be wrong. If you have chosen Wi-Fi-certified equipment, your investment should be sound, even if you switch to a different AP manufacturer midstream. You may have to forgo proprietary enhancements, but doing so may be an acceptable price in exchange for reliable support from the vendor.

Adequate Network Capacity

Use the site survey (discussed in Chapter 4) to calculate how many APs you need to install to ensure adequate network capacity. In some situations, however, you may not be able to accurately predict the peak loads. In a college environment, for example, when a class is meeting, a surge in the load of the nearest AP may suddenly occur. You need to be confident that the surge won't shut down that segment of the WLAN altogether. In locations where you expect that the load could grow rapidly, either provide excess capacity from the start or plan for quickly adding capacity should the need arise.

At a minimum, check the manufacturer's stated maximum number of simultaneous users. If practical, you can overlap AP coverage areas to double the capacity where usage will potentially saturate a single cell. Be careful, however, to choose DSSS channels that are sufficiently separated so that they don't interfere with each other (usually at least 30 MHz of separation, although you may be able to get away with 25 MHz).

Determine whether there is a provision for adding a second radio (that is, a PC card) to the AP. A second radio, set to a noninterfering channel, should double the AP's capacity by effectively creating two concentric cells. As an added benefit, some APs, such as the ORiNOCO AP-2000, can support a second radio that complies with the 54 Mbps 802.11a standard, providing a nice upgrade path.

Range and Coverage

Another goal of the site survey is to ensure adequate range and coverage. The site survey, however, is based on assumed minimums for AP range and coverage. When you select a line of APs for a WLAN, make sure that the actual capabilities of the APs match your site survey assumptions.

Try to narrow your choice down to two or three AP candidates, and then perform a "shoot out" to test range and coverage in a real-world environment. If possible, hold all other variables constant, such as the wireless network card that you use in the test laptop and the exact position of the AP that you are testing. Reception can vary between wireless network cards, and moving an AP just a few feet can change the signal pattern.

You will probably find that APs with external antennas outperform APs with internal antennas, and APs with dual antennas (shown in Figure 5-4) outperform single-antenna models. Dual-antenna units, with the diversity feature activated, continually sample the signal that each antenna receives from a particular station and select the best signal. If the AP doesn't come with external antennas, determine whether they are available as an option.

The important question is whether the real performance of each AP matches your plan. Reject any AP that does not provide the coverage you have planned for. Keep in mind that moving an AP a few feet one way or the other can make a significant difference in how far the signal reaches in the proposed cell.

Sometimes the coverage you get may be more than you need. For example, one cell may bleed into another, causing interference; or perhaps you want to reduce the strength of the signal that emanates outside your company's building walls. In these situations, consider using a directional antenna to control where the signal propagates. Even better, a few of the best APs enable you to adjust the power output, giving you better control over signal strength and coverage. You can configure the Cisco Aironet 350 series, for example, to transmit at 1, 4, 20, 30, 50, or 100 mW as needed to control coverage or minimize interference.

Security

The fact that the WEP security feature of 802.11b networks can be "hacked" has probably been much overblown. It is seldom reported that regular changing of keys greatly reduces the risk of a successful WEP attack. Nonetheless, several of the high-end (and high-priced) AP vendors offer sophisticated key-management programs to help you change encryption keys frequently. However, in a large installation, even with the aid of software, frequent reconfiguring APs and station cards can become a major headache.

You take a much greater security risk if you don't use WEP at all. Even so, concerns about the perceived weaknesses in WEP have caused some companies to put off the decision to install a wireless LAN. To address these concerns, the IEEE 802.11 committee is actively working on an "official" solution, and several leading hardware manufacturers, including Cisco and ORiNOCO, are shipping products that include their own proprietary solutions. If your company plans to secure the WLAN by creating a VPN (using IPSec, for example), WEP is not really a concern. However, if your only means of keeping prying eyes away from your network is WEP, consider using one of these proprietary solutions. Although these proprietary WEP enhancements are usually backward compatible—that is, they still support plain old WEP—keep in mind that the wireless adapters used by each workstation must also be from the same manufacturer in order to use the enhanced WEP.

A *MAC filter* is a security feature of a different sort that is available in many AP implementations. Because communication between the AP and the stations that belong to the same ESS (extended service set) occurs at the MAC address level, the AP can theoretically set up a filter that can either block certain MAC addresses or permit a given list of MAC addresses to access the WLAN. The latter type of filter is the preferred feature. If you have a finite set of users who will need access to each given segment, look for an AP that enables you to enter this list of MAC addresses in a filter table. Wireless stations with any other MAC address will not be added to the ESS.

CAUTION

Although the MAC filter feature is a desirable security enhancement, it should not be used as the only form of security. A determined hacker may discover the MAC address of a legitimate user and then use software to masquerade as that MAC address. The AP would permit the hacker to join the network. This is called a *spoof attack*.

Small Business/Home Gateways

The access point requirements for a small business or home network differ somewhat from those of larger businesses. If your home or business establishment is approximately less than three thousand square feet in size, you can probably make do with a single AP—depending, of course, on the physical layout and construction materials. Larger homes and businesses (up to about ten thousand square feet) will need two or three APs to do the job. Because the number of APs is so small, you don't need to be as careful about ease of installation, setup, and maintenance. You still want good technical support, but only if it is available free-of-charge (over a toll-free tech support line or through an online chat session).

Range and coverage will be important to you even if you are covering a small facility. Look for APs with external antennas, preferably two. After you buy an AP, you may have to experiment a little to find the best placement. If you can get a good signal in portions of your home or office, but not in others within the same radius from the AP, try repositioning the AP to a spot with smaller "shadows" cast by walls and other solid objects. The fewer walls the signal has to pass through, the stronger the signal will be. Also, consider adding a better antenna. Figure 5-5 shows a picture of an external antenna that is designed to replace one of the "rubber ducky"-style antennas that come installed on most APs with external antennas. Using such an antenna can significantly increase the strength of the signal, as well as its range.

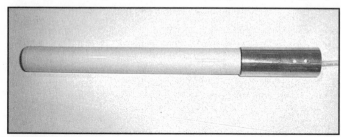

Figure 5-5: An external antenna

In a home or small office network, you may need to consider the necessity of a *Dynamic Host Configuration Protocol (DHCP) server* and an Internet gateway. Most likely, a business of any size already has a wired network with one or more DHCP servers and existing Internet service. However, many homes and small businesses are only now being wired for fast Internet access and are adding local area networks. These homes and businesses have neither a DHCP server nor a shared Internet connection.

A DHCP server dynamically assigns IP addresses to the client computers in a network segment. These temporary IP addresses are *leased* to each station for a set time (72 hours) and periodically renewed or released. A DHCP server relieves the network administrator from having to keep track of all the devices on the network and from having to assign addresses to each one. The DHCP server maintains a database of all the current DHCP clients, issuing new addresses as requested.

An Internet Gateway enables multiple computers to share the same connection to the Internet—that is, the same IP address. This function is often performed by a router that provides a service called *network address translation (NAT)*. The NAT service communicates with each station on the network using the private IP addresses assigned by the DHCP server, but uses a single IP address—the one assigned by the *Internet Service Provider* (ISP), which may have also been assigned by the ISP's DHCP server—in packets intended for the Internet.

In a small network or home network, it is very convenient to combine the DHCP and Internet gateway functions into one device. It's even better if these functions can be combined with the wireless networking AP function. Not surprisingly, several manufacturers have developed products that nicely fit this description. These one-stop combination AP/DHCP/routers are sometimes called *residential gateways* because they are frequently marketed to the home user. If you are planning to add a WLAN to your home or small office, take a close look at the residential gateways. The AP in Figure 5-5 is an example of such a device. In fact, the unit shown in the picture, a product from Linksys, also includes a switched hub that can handle up to four wired connections in addition to an unspecified number of wireless stations. By using one of these devices, all the computers in your home or business will be able to share files and printers, as well as an Internet connection.

Software-Based Access Points

In addition to hardware-based access points, software-based access points are also available. It is possible to create an access point using one of the existing wireless NIC cards as the radio and a PC to run the access point controller software. This design seems like a good idea because of the computing power available in modern PCs. You should be able to get more capacity, range, and throughput out of a 1.5 GHz PC than a $200 standalone access point device.

However, although some AP management functions probably run more rapidly in a fast PC, in the final analysis, software-based APs are the best solution only in limited circumstances.

The major drawback to using a PC to run AP software is the likelihood that you will use this PC to do other work as well. If you ever need to reboot the computer, or someone turns it off to conserve power, the WLAN that this AP is serving also goes down.

Second, you cannot easily position an AP-in-a-PC in the optimum position for maximizing radio reception. Rather, you will place the PC wherever you otherwise need to use it, and the AP function will tag along.

Finally, the cost of purchasing the wireless NIC should be included in the actual cost of building a software-based AP. When you add the price of the software to the price of the NIC, the total may actually exceed the cost of a comparable standalone access point device.

In a few situations, however, you may find a software-based AP quite a good deal. If you have already purchased a wireless network adapter that is compatible with the AP software, the cost of acquisition is now only the cost of the software. This cost may be less than buying a standalone AP. In a home or small office environment, you may want to add only one or two additional computers to a network. The drawbacks previously described may not really apply to your situation. In fact, you may already have the software—as in the case of the Base Station software that ships with Apple Airport wireless adapters—so you might as well use it.

Even if you aren't prepared to purchase software-based access points, you may want to evaluate a few of them.

♦ ZoomAir 11 Mbps Access Point Software from Zoom Telephonics and Compaq's WL300 Wireless LAN Software Access Point both enable you to use a Windows PC as an access point. In order to use either of these products, you must also have a wireless network adapter installed in the PC—ostensibly from the same manufacturer. The wireless NICs explicitly supported by these products are PRISM-based cards, so you could potentially use this software with any PRISM wireless NIC. Compaq's most current wireless networking offerings, however, are OEM'd Lucent products; so Compaq no longer promotes this PRISM-based software AP.

Both ZoomAir and Compaq WL300 have very basic features, but are probably adequate for home use or even for a small office. Unless you can find this software at a very good price (the Compaq product is available online for as little as $49.99, but the ZoomAir product costs over $150 at press time), you will probably do better with a standalone product.

♦ IP NetRouter from Sustainable Softworks is an inexpensive product that enables a Mac to act as an access point and router. Apple licenses a version of this software under the name Software Base Station and includes it free with its Airport products. The full IP NetRouter provides more configuration options and documentation that is more complete than the Apple version. It also includes a DHCP server, NAT services, and IP filtering.

♦ If you want to use a Linux-based system to build a software-based AP, consider a free software product written by Jouni Malinen and available for download at www.epitest.fi/Prism2. This product was developed to run in the Linux 2.4x environment, but may also work with Linux 2.2x kernels. As you may have guessed, this product supports only wireless PC cards build on the PRISM II chipset. It is licensed under the GNU General Public License Version 2, as published by the Free Software Foundation.

Network Interface Adapters for Client Stations

By now, you should know the most important issues relating to the selection of wireless network interface cards (NICs) for client stations:

♦ Wi-Fi certification

♦ The chip set on which the card is based

♦ Compatability with proprietary extended features that are supported by the WLAN's access points

At a minimum, all wireless NICs in a WLAN should be Wi-Fi-certified to ensure a minimum level of interoperability. Even better, all cards should come from the same company that manufactured the access points used in the WLAN to ensure maximum interoperability and to take full advantage of any extended features that the APs offer.

In addition, a few other factors should be considered when deciding on wireless NICs.

PC Cards

Probably because the concept of wireless networking is associated with portability, most wireless NICs are built as *Personal Computer Memory Card International Association* (PCMIA) cards (also called *PC cards*, or *PC bus cards*; previously shown in Figures 5-2 and 5-3). Nearly all Windows and some Mac notebook/laptops have PCMCIA ports that are compatible with these cards.

AN AIRPORT CARD IS NOT A PC CARD

Apple Macintosh computers were the first to have wireless networking capability. All new Macs come either with built-in 802.11b wireless connectivity or with an Airport slot ready to receive an Airport card — which is not the same as a PC card slot. Some Mac laptops have both an Airport slot and a PC card slot. Apple computers that are equipped with an Airport slot also have built-in antennas; therefore, in contrast with wireless PC cards, nothing protrudes from the Mac when an Airport card is inserted. Older Macs, built before the introduction of the Airport, have neither an Airport slot nor a PC card slot.

Most laptops have two type-II PC card slots and one type-III slot. Most wireless PC cards are built in the type-II form factor. All wireless PC cards must have an antenna so that the built-in radio can communicate with an AP. Most have a built-in *patch* antenna that is enclosed in a plastic casing that protrudes from the PC while the card is fully inserted. One manufacturer offers a retractable antenna that is less likely to get damaged when not in use.

Many brands of PC cards include antennas that are enclosed in a casing that is thicker than the type II card. The card still fits in the type II slot, but the antenna may block the other type II slot. For most users, this should not pose a serious problem, however. In cases where a user needs to have two PC cards inserted at the same time, he or she can insert the wireless NIC in the top slot, leaving the bottom slot unimpeded. If you feel that the thickness of the antenna casing is an issue, several manufacturers offer wireless PC cards that have antenna casings no thicker than the rest of the card.

A larger concern is the reception achievable by the antennas embedded in wireless PC cards. Antennas work best when oriented vertically (that is, placed at least at a 90-degree angle to the ground). Patch antennas embedded in a PC card will always be oriented horizontally. Consequently, these cards are working from a built-in disadvantage. Some brands of wireless NICs don't receive a signal as well as others. Make sure that the cards you choose will provide the reception that the WLAN users expect.

Before you make a big investment in these devices, narrow your choices to a few options and then compare them in a real-world test, holding the AP constant and varying the NICs to determine which brand gives the best reception and throughput.

Some manufacturers offer two versions of the same card—one with 64-bit WEP encryption and the other with 128-bit encryption. As my father would say, "You pay your money and you make your choice." For my money, I'd go with the most robust-featured set available, unless the cost differential is prohibitive.

The current generation of wireless PC cards supports Windows 9*x*, Windows NT, and Windows 2000. At the time Windows XP shipped, however, drivers for only a few wireless PC cards were included "in the box" (on the installation CD). If you expect to install wireless PC cards in PCs running Windows XP, check with the manufacturer of the cards you select to make sure a driver is or soon will be available.

NOTE

Both the Lucent and Intersil chip sets support the Mac OS and Linux, but most wireless PC card manufacturers include only drivers for Windows with their products. Several cards are available, however, for the Mac OS (such as the SkyLine PC card from Proxim—formerly Farallon) as well as for Linux (such as the ORiNOCO PC card).

PCI Adapters

In situations where the WLAN is the only way to connect users to the network, you need to install a wireless NIC in every PC, including the desktop PCs. Nearly all desktop PCs are without a PC card slot, but all new PCs should have at least one *Peripheral Component Interconnect (PCI) slot*. Consequently, most wireless NIC manufacturers offer a wireless PCI adapter—a version of their product that can be installed in a PCI slot (see Figure 5-6).

Most wireless PCI adapters are cards that adapt a PC card for use in a PCI slot. In most designs, the PC card's built-in antenna casing protrudes from the back of the computer case. Some designs completely enclose the PC card inside the computer case and include a larger dipole antenna that is attached to the back of the computer case.

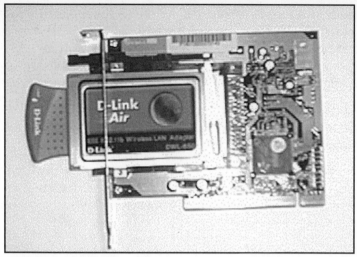

Figure 5-6: A wireless PCI adapter

Even though newer versions of Apple Macintosh computers contain PCI slots and both the Lucent and Intersil chip sets support the Mac, most wireless PCI adapters will not work in a Mac. To my knowledge, the Skyline PCI card from Proxim (formerly Farallon) is the only PCI card that enables you to add a wireless NIC to a Mac that doesn't have either a PC card slot or an Airport slot.

> **CAUTION**
>
> Although many wireless PCI adapters look something like a general-purpose PCMCIA slot for a desktop PC, they are not. They are designed only to support a wireless PC card, and then only from the same manufacturer (although I suspect that many are from the same OEM and would work with PC cards from several manufacturers). You should not insert or remove a wireless PC card while the computer is running—something that is permitted in real PCMCIA slots. If you want to remove the PC card so that you can use it in a laptop computer, first shut down the computer and make sure the power has been turned off.

USB Adapters

In the last couple of years, the *Universal Serial Bus (USB) standard* has become the most ubiquitous method of connecting peripherals to a PC. First popularized in the Apple iMac, USB supports a data transfer rate of 480 Mbps, many times faster than the fastest wireless network transmission rate. USB is, therefore, a good candidate for connecting an external wireless network adapter to either a laptop or a desktop PC. Several wireless networking hardware vendors offer USB wireless network adapters.

USB's popularity has grown rapidly because it simplifies the procedure for connecting a device to a PC. This holds true for wireless NICs. USB wireless NICs are sometimes a better choice than PC Cards or PCI cards. If a computer doesn't have a PC card slot, but does have a USB port, you either need to install a PCI adapter or select a USB wireless network adapter.

As with PC cards and PCI cards, it is ideal to use the same brand of USB wireless network adapter as the AP; however, any Wi-Fi-certified USB adapter is interoperable with any 802.11b AP.

In addition to their plug-and-play convenience, another advantage that USB adapters sometimes have over PC cards and PCI cards is the size and orientation of their antennas. The ORiNOCO USB adapter, for example, is oriented vertically to enable the embedded antenna to be positioned vertically.

Oddly enough, even though the Mac was the first to use USB, no manufacturer is currently offering a USB wireless network adapter for Macintosh computers.

CF Cards

The newest addition category of wireless network adapters uses a *Compact Flash (CF) interface* to enable connection to PDAs and other devices. Using a CF device, such as the Spectrum24 High Rate Wireless Networker CompactFlash Card from Symbol Technologies, for example, you can connect a Pocket PC to a WLAN. At least one vendor (D-Link) offers an adapter for the CF card that converts the CF wireless NIC into a PC card.

Only time and the marketplace will determine whether 802.11-based technology, Bluetooth, or some yet unidentified technology will become the dominant method of connecting PDAs and other small devices to local area networks. The list of potential applications of wireless technology to handheld electronic devices is virtually limitless.

External Antennas

If there is a single weak link in the wireless networking suite of products, it is probably the poor antennas built into most wireless NICs. As previously noted in the section on APs, an external antenna usually performs better than an internal antenna. Unfortunately, neither the 802.11b standard nor the

Wi-Fi interoperability tests specify a standard connector for external antennas; so there is no generic antenna that will work with all wireless NICs. There are, however, external antennas available for some wireless PC cards from the card manufacturers.

If a user is having difficulty getting good reception, adding an external antenna may greatly improve the situation. The external antenna will naturally have better reception because of its size, but because it connects by a cable to the PC card, it will also enable the user to fine tune the antenna's positioning to get the best reception—reminiscent of the old rabbit-ear TV antennas.

Wireless PC cards built by Lucent have a connector at the end of the antenna casing into which you can plug an external *range extender* antenna cable. Lucent (under its various brand names) sells an antenna to attach to the cable.

Some wireless PCI adapters have connectors for external antennas. Because PCI adapters are typically used in desktop computers, you may need to run a feed cable from the antenna connector at the back of the computer. This enables you to mount the external antenna in a spot with a clear line of sight to the AP's antenna in order to get the best reception.

In addition to optional antennas offered by the wireless NIC's manufacturer, you should be able to find third-party cables that are terminated in a generic antenna connector. These cables will give you the most flexibility to add third-party antennas.

Planning Ahead

The discussion of IEEE 802.11 in Chapter 2 describes several faster alternatives to the 802.11b technology that will soon be available. If you are in the process of selecting hardware for a wireless network and can't wait for the arrival of these new standards, you should at least plan a migration path.

Planning for 802.11a

Products based on the IEEE 802.11a standard are the first available standards-based WLAN products to have faster transmission speeds (up to 54 Mbps) than the current market-leading 802.11b products. Proxim was the first to ship 802.11a products, with many competitors' products following.

The introduction of 802.11a products is following a similar pattern to that of 802.11b products. WECA has announced that 802.11a products that pass the suite of interoperability tests will carry a new Wi-Fi5 logo to distinguish them from the 802.11b/Wi-Fi products. Many of the same companies that lead the Wi-Fi pack are at the head of the Wi-Fi5 pack as well. Several chip sets are already available.

The first company to ship 802.11a-based products, Proxim, bases its products on the AR5000 chip set from Atheros, the first company to receive the Microsoft Designed for Windows XP Logo Program certification for an 802.11a wireless networking solution.

In addition to the Atheros chip set, Intersil is ready with its own chip set based on the 802.11a standard, the PRISM Indigo 54 Mbps 5 GHz chip set. The Intersil chip set will also support the very similar ETSI HIPERLAN/2 standard. Both the Atheros chip set and the Intersil chip set are available in a small enough form factor to facilitate use in both PC cards and CF cards.

Much has been said in the computer trade press about the lack of compatibility between 802.11a and 802.11b products. These two standards operate in different ISM frequency bands. There are, however, a couple of ways to deal with the likelihood that you will eventually have Wi-Fi5 wireless stations that need to connect to your WLAN.

Both Proxim and Agere ORiNOCO now offer access points that can support both 802.11a and 802.11b. If you are about to implement an 802.11b WLAN and you are concerned that you will soon need to support 802.11a devices as well, consider adopting one of these products. The Agere product, for example, enables you to upgrade a particular AP to 802.11a support by simply inserting an 802.11a PC card to the AP into the available PC bus slot.

Another approach, not tied to a specific vendor, is to install another access point in any portion of the WLAN that needs 802.11a support. Because 802.11a and 802.11b are compatible at the LLC layer, you can use a mix of both types of APs on the same WLAN. Each will be on a separate wireless segment of the WLAN, which will help to balance the network load. Because 802.11a segments will not interfere with any existing 802.11b segments, this upgrade should be easy to implement. (Of course, if you have many APs in the system, the upgrade could also get expensive.)

Ideally, the 802.11a wireless NICs would be backward compatible with 802.11b APs so that IS departments could upgrade APs at their own pace without having to worry that 802.11a stations won't have network access. Dual-mode wireless cards will certainly be introduced by one or more of the many companies competing in this market. The 802.11a standard, however, does not mandate this capability, so it won't be uniformly available for some time (at least until 802.11g-based products come along).

Planning for 802.11g

The IEEE 802.11g standard is still a work in progress. The proposed standard mandates the use of *Orthogonal Frequency Division Multiplexing* (OFDM) but also includes *Complementary Code Keying* (CCK)-OFDM (from Intersil) and *Packet Binary Convolutional Coding* (PBCC) (from Texas Instruments) as options. The full details of the specification and a timetable for the arrival of products have yet to be determined. The big news on the 802.11g front is that it will be backward compatible with 802.11b wireless LAN technology but will still deliver the same transmission speeds as 802.11a—up to 54 Mbps. The fact that market-leading Intersil, as well as Texas Instruments, is already supporting the underlying technology bodes well for swift industry adoption as soon as the standard is fully approved.

The high probability that 802.11g products will be developed and released in the not-so-distant future obviates the concern that 802.11b WLANs will not be able to support the 54 Mbps transmission speed offered by the new 802.11a WLANs. Products based on 802.11g could be on the market by mid-2002.

Summary

This chapter explores Wi-Fi certification, selecting access-point hardware, selecting wireless network-interface cards, and the upcoming products based on IEEE standards 802.11a and 802.11g. After you have made your decision on the hardware you will use in your wireless network, you are ready to begin installation.

Chapter 6 covers issues that are unique to home-based LANs. If you are installing a network in your home, turn directly to this chapter. IS professionals, on the other hand, should turn to Part II that covers the installation of a wireless network. You may want to start with Chapter 7, "Installing Access Points," for a few tips on setting up and configuring the APs in your wireless network.

Chapter 6

Planning a Home Wireless Network

In This Chapter

This chapter covers the following topics:

- Budgeting
- Performing a site survey
- Interoperability with an office WLAN
- Connecting to the Internet
- Residential gateways
- Security

This book should serve the needs of home wireless local area network (WLAN) users as well as those of corporate IS departments responsible for setting up and maintaining business WLANs. That said, even a corporate IS department may want to set up a home WLAN. Most top corporate executives need continuous connectivity to their company's information infrastructure. Any IS director who can provide this capability to a CEO, CFO, or CIO in his home, without having to run any cables, will probably be considered a hero.

Increasingly, employees and entrepreneurs of all types are obtaining high-speed Internet connections for their homes. The natural next step is to network several of their home computers to share printers and the Internet connection. If they haven't already wired their homes for networking, building a WLAN may be the perfect solution. Indeed, wireless local area networks may offer more advantages to home users than to any other group of potential users. Although corporate WLANs currently outnumber home WLANs two to one, at least one market research firm predicts that the number of home WLANs will exceed office WLANs within the next four years.

This chapter shows you how to budget for a home WLAN, walks you through the process of performing a site survey, helps you ensure compatibility with office WLANs, and discusses other considerations, such as security, connecting your computer to the office LAN, and sharing Internet connections with the neighbors.

Budgeting for a WLAN

The out-of-pocket costs required to set up a wireless network are an important consideration for any consumer, but especially so for the home user because home-network budgets are usually much smaller than their corporate counterparts.

Wireless networking hardware is available at a wide range of prices:

♦ Basic wireless access points (APs), sometimes called *base stations,* range in price from about $150 (street price) to around $300. (*Street price* is the price at which you can purchase the product from a retail outlet such as a computer-electronics retail store, or an online retailer—the *suggested retail price* is often higher).

♦ Multifunction access points that facilitate connecting multiple computers to the Internet (sometimes called *gateways* or *home gateways)* range in price from about $200 to $350.

♦ Small business access points range in price from about $400 to $750.

♦ Enterprise-class access points range in price from $800 to over $1,000.

When planning to purchase an AP for home use, you should budget at least $250, although you will probably find what you need for $200 or less.

Wireless network interface cards (NICs) range in price from $100 to $200 for PC card varieties—those used primarily in laptop computers. I would budget at least $150.

If you plan to connect a desktop computer, you will need a PCI or ISA adapter—available as a card into which you plug a wireless PC card, as an adapter that comes with the PC card, or as an adapter card that comes with an external antenna installed. Prices for these products range from $150 to almost $300. Budget at least $225.

If your setup, for example, involves a cable modem Internet connection, two laptop computers, and a home desktop computer that you want to connect via a wireless LAN, your hardware budget may resemble that shown in Table 6-1.

Table 6-1: Home Wireless LAN Budget

Item	Low Price	High Price	Budgeted Expense	Quantity	Total Expense
AP	$200	$300	$250	1	$250
PC card	$100	$200	$150	2	$300
PCI adapter	$150	$300	$225	1	$225
					$775

To be safe, budget at least another $100 for miscellaneous items, such as category 5 twisted-pair cable to run from the cable modem to the AP, installation hardware, and tools.

The budgeted expense detailed in Table 6-1 for setting up a home wireless LAN does not cover the cost of buying or renting the cable modem.

Performing a Site Survey

Chapter 4 describes the process of performing site surveys for a business WLAN. You can follow a similar approach for a home WLAN. You may recall the four areas of focus for a site survey:

♦ Signal coverage and range

♦ Network capacity

♦ RF interference

♦ Power requirements

Note that *network capacity* probably won't be an issue with home WLANs the way it is with business WLANs. Even the least expensive APs can handle as many as 32 wireless stations at once.

The following sections address the other three areas of focus for your home site survey.

Signal Coverage and Range

The most important aspect of a home WLAN site survey is evaluation of signal coverage and range. Keep in mind that your evaluation will be most effective if you take a common sense approach to determining the best placement of an AP. If you have a drawing of your house plan, make a couple of photocopies to use for sketching tentative WLAN plans.

Start with the assumption that you will use an omnidirectional antenna, which propagates a signal in a spherical shape. Most AP manufacturers claim a range of 100 feet indoors, at 11 Mbps. To be conservative, assume a range of 60 feet laterally and one floor above or below the AP. With this information in mind, you should be able to answer the following questions:

1. Will one AP be sufficient?
2. Where should the AP(s) be placed?

The signal pattern that radiates from an AP is shaped like a fat doughnut with a tiny hole in the middle. The hole is directly above and below the antenna. Due to this signal pattern, the AP should be placed as close to the very center of the house as is practically possible. Use the drawing of your house plan to locate the center of the house. This spot will be your first trial AP location. The signal radiates from the antenna to the floor above and the floor below, as well as to the floor on which the AP is located; so if your house has multiple floors, try the second floor first.

Draw a circle with a 60-foot radius on your house plan, using the trial AP location as the center of the circle. If your entire house falls inside the circle, one AP will probably do the job. Conversely, if some portion of the house is outside the circle, coverage may be weaker in that area.

If you determine that one AP will not cover your house, you need to decide how best to place two APs (or even three, as necessary). The design of your house will determine the best placement. For a one-level design, start at one end of the house and determine the best location for a 60-foot radius circle that will cover all the way to the walls. The center of this circle is the location of the first AP. Then move toward the other end of the house, drawing 60-foot radius circles until the house is covered. The center of each circle will be a trial location of an AP. If possible, don't leave any area in the house uncovered.

CONSIDER USING AN EXTERNAL ANTENNA

On Internet newsgroups and mailing lists, the most frequent complaint about wireless networks is the poor quality of the signal. Although some users don't experience any problems, others seem to have an inordinate number. The fact is, external antennas, which are larger than internal antennas, normally get better reception. Furthermore, because external antennas connect by cable to the PC card, the user can finetune the antenna's positioning to get the best reception. External antennas are available for some wireless PC cards and wireless PCI adapters. Keep that in mind when choosing a hardware vendor.

RF Interference

Microwave ovens and portable (cordless) telephones are the two most likely sources of 2.4-GHz RF interference in the home. The best way to avoid this interference is to keep AP placement and wireless station placement at least six feet away from the microwave and the base station of any portable phone that uses the 2.4-GHz band.

Bluetooth devices also use the 2.4 GHz band, but the hop pattern of the Bluetooth modulation protocol all but ensures that any interference will be short enough in duration to be negligible.

Power Requirements

Only the more expensive APs can be powered over the Ethernet cable. Most likely, you will need to place your AP near a power outlet. Examine the tentative AP locations in your home WLAN to determine whether each AP's electrical cord is within reach of an electrical outlet. If not, adjust the location of the AP.

Ideally, your AP would be suspended from the ceiling. However, ceilings usually don't contain electrical outlets (except perhaps in the garage, for a garage door opener). Furthermore, an AP on the ceiling would be unsightly. A better solution is to place the AP on top of a desk, or even a bookcase—the higher the better—that is both near the center of the house (or portion of the house that you are covering), and near an electrical outlet.

Ethernet Connection

If you intend to use the WLAN to share a DSL or cable modem, you will also have to run an Ethernet (category 5) cable from the modem to the AP. The modem may already be located in the same spot, but if not, decide how you will run the cable to the AP.

CROSS-REFERENCE

Refer to Chapter 10 for a few suggestions on running the cable, for an RJ-45 color chart, and for instructions on crimping the cable connectors.

Ensuring Interoperability with Office WLANs

In some cases, individuals decide to install a wireless network at home after experience with one at the office. Connecting to your home network or the office network is then as easy as turning on the computer—no cables to deal with, and not tied to a desk. If your office WLAN is Wi-Fi-certified and you purchase only Wi-Fi-certified products for your home WLAN, you should feel confident that your office laptop will be able to communicate with your home WLAN. The only issue may be the SSID. If your office WLAN's network administrator has specified that all stations connecting to the WLAN must use a particular SSID, you may have to assign the same SSID to your home WLAN. Even if your home WLAN has a different SSID than your office WLAN, connecting at each location is still very simple. If your computer uses the Windows XP operating system, you can configure both SSIDs in your computer so that your computer will automatically connect to either your office AP or your home AP, depending on which signal your computer's radio detects.

TIP

With most brands of wireless NICs, if you use the SSID set to "any," you can connect to *any* SSID. Therefore, the SSID is not a security feature. If your laptop can connect to both the office WLAN and the home WLAN with the SSID set to "any", the two WLANs can have different SSIDs.

The Alternatives to Wi-Fi

Many different types of networking technology are available for the home. So, before you invest in a wireless network, consider several alternatives to Wi-Fi. Wired Ethernet, for example, is the de facto standard for office networking. Presumably, you have already decided that you don't want to run category 5 networking cable all over your house; however, if you are willing to go to that kind of trouble and expense, you will have a cheap, fast connection wherever you install a network jack. Current Ethernet technology routinely delivers 100 Mbps, and the newest version of Ethernet can achieve 1-Gbps transmission speeds. You won't need that kind of speed to surf the Web (your DSL or cable modem connection is no faster than 1.5 Mbps), but when it comes to playing multiplayer video games, watching DVD movies, or listening to digital music, faster speeds make a noticeable difference.

Ethernet over category 5 cable is the dominant standard for the office, but the technologies, HomePNA, HomeRF, and HomePLUG, are specifically intended for the home networking market. When you plan your WLAN, consider these alternatives:

♦ *HomePNA* (also known as *HPNA*) is a de facto standard promoted by the Home Phoneline Networking Alliance, an industry association working to ensure adoption of a single, unified phoneline networking standard. HPNA is built on Ethernet and enables home computers to use existing telephone wiring to be networked, obviating the need to run category 5 cabling. Many of the same companies that produce Wi-Fi products also produce HomePNA products. As with category 5 cabling, the location of workstations is tied to the location of phone jacks.

♦ *HomeRF* (discussed in Chapter 3) is sponsored by the Home Radio Frequency Working Group (HomeRF WG), which was launched in March 1998. With transmission speeds up to 10 Mbps, this wireless networking standard is a direct competitor to the 802.11 standard. To date, HomeRF has found the majority of its following in Europe. Wi-Fi retains a strong foothold in the U.S. market, and it doesn't appear likely that this market leadership will change any time soon.

♦ *HomePlug* is a new, as yet unproven (in the marketplace, that is), technology that enables home networks to use preexisting electrical wiring as a networking medium to deliver speeds as fast as 14 Mbps. This HomePlug initiative is also backed by an industry group, the HomePlug Powerline Alliance. Intellon Corp. has been shipping a chipset supporting this de facto standard since May 2001. Several network hardware companies have announced products, but their products based on HomePlug technology are not yet being shipped.

Sharing Internet Connections over Residential Gateways

Only two or three years ago, people were still debating the benefits of Internet access in the home. Today, if you are in any type of business, have school-aged children, watch the stock market, or just want to communicate regularly with friends and family, your Internet connection gets used as often as your telephone—if not more.

You can access the Internet from a home computer in three ways:

♦ Over a dial-up telephone connection

♦ By DSL

♦ By cable modem

In most modern homes, at least one phone jack is located in every bedroom, and in several other strategic places within the house. Consequently, you can usually find a phone jack for your modem, enabling you to dial out for an Internet connection.

As soon as you splurge for a DSL or cable modem connection, the PC nearest the modem is at a distinct advantage because it will be the easiest computer to connect to the modem and, therefore, to the Internet Most DSL and cable modems connect to the PC through an Ethernet network adapter card. Many end users network all the computers in the household primarily because it is easier to share a DSL or cable modem Internet connection.

There are two ways to share an Internet connection over the network:

♦ **Software.** Windows 98 and later versions of Windows enable Internet-connection sharing. Each computer in the network must be set up to connect to the Internet through the computer that is connected to the high-speed modem. The disadvantage with this system is that you can't turn off or remove the computer that is connected to the modem without disconnecting all computers from the Internet. In addition, simultaneous usage (for example, several people on the network using the Internet at once) may negatively impact the processing speed of the computer providing the connection.

♦ **Hardware.** By connecting a device called an *Internet Gateway* between the high-speed modem and the home network, all computers can access the Internet directly. The Internet connection no longer depends on any computer on the network.

An Internet Gateway enables multiple computers to share the same IP address on the Internet. This capability is provided by a service called *network address translation* (NAT). The NAT service communicates with each station on the network using a private IP address assigned to each computer on your network, but uses a single IP address—the one assigned by your *Internet Service Provider* (ISP)—in packets intended for the Internet.

The function of a *Dynamic Host Configuration Protocol* (DHCP) server is to dynamically assign private IP addresses to the client computers in a network segment so that they can communicate. You could manually assign an IP address to each computer, but that process is tedious and much less flexible than automatic address assignment. Automatic IP address assignment also enables you to easily use, on your home WLAN, a computer that you've brought home from the office. When you are using the computer at the office, a DHCP server attached to your office network will assign an IP address to the computer. Similarly, when you are using the same computer on your home WLAN, the DHCP server attached to your home network will assign a different IP address. In neither case are you required to manually assign an IP address.

As discussed in Chapter 5, it may be convenient for you to choose an access point device that also performs several other network-oriented services. Combining the DHCP and Internet Gateway functions into one device is advantageous in a home network. When setting up a wireless LAN, it is even more expedient to combine the DHCP, gateway, and access point functions into a single device, called a *residential gateway*. Sometimes residential gateways are also switched hubs, and/or print servers. Some even have built-in dial-up modems to facilitate sharing a dial-up Internet connection.

Figure 6-1 depicts the network design of a typical home wireless local area network using a device that combines AP, DHCP, and NAT/gateway functions into a single standalone unit. The residential gateway device then conn ects to the DSL or cable modem, which in turn connects to the Internet.

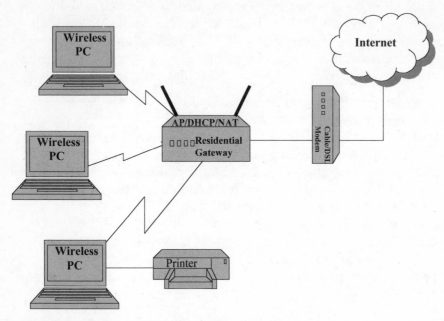

Figure 6-1: A typical home WLAN using a residental gateway device

If you already have a wired network, and have purchased a gateway device without the AP function, you don't have to replace the existing device. Instead, you need only purchase a wireless access point. Figure 6-2 depicts the network design of a typical home wired network with an AP and wireless stations added. Each PC in the wired network is connected to a hub. By connecting the AP to the hub, the AP acts as a *bridge* between the wireless *network segment* and the existing wired network. In your home LAN, you may want to use a single device that acts as a combined DHCP server, NAT, and hub; or you may have a separate hub, as shown in Figure 6-2. Either configuration will work.

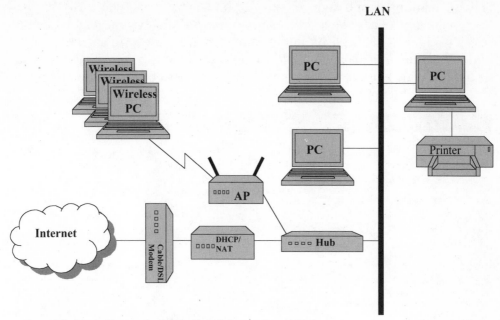

Figure 6-2: A typical home wired LAN with a wireless segment added

Adding Security

No type of network is immune to hackers. However, WLANs are more vulnerable to attack because hackers can more easily gain access to a wireless network through the air than gain physical access to a wired network. Home WLANs may not seem as vulnerable, but anyone with a portable PC, wireless network adapter, and an external antenna can sit in the house next door, or in a car a block away from your house, and have a reasonable chance of accessing your WLAN. The radio waves that radiate from an AP don't stop at the boundary of your property. Even if these radio waves are too weak to be used by a wireless PC card alone, by adding a sensitive external antenna, a potential hacker can boost the capability of his PC card to read the signal. Fortunately, the Wi-Fi specification includes an encryption method to protect the privacy of your data.

Much has been written in the computer trade press about weaknesses in the Wi-Fi encryption technology called *Wireless Equivalent Privacy* (WEP) that is intended to keep data transmitted over the WLAN private. WEP uses the *Rivest Cipher 4* (RC4) streaming data cipher.

When WEP is used to ensure privacy in an 802.11b wireless network, the network administrator assigns either a 40-bit encryption key or a 104-bit encryption key. (These keys are usually called 64-bit keys and 128-bit keys, respectively, because a 24-bit initialization vector is added to each key.) A wireless station (client) is only allowed to connect to the WLAN and receive data if the same key is entered in the client's wireless NIC configuration software (see Figure 6-3).

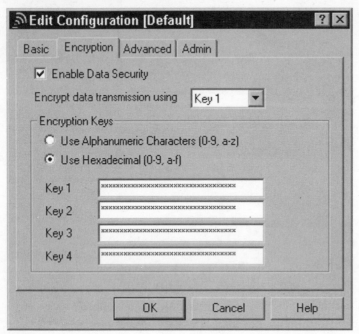

Figure 6-3: A client configuration dialog box for entering the WEP 40-bit key

WEP's inherent weakness is that this privacy protocol can be broken by a hacker if the hacker can intercept a large enough volume of data that has been encrypted with the same key.

A much bigger risk to your data than the flaw in WEP is to not use WEP (or something in place of it) at all. Several recent experiments have shown that nearly half the wireless networks already installed in this country fail to use any type of encryption. In other words, these wireless networks are "wide open" to hackers.

Some of the Wi-Fi wireless networking equipment available on the market provides only the 64-bit option as a less expensive alternative to the 128-bit version of WEP. In addition, in some implementations, using the 128-bit key can slow down the throughput. Whether you decide to save a few dollars and get only the 64-bit version, or whether you decide to splurge on 128-bit keys, you should always use WEP.

CROSS-REFERENCE

Refer to Chapters 12 and 13 for more in-depth coverage of the wireless security issue.

Adding Printers

Next to sharing an Internet connection, printer sharing is probably the most cost-effective reason to network home computers. Rather than buying a printer for every PC, everyone in the house can share one printer.

As with Internet sharing, you can set up your network for printer sharing in two ways:

♦ **Software.** Windows enables you to share any printer connected to any Windows computer on the network. The computer to which the printer is connected must be running and be connected to your network.

♦ **Hardware.** Several hardware manufacturers produce print server devices that enable you to connect one or more printers directly to the network. Some of these devices connect via a network cable, and others are wireless. Some high-end printers even have print server options that install inside the printer cabinet. For home use, network print servers are a bit pricey. Perhaps the most reasonably priced print server for use on a home network is the type that is bundled in a residential or Internet gateway.

Figure 6-4 depicts a home WLAN with a residential gateway and bundled print server.

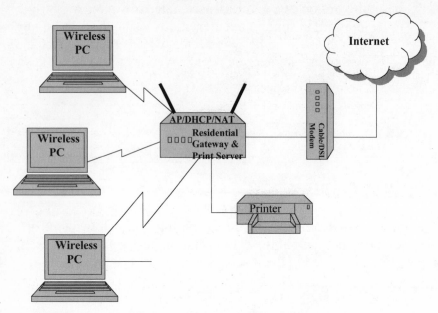

Figure 6-4: A home WLAN with residential gateway and bundled print server

At first, you may not see the usefulness of connecting your printer to the access point device. Nevertheless, a print server is advantageous because it permits the printer to stand alone on the network, untethered from any specific computer.

Connecting to the Office LAN

If you plan to use the same computer at home that you use at work, you may want the ability to access office network resources from home. Perhaps you need full access to the company network because you routinely telecommute, or maybe you just want to periodically connect to the company intranet or to your office e-mail. Whatever the reason, there are several ways you can connect your home computer to your office network.

Point-to-point Wireless

The most exotic way to connect your home computer to the office network is to establish a long-distance *point-to-point* wireless connection. This may seem absurd at first, because Wi-Fi networks are designed to transmit a few hundred feet, not miles. However, with the right equipment and physical environment, it is quite possible to wirelessly telecommute to the office.

There's a catch, of course. To establish a wireless connection at this distance, you must have a special antenna and a "line of sight" from your home to your office—in other words, a line of sight from an antenna tower on your roof or in your back yard to an antenna tower at your office building.

CROSS-REFERENCE

If you find the concept of using wirless netoworking equipment to connect computers that are miles apart interesting, turn to Chapters 19 and 20 for a more detailed discussion.

Virtual Private Network

If you plan to connect your home WLAN to the Internet, you may be able to access your office network over the Internet. However, your company's IS department has probably hidden your office network behind a *firewall* so that it isn't "visible" (accessible) directly from the Internet. Nonetheless, it is possible that your company also has a *virtual private network* that you can use to access the office network.

As its name implies, a *virtual private network (VPN)* is a private network connection that you can access over a public network—for example, the Internet. In general, a VPN creates an encrypted "tunnel" through the Internet to a VPN server behind your office network's firewall. There are many different ways and products that your IS department can use to set up a VPN. Check with your IS department for details.

Another reason to use a VPN is to add an extra layer of security between a wireless LAN and a wired LAN.

CROSS-REFERENCE

Chapter 13 discusses how VPNs provide a secure method of connecting wireless PCs to a LAN.

Sharing with the Neighbors

Considering the potential range of the wireless signal that emanates from a Wi-Fi access point, chances are good that the signal from your home WLAN may reach beyond the boundaries of your property into your neighbor's house. Chances are even greater if your neighbor has a Wi-Fi network card and a good antenna. This fact may or may not tempt neighbors to share an Internet connection.

However, before you rush over to your neighbor's house or apartment to tell him the good news, you may want to review your Internet Service Provider's subscriber agreement. Most ISPs believe that the sharing of network connections between residential neighbors violates their subscriber agreements.

Keep in mind that the wireless signal transmitted by your wireless network does not automatically stop at your home's outside walls or even at the edge of your property. The signal is like ripples in a pond — it keeps going and going and going, in a weaker and weaker form, until it hits something solid enough to stop it. Sensitive antennas can pick up the signal well beyond the point where your standard issue PC card will operate. For this reason, always use the WEP encryption feature to add a measure of privacy to your WLAN.

Summary

The focus of this chapter is budgeting and planning for the installation of a wireless local area network (WLAN) in the home. It explores how to perform a simple site survey, and how to plan a wireless network that will enable multiple computers in your home to share a single Internet connection and printer.

This chapter concludes Part I, the planning portion of the book. You should now have the tools you need to begin installing your WLAN. Turn now to Part II, "Installing a Wireless Network," to get started.

Part II

Installing a Wireless Network

Chapter 7

Installing Access Points

In This Chapter

This chapter discusses the following topics:

♦ Implementation of your WLAN plan

♦ Network wiring issues

♦ Installing APs in various locations, including ceilings, walls, and tabletops

♦ Powering APs over Ethernet and other power considerations

♦ AP configuration in infrastructure mode

Assuming you have completed the planning for a wireless local area network, this chapter assists you in installing access points, the heart of any WLAN. It also explores powering APs over the Ethernet cable (for those APs that have such an option) and configuring an AP for infrastructure mode.

Implementing the Plan

As Colonel "Hannibal" Smith was fond of saying in the popular 1980s TV show *The A-Team*, "I love it when a plan comes together!" At this point, you should be armed with a fully annotated set of floor plans that show the location of all APs, as well as other devices that will constitute your wireless local area network. You should have included enough testing in the site survey to be confident that you have identified the optimum location for each AP.

The following sections provide some pointers on the practical aspects of installing APs, a task that constitutes the majority of work involved in a WLAN installation.

CROSS-REFERENCE

Chapter 8 describes how to set up client workstations on the WLAN, and Chapter 9 covers some testing that you can do to fine tune the network. If you are installing a WLAN in your home, you should also look at Chapter 10. Chapter 11 covers issues that will be of particular interest if you are installing a WLAN on a college campus.

Network Wiring

Almost every wireless network is connected in some way to a wired network. In most business installations, a WLAN is a segment of a larger network, with each access point attached to the wired network and acting as a bridge from the wireless segment to the LAN. Even if you don't plan to attach any computers directly to a wired LAN, you will need to run networking cable between access points. Similarly, you will probably want Internet connectivity, which requires network wiring of some type.

If you have a lot of cable to run, you may decide to hire an electrician. If you plan to pull the cable yourself, however, make sure you are familiar with local building and electrical codes. For example, use only plenum-rated cable in areas of the building where air circulates, such as in the area above dropped-ceiling tile.

Even if someone else runs the cable for you, you should know how to connect the most common type of network cable, because every AP is connected to it.

Cat 5 Cable

Several different types of cable could be used for network cabling in your building, but the most common type is *category 5 unshielded twisted pair (UTP)*—often called *cat 5 cable* (see Figure 7-1). If your facility uses a different type of cable, such as fiber optic cable, you will need to obtain adapters that enable you to connect the network cable to each AP that you install. Most APs are set up to accept cat 5 cable.

Category 5 cable has four pairs of wires inside the jacket (outer cover). In other words, eight individually jacketed wires are twisted into four pairs, and then these four pairs are twisted together. The number of twists per foot is one aspect of the cable specification that gives it the category 5 rating, a rating scheme established by the *Telecommunication Industry Association/Electronic Industry Association* (TIA/EIA) standards group.

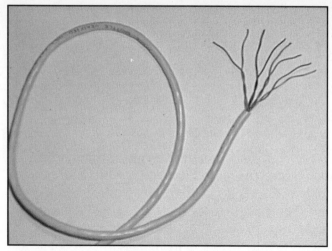

Figure 7-1: Category 5 unshielded twisted pair cable

Category 5 cable is used for LANs because it can support faster transmission speeds than cable with a lower rating. Telephone wire is often category 1 cable. A few years ago, category 3 UTP was commonly used for network cabling because it supports the 10 Mbps transmission speed of the original Ethernet standard. However, because of the unique electro-magnetic properties of low voltage signals moving through twisted cable, you need category 5 cable, with more twists per inch, to support 100 Mbps (Fast Ethernet) and the newest 1 Gbps Ethernet speeds.

The specification for cable that supports data transmission at 10 Mbps on a baseband signal (that is, standard Ethernet) over twisted pair cable is called *10BaseT* (for *10* Mbps, *Base*band, *Twisted* pair). The specification for 100 Mbps on a baseband signal over twisted pair is called *100BaseT*.

RJ-45 Connectors

To connect cat 5 cable to an Ethernet network adapter card or to an access point, you use a *registered jack-45* (RJ-45) connector (see Figure 7-2). This type of connector resembles an RJ-11 connector typically used on home telephone lines. RJ-11 jacks, however, can accommodate only four wires, whereas RJ-45 jacks can handle eight.

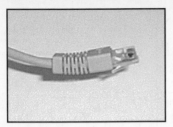

Figure 7-2: An RJ-45 connector at the end of a category 5 unshielded twisted pair cable

You can purchase cat 5 cable with RJ-45 connectors preinstalled at both ends, but not at the lengths needed to connect each AP to the network. Ethernet UTP cable can extend as much as 100 meters without requiring a repeater to boost the signal. Therefore, you can install each AP up to 100 meters from the nearest network hub. You will need to add a connector to the end of the cable that connects to the AP and to the other end that connects to the hub.

Adding an RJ-45 connector is easy. You just have to be careful to place the eight wires in the correct order, and to use a good crimping tool (see Figure 7-3). Category 5 cable, RJ-45 connectors, and crimping tools are readily available in electronic supply stores, hardware stores, and through online retailers.

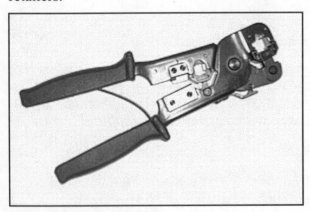

Figure 7-3: An RJ-45 crimping tool

Table 7-1 lists the RJ-45 color code that you should use to line up the wires. This wiring configuration follows the TIA/EIA T568B commercial building standard for telecommunications cabling standard and is the configuration most widely used worldwide for new data installations. It is also specified by the IEEE 802.3 standard as the configuration to use for10BaseT Ethernet over twisted pair cable.

With the tip of the connector (the part that goes in the jack first) facing away from you, and the copper side facing up (and the flexible plastic clip facing down), wire (sometimes called *pin*) number 1 is on the far left and wire number 8 is on the far right.

Table 7-1: The RJ-45 Color Code

Wire	Color
1	White with orange stripe
2	Orange
3	White with green stripe
4	Blue
5	White with blue stripe
6	Green
7	White with brown stripe
8	Brown

The RJ-45 connectors on both ends of the cable should be wired in exactly the same way. A cable that is wired the same on both ends is sometimes called a *straight-through* cable. Ethernet uses only wires 1, 2, 3, and 6, but it is customary to use all eight wires in the RJ-45 connector at both ends of a straight-through cat 5 cable.

> **TIP**
>
> From time to time, you may need to create a *cross-over* cable, which connects two computers together by running a UTP cable between the network adapter cards in each computer without using a hub. You may also need a cross-over cable to connect two network hubs together. Cross-over cables are not wired the same at both ends. Standard RJ-45 wiring is used on one end, but on the other end, wires 1 and 3 switch positions and wires 2 and 6 switch positions. This configuration connects the pins that send the signal on one end of the cable to the pins that receive the signal on the other end. When you use a network hub, you must use straight-through cables because the hub internally takes care of this cross-over.

To attach the connector to the cable, follow this procedure:

1. Remove about an inch to an inch-and-a-half of the outer jacket from the end of the cable, exposing the four twisted pairs of wires. Do not strip the jackets from any of the eight individual wires.

2. Using the color code in Table 7-1, line up the wires between the thumb and forefinger of one of your hands. Make sure the ends of the wires are pointing away from you. Wire 1 is on the left, and wire 8 is on the right.

3. Holding the wires firmly between your thumb and forefinger, use wire cutters (often included as part of the crimping tool) to cut all wires the same length—about one-half inch from the portion of the cable still covered by the outer jacket.

4. Using your other hand, slide the RJ-45 connector onto the eight wires. With the tip of the connector facing away from you and the copper side facing up, wire number 1 (white with orange stripe) should be on the far left and wire number 8 (brown) on the far right.

5. Slide the connector into the crimping tool and squeeze the tool handle firmly. You may hear a faint "click" as the tool crimps the plastic connector.

Notice that you never have to strip the jackets from the eight wires. The process of crimping the connector pierces each jacket and makes the necessary connections to the pins inside the connector.

When you intend to install the network cable inside a wall, you should terminate the cable with an RJ-45 jack that you install in an outlet plate in the wall. Wall jacks are convenient in a home or office for the same reasons that telephone jacks are convenient. If you install at least one in each room, you will always be able to easily connect a device to the network. Using an RJ-45 outlet plate even when you are installing an AP at the ceiling also makes for a professional-looking installation. You can then use a short straight-through RJ-45 cable, usually called a *patch* cable, to connect the AP to the jack. Make sure you follow the color code from Table 7-1 when you connect the cat 5 cable to the jack.

Mounting the AP

Most of the effort to install a wireless local area network is spent mounting and configuring the access points. In an ideal situation, where you have already identified the best location for an AP in each section of the building that will be covered by the WLAN, your task should be as simple as mounting the APs into position. In a business or institutional setting, however, a wireless network is part of the infrastructure that the people who use the facility take for granted. When you install access points in this type of environment, they should be as unobtrusive as possible, while still delivering the service for which they are intended. Accomplishing both of these goals can be tricky.

Most enterprise-class access points are designed for mounting on a wall or on the ceiling. They often have either a metal or plastic mounting bracket integrated into their physical design.

Some manufacturers recommend against mounting the AP on the ceiling. They suggest that you either mount the AP vertically against a wall or sit it flat on a desk or table (if it comes with a stand, you may even be able to position it vertically on the table- or desktop). Access points intended for the home or small office are typically designed to work best on a table or desk (see Figure 7-4).

Figure 7-4: A typical home/small office AP sitting on a desk

Stations will always get the best reception if they have an unobstructed line of sight to the AP. In virtually any office, cubicles, furniture, copy machines, water coolers, and people will be least prohibitive if the AP is mounted at the ceiling level. Thus, the best place to install each AP in a business setting is at or near the ceiling.

If you decide to mount an AP on the ceiling, make sure it is securely fastened. Various elements in a building can cause vibrations that may cause the AP to slide off its mounting screws or bracket, falling on someone and/or damaging the access point or other equipment. If the AP attaches to a mounting bracket by clips or tabs that are not secured by screws, don't attach it to the ceiling.

Many modern office buildings have large metal beams exposed above the ceiling tiles. Some installers secure each AP to the side of a metal beam. If you use this type of installation, however, you should add a short extension cable between the AP and its antenna so that the metal beam doesn't block the signal.

You may be able to install the AP above the ceiling tiles, but make sure the RF signal isn't significantly attenuated by this placement. Some manufacturers sell kits that include an extension cable and a metal drop-ceiling fascia. Using such a kit, you can extend the antenna that is normally attached to the AP through the ceiling tile. Your testing may demonstrate, however, that the signal is still strong enough for your purposes without the extension cable and drop-ceiling fascia, even when transmitting through the ceiling tiles.

It may be advantageous to mount the AP above dropped-ceiling tiles, but the area above a dropped ceiling, called a *plenum* space, is used for air circulation in heating and air conditioning systems. Any equipment or cable that is installed in a plenum space must be manufactured from a fire-retardant material that won't emit noxious fumes in the event of a fire. For similar reasons, building codes may not permit you to run UTP cable in a plenum area if it is carrying electrical power. If you plan to use power injectors to get electrical power to each AP over the Ethernet cable, check with local building and electrical codes before installing APs above the ceiling tiles. Similarly, APs made from certain plastics may not be permitted.

The easiest type of permanent AP mounting is on the wall—not much more difficult, in fact, than hanging a picture. The hard part, once again, is running Ethernet and power to the AP. Be sure to follow the instructions that come with each AP to attach the AP securely to the wall. Figure 7-5 shows an AP attached to a wall.

One disadvantage of installing an AP on a wall is that the wall will attenuate the signal that attempts to penetrate the wall. Depending on the type of building material, a useful signal may not extend as far on the other side of the wall as it does on the inside. Make sure to take this attenuation into account when you determine on which wall to mount the AP.

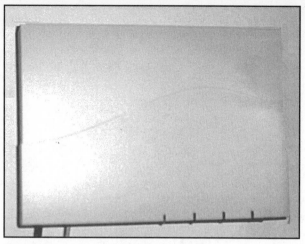

Figure 7-5: An access point mounted on a wall

TIP

Signal amplifiers are available for 2.4 GHz radio transmissions that could enable you to "blast" the signal through most walls, but you are limited by the FCC to less than one watt of power without having to obtain a license. In most office situations, however, you will run up against a throughput ceiling if you try to spread a WLAN cell too far. Most APs provide maximum throughput—the quantity of data that can flow through the AP to all stations—sufficient to handle only about 30 users at any one time on a single channel. You will typically have to add more APs as often to handle throughput as to provide adequate signal coverage.

Power Considerations

Unless you are installing APs in a new building that has been specifically wired to support wireless APs in the ceiling, you will probably have to hire an electrician to install an electrical outlet for you at each location where you decide to install an AP. Even if you hire an electrician to run the network cable, installing electrical power will probably more than double the cost when compared to running network cable by yourself. What's more, many states require two different licenses and sometimes two different unions to install both electrical power outlets and network cable to the same locations.

If you plan to connect several APs together, and/or connect each AP to a wired LAN, you will always need to run the network cable to each location where you plan to install an AP. If you have the forethought to select a line of APs that has the option of powering the APs over the Ethernet cable, you can save the cost and delay of installing power outlets. By some estimates, using an AP that can be powered over the Ethernet cable can save you as much as $1,000 per access point.

To power the APs over the network cable, install a device called a *power injector* in the same location as the network hub. Some manufacturers sell multiport power patch panels that can be used to power several APs from the same device. Power injectors cost between $50 and $100 per AP; however, if you save anywhere close to $1,000 by eliminating the need for a power outlet, you still realize a substantial savings by using power over Ethernet.

CAUTION

Only the newer models of high-end access points are designed to be powered over the Ethernet cable. In some cases, attaching an old AP to a network cable into which you have injected power can significantly damage the AP. In other cases, the PoE device is "smart" enough to be able to determine whether an AP supports PoE before it sends a damaging signal to the AP. Be careful to clearly label the end of any Ethernet cable that carries power so that later installers can quickly identify the cable.

Configuring an AP in Infrastructure Mode

Each access point from a vendor is going to have a *default* configuration — the configuration that results if you *reboot* or *reset* your system, erasing your custom settings. Some APs also have a *factory set* configuration that enables each AP to work out-of-the-box. Nonetheless, to use an AP in your wireless network, you will certainly need to make a few changes to either the default or the factory set configuration.

In most cases, you will use each AP to manage an *extended service set* or *cell* of a wireless network. If so, you need to set up each AP in infrastructure mode. Some APs can alternatively be set up for point-to-point communication between two networks, with two APs acting as a wireless bridge. In addition, some APs can be configured to bridge to several other APs at one time, a configuration called *point-to-multipoint*.

CROSS-REFERENCE

For further discussion of configuring APs for point-to-point and point-to-multipoint bridging, refer to Chapters 19 and 20.

Each brand of access point has its own configuration software. Some products provide several methods of configuration. The following are the most common types of configuration tools:

♦ **Terminal-based.** To use this method of configuring an AP, you either connect a terminal or a PC running terminal emulation software directly to the AP through the AP's Ethernet port or using a serial port (if the AP has a serial port).

♦ **Management-software-based.** Some APs come with access point
management software that runs on a workstation and enables you to
configure each AP over the Ethernet cable. Figure 7-6 shows a list of
APs that can be configured using ORiNOCO's AP Manager software.
You should avoid making changes to an AP's configuration from a
wireless client computer, because you may make a change that results in
the wireless station's disconnection—one that you won't be able to
correct until you regain access from a wired connection. AP
management software is often based on *Simple Network Management
Protocol* (SNMP). Some AP management utilities can be run over a
USB cable connected directly from a workstation to an AP.

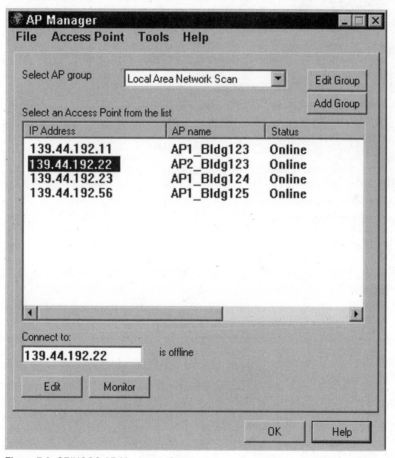

Figure 7-6: ORiNOCO AP Manager software

♦ **HTML-based.** Most of the new lines of APs have a series of HTML forms stored in firmware that enable you to configure each AP, as shown in Figure 7-7. You can access these forms over the Ethernet cable using a Web browser if you know the AP's IP address.

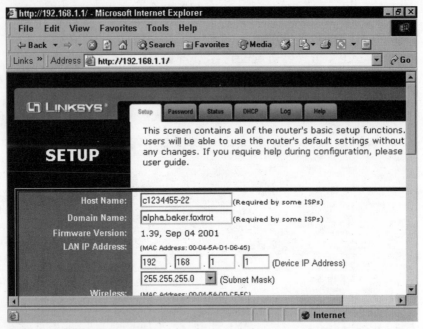

Figure 7-7: HTML-based configuration software stored in the firmware of a Linksys AP

Regardless of the utility that you use, you will need to record and/or set the following parameters in the access point:

♦ **MAC address.** This is the physical address of the AP, which should be printed on the label attached to the device. If the AP uses a PC card as its radio, the MAC address for the AP is sometimes printed on the back of the PC card.

NOTE

The AP's Ethernet connection to the wired network also has a MAC address that is different from the MAC address of the radio in the AP.

♦ **Local IP address.** In some cases, you will need this IP address to make any changes to the AP's configuration. If your network has a DHCP server, many AP models will be able to lease the IP address automatically each time they power up while connected to the network Ethernet cable. If this feature is enabled by default in the AP's configuration, you may need to obtain the leased IP address before you can make any changes to the configuration. DHCP server products enable you to access a table of active IP addresses, along with the corresponding MAC address of each device. After you have attached the AP to the network and powered it up, the DHCP server will assign an IP address to the AP and add this address to the active IP table. You will be able to look up this IP address in the table.

With several brands of AP you can also use a utility program to scan the network for the IP address(es) of any AP(s) attached to the network. In addition, some APs have a serial port to which you can connect a PC or terminal device to access a utility progam stored in the AP's firmware. Using this utility program, you can either determine the AP's DHCP server-assigned IP address, or assign a static IP address manually.

The best practice, however, is to assign a static IP address to each AP, rather than using a DHCP-assigned address. This way, you ensure that the address will not change if you need to make configuration changes from time to time. If you assign addresses yourself, make sure that each device has a unique IP address and that you follow the addressing scheme used for the rest of the LAN. You will compromise your WLAN's security if you fail to change the automatic IP address that was set at the factory, because every other AP from the same manufacturer probably has the same factory-set address.

> **TIP**
>
> Larger networks are sometimes configured as multiple subnets separated by routers or gateways. If you are adding a WLAN to such a network, make sure that all access points within "roaming distance" of one another are on the same subnet. Otherwise, as a mobile wireles station roams from one subnet to another, it may lose its connection.

♦ **Subnet Mask.** This value will probably be either 255.255.0.0 or 255.255.255.0, depending on the number of segments and hosts you plan to use and on whether your LAN is set up as a class B or class C address scheme. If your network has a DHCP server and you use this feature, the appropriate subnet mask will also be supplied when the DHCP server leases an IP address to the AP. All APs in the WLAN should have the same subnet mask.

♦ **SSID.** The *service set identifier,* sometimes called the *extended service set identifier* (ESSID, or *network name*),can be any alphanumeric string, including uppercase and lowercase letters, up to 32 characters in length.

Some APs can be configured for so-called *secure access*, a setting that prevents the AP from broadcasting its SSID. This setting also requires each wireless station to use the correct SSID to gain access to the WLAN. If this feature is not available, or not enabled, stations with a blank SSID or that have the word "ANY" will be permitted access, along with stations that have the designated SSID. This quasi-security feature is independent of WEP encryption.

If you use the SSID "security" feature, all APs in the same *extended service set* (ESS) should have the same SSID. You should always use the same ESSID for APs in the same WLAN and require stations to use the same name. Following this practice gives you the flexibility to turn on the secure access feature whenever you feel it is needed, without having to reconfigure all APs and client equipment.

♦ **Channel.** This is the DSSS channel over which the AP will communicate. There are 14 available 5 MHz channels. However, because DSSS signals occupy 22 MHz, you can really only use up to three channels (typically, 1, 6, and 11) in a given WLAN.

♦ **SNMP parameters.** APs may support *Simple Network Management Protocol* (SNMP), enabling you to use SNMP-compliant network management software, such as IBM's NetView, to manage many APs at once. If the AP supports SNMP, you will need to know the SNMP read/write *community name* in order to save any changes you make to the configuration. If you are setting up a brand new AP, make sure to change the community name (a password) from its default value. For example, some AP manufacturers assign the word "PUBLIC" as the default community name. Every AP from that manfacturer has the same community name/password, so you should always change it to a different community name—one you can remember because, without it, you won't be able to change the AP's configuration.

♦ **WEP Keys.** In nearly all typical business environments, you should use 802.11b's built-in WEP encryption. Only a determined hacker with the proper equipment and software will be able to crack the key. However, if you don't use WEP, any nosey "war driver" with a laptop, wireless PC card, range-extender antenna, and software (that is freely available on the Internet) can see and access your WLAN from the highway, driving by your building at top speed. Whenever you use WEP, all users on the WLAN must use the same key. Several vendors make key mangement software available, which eases the chore of continually changing the WEP key. A newer, more secure version of WEP is scheduled for availability some time in 2002.

This list covers the AP parameters that you will most often encounter and need to configure, but it is not comprehensive. In addition to these configuration settings, you may need to address additional security features, such as creating a list of MAC addresses that are permitted to access the WLAN, and employing a RADIUS server for user and station authentication.

Other settings that you probably don't need to change include the transmission rate—which normally adjusts automatically to give the best throughput—RTS/CTS protocol settings, the beacon interval, and the fragmentation threshold.

The *preamble type* setting is one setting that can sometimes cause problems. This is particularly true when you are using a wireless NIC from one manufacturer and an AP from another. The majority of WLAN manufacturers set the *preamble type* to "Long" by default. If you are having trouble getting a particular PC card or other wireless station to work with the AP, check to see if the preamble type in the AP matches what the wireless station is expecting.

TIP

As you configure each AP, record all the settings on a separate form designed for that purpose and store all the forms together in your office. Any time you make a change to a configuration, update the form. These documents may later save you many headaches when you need to add and change equipment on your WLAN. Many AP management utilities also enable you to save all the configuation options as a file that can be reloaded later should the AP lose its configuration through a power loss or other occurrence.

Summary

This chapter discusses the implementation of the WLAN plan that you developed through your site survey. It covers network-wiring issues, installing APs in various locations (including ceilings, walls, and tabletops), powering APs over Ethernet, and configuring an AP for use in infrastructure mode. Turn now to Chapter 8, where the topic of setting up wireless client stations is discussed.

Setting Up Client Stations

In This Chapter

This chapter discusses the following:

♦ Installing PC cards

♦ Installing PCI and ISA wireless adapter cards

♦ Installing USB adapters

♦ Setting up wireless PCs running Windows, Windows XP, Mac OS, and Linux

Although the access point is the heart of each cell of a wireless network, don't forget the other half of each network connection: the wireless radio that is installed in the client computer. In addition to installing the access points for your WLAN, you will probably need to install a wireless network interface card and client configuration software in each computer or device that will access the WLAN. Proper installation and configuration of these client wireless networking devices is crucial to getting the WLAN up and running.

This chapter helps you install and configure wireless network adapters, including PC cards, PCI adapters, ISA adapters, and USB adapters. Because many different types of computers can communicate over a wireless LAN, this chapter examines wireless stations running under Windows, Apple Mac OS, and Linux.

Read the Docs First!

I have had to learn the hard way to read installation instructions before I start a project, rather than waiting until problems arise. In general, you can save yourself a lot of time and frustration if you read the directions before you start installing wireless networking equipment in your computer. The next few paragraphs explain why.

Most of the wireless network adapters currently available are either PC cards (also known as PCMCIA cards) or adapters that plug into a PCI slot in a desktop computer. The PCI adapters are most often a carrier for a PC card. If you have experience installing PC cards, you may assume that you know what to do with a PC card wireless networking adapter—but you may be wrong.

When you read the installation instructions before beginning the installation process, you may find that you need to install software before installing the hardware. You may also need to uninstall old software before installing new software. Undoing a faulty installation is often much more difficult than following the proper steps in the first place.

Hardware and Software

Installation of a wireless networking adapter always includes installing both hardware and software. If you keep that point in mind, the installation process will seem more logical. Depending on the type of adapter you are installing—PC card, PCI adapter, ISA adapter, or USB adapter, you will need to install either one or two hardware drivers so the adapter can communicate with the computer's operating system. In addition, because the wireless NIC communicates with the wireless access point(s), you will need to install and configure client wireless station software. (If you are setting up an iMac, iBook, or G4 with an AirPort slot, the hardware drivers and other AirPort software may have already been installed.)

The next few sections of this chapter examine potential installation and setup issues that are related to the different types of wireless NICs. Because the majority of stations run one of the Windows operating systems, the general instructions in this chapter assume a Windows computer. The installation process for Windows 95 through Windows 2000 is very similar. Later sections in the chapter explore issues that are unique to Windows XP, as well as Mac OS and Linux. Keep in mind that the exact wireless NIC installation and configuration procedure that you should follow depend on the brand and model of adapter. Be sure to read all included documentation, printed and on disk, *before* installing the products.

Before You Start

Before you install a wireless NIC, you require certain information, or parameters, that you will enter during the installation and setup process. You can change a number of other settings later, but these parameters are required to either establish communication between a wireless station and an access point or between two wireless stations:

♦ **Ad Hoc or Infrastructure.** Whenever you plan to use the wireless NIC to access a WLAN, you usually intend to have the wireless NIC communicate with one or more access points in the WLAN. This type of wireless communication is called *infrastructure mode*. By contrast, if you are setting up a wireless NIC solely for the purpose of communicating with other wireless NICs, in a peer-to-peer fashion, you need to set up the device for *ad hoc mode*.

If you are using wireless NICs from different manufacturers, different terminology may be used for the same mode. For example, one manufacturer's configuration software may refer to *Ad Hoc mode*, whereas another's may call it *Peer-to-Peer mode*. At least one manufacturer uses the term *ad hoc* to refer to a proprietary mode that communicates only with other cards from the same company and uses the term *802.11 ad hoc mode* to refer to the mode that interoperates with cards from other manufacturers.

> **TIP**
>
> Recall from the discussion in Chapter 2 that communication between a wireless NIC and an AP, or between two wireless NICs, takes place at the lowest two layers of the OSI model, the Physical and Data Link layers. Therefore, it is possible to make a connection between two wireless devices but still not successfully transfer data. You also have to connect at the higher levels for meaningful data transfer to take place.

♦ **SSID.** The *service set identifier* (SSID), or *network name,* identifies the wireless network. The SSID should already be entered in the configuration settings for each access point in the WLAN. You should have selected the same SSID for all the APs that will be communicating with mobile wireless stations.

Some APs have a configuration option that turns this identifier into a security feature of sorts by requiring that each wireless station use the correct SSID to obtain access to the WLAN. Unless this security feature is available and enabled in the APs in your WLAN, however, the best alternative for each wireless station may be to leave the SSID blank. Leaving the SSID blank typically permits the wireless station to access any service set (that is, a wireless LAN) regardless of the SSID assigned to each service set. Entering the SSID "any" or "ANY" will usually give you the same result. If you do choose to enter a specific SSID in the configuration for each wireless station, it has to match the one used by the APs with which the station will communicate.

♦ **WEP encryption key.** Every Wi-Fi-certified WLAN has the capability to use WEP encryption to protect the privacy of the data that is transmitted wirelessly over the WLAN. Unless your network is truly a public network, you should have this feature enabled at all times in all APs. If the APs are using WEP, all wireless NICs must also use WEP and the same WEP key in order to gain access to the network.

WEP is another feature that may not appear to be implemented in the same way by different manufacturers. All Wi-Fi-certified PC cards must support WEP and be able to interoperate with one another. Nevertheless, the user interface for entering the WEP key can differ greatly from one manufacturer to the next.

The configuration software that accompanies Prism-based cards enables you to type a *passphrase* up to 31 characters in length. You then click a Generate button to generate four 40-bit keys (see Figure 8-1). As an alternative, you can manually type four ten-character hexadecimal key sequences, each of which represents five hexadecimal numbers. Each hexadecimal number represents an eight-bit ASCII character—eight bits times five characters results in a 40-bit key in each line. Note that 40-bit encryption is another name for so-called 64-bit encyption, which uses a 24-bit initialization vector plus the 40-bit key.

If you choose to use 128-bit encryption, some configuration software permits you to generate a key with a passphrase, and some software requires that you type a 26-character hexadecimal code representing 13 hexadecimal characters (13 x 8 bits = 104 bits +24 bits = 128 bits).

The configuration software from some manufacturers—such as those that use the Lucent chip set—requires that you enter the key either as four rows of five alphanumeric characters or four rows of five two-digit hexidecimal numbers. Figure 8-2 shows the same 64-bit (actually, 40-bit) hexadecimal keys that were generated by the passphase shown in Figure 8-1.

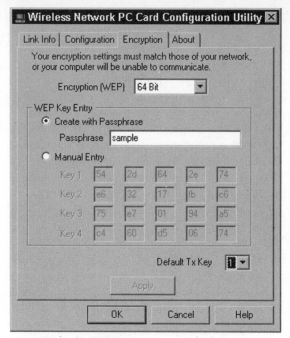

Figure 8-1: Using a passphrase to generate four 40-bit keys

Refer to the sections later in this chapter that discuss adding a wireless NIC to a PC that runs Windows XP and to an Apple Macintosh computer. The configuration software available on these two systems is different enough from the other products to require an additional discussion. A later section also briefly examines adding a wireless card to Linux, a task that is quite a bit more complicated that any of the other cases covered.

In addition to the parameters described in the preceding paragraphs, you should also have handy a CD-ROM containing the Windows operating system that is installed on the computer to which you are adding the wireless NIC. During the installation process, Windows may need to copy files from this CD (or from the \Windows\Options\Cabs folder on the computer's hard drive — many business computers have a copy of the Windows installation files stored in that location).

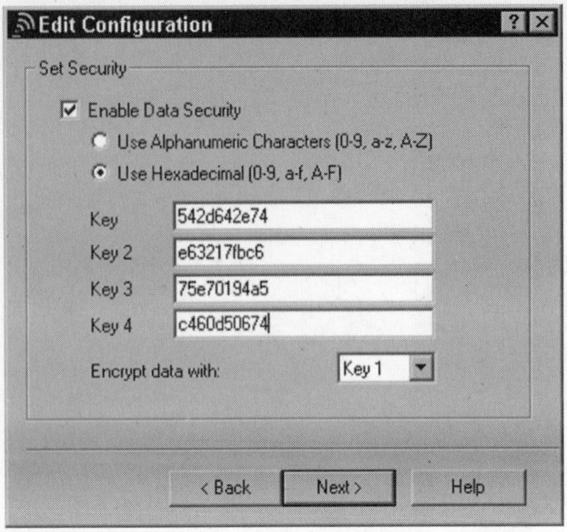

Figure 8-2: Manually entering four 40-bit keys

PC Cards

As pointed out in Chapter 5, most wireless NICs are PC cards. Nearly all Windows laptops and some Mac laptop computers have PC card ports that are compatible with these cards. If you are installing a PC card in a computer with a PC card slot, use the following general guidelines. Once again, refer to the documentation that comes with the card for detailed instructions.

The general guidelines for installing a PC card wireless NIC are as follows:

1. Insert the CD that accompanied the PC card into the CD-ROM drive. If the CD's auto run feature doesn't cause the setup program to start, use the Run command from the Start button (in Windows) or Windows Explorer to run the Setup.exe program on the CD.

2. Install the wireless station (client) software. During this installation, you may be asked to indicate whether you want the PC card to be set to infrastructure (Access Point) mode or to Ad Hoc (Peer-to-Peer) mode, for the SSID (network name), and to indicate whether you will use WEP encryption.

3. After the wireless station software is installed, restart the computer.

4. As the computer restarts, insert the PC card wireless network adapter into the available PC card slot (type II or type III). Windows 95, Windows 98, Windows Me, and Windows 2000 are *plug-and-play-compliant*, so they should recognize that you have inserted a new device in the PC card slot and will automatically search the hard disk for the driver. If Windows finds the driver, it will enable the driver for the card. If Windows can't find the driver, it will start the Found New Hardware wizard (see Figure 8-3).

Figure 8-3: The Found New Hardware wizard

5. Click Next. On the screens that follow, guide Windows through the process of searching for the drivers on the CD-ROM.

6. After Windows finds and installs the driver, you will need to reboot the computer.

If you did not receive a CD with the PC card or you suspect that it may not contain the most up-to-date software, check the manufacturer's Web site for the most recent drivers and client station software. In some cases, software that is included with the operating system has been updated by the manufacturer to correct bugs or to add features. Wireless networking technology is still evolving, so it is important that you keep up with the changes. For example, to address the security flaws in WEP, a new version of the encryption protocol is currently in beta testing. By the time this book is published, it should be available for download from most wireless PC card manufacturers.

Some PC card wireless NIC adapter manufacturers periodically post on their Web site software that enables you to update the *firmware* that is stored in the circuitry inside the card. In most cases, firmware updates address-specific hardware or software issues. If you aren't aware of a problem with the card, you should probably leave well enough alone. Nonetheless, you may sometimes see a new feature included in a firmware update that is worth adding—even if there is a risk that something will go wrong during the update process.

With many other types of PC cards, installation consists of plugging the card into the PC card slot and supplying a disk or CD when prompted to do so. With most PC card wireless NICs, however, it is important to install the software drivers *before* inserting the PC card for the first time. This ensures that the correct driver will be present on the computer when the operating system recognizes that you have inserted a PC card. Installing the drivers first also ensures that you can configure the software as you install the device.

PCI and ISA Cards

Very few, if any, desktop PCs come with PC card slots, but there may be times when you want to connect a desktop computer to a wireless LAN. Consequently, wireless networking hardware manufacturers sell special adapters for use in PCI or ISA slots that enable you to install a PC card in a desktop computer. These adapters are not intended as general-purpose PCMCIA slots. Rather, they should only be used with a PC card wireless NIC from the same manufacturer. Using them with any other PC card could damage your computer.

TIP

Not surprisingly, several PC card manufacturers use identical PCI or ISA adapters. At least one manufacturer acknowledges that you may be able to use its adapter with other PC cards. All manufacturers explicitly state that they only support use with their own products. Some manufacturers specifically warn that you could damage your computer if you use their PCI adapters for any PC cards other than the ones they specify.

Some brands of wireless networking PCI card adapters do not support "hot swapping." That is, you must turn off the computer before inserting or removing the PC card or risk damaging the computer, the PC card, or both. Other wireless networking PCI cards operate more like a typical PCMCIA slot, allowing you to insert and remove a PC card while the computer is running. Before you make any assumptions about how the PC card works, read the product documentation carefully. If you don't have any documentation, most manufacturers store up-to-date versions of the product documentation on their Web sites.

Follow these general guidelines for installing a PCI or ISA adapter card:

1. Insert the CD that accompanied the PCI or ISA card into the CD-ROM drive. If the CD's auto-run feature doesn't cause the setup program to start, use the Run command from the Start button (in Windows) or Windows Explorer to run the Setup.exe program on the CD.

2. Select the option for installing the PCI or ISA card driver software. At this point, the driver will only be copied to the computer's hard drive. The driver will be added to the operating system in a later step.

3. If prompted to restart the computer, select "No, I will restart my computer."

4. Install the PC card wireless station (client) software. In some cases, Step 2 and Step 4 will be accomplished in a single software-installation step. In other cases, you will only install the wireless station software at this point.

5. During the installation of the wireless station software, you may be asked to indicate whether you want the PC card to be set to infrastructure (Access Point) mode or to Ad Hoc (Peer-to-Peer) mode. You may also be asked for the SSID (network name) and to indicate whether you will use WEP encryption.

6. After both the PCI card or ISA card driver and the wireless station software are installed, shut down the computer.

7. Unplug the computer and install the PCI or ISA card in an available slot. Insert the PC card before installing the PCI or ISA card in the computer, if the documentation instructs you to do so.

8. Restart the computer. Windows will recognize that you have installed new hardware and will automatically search the hard disk for the driver. If Windows finds the driver, it will enable the driver for the adapter. If Windows can't find the driver, it will start the Found New Hardware wizard. If Windows does not recognize that you have installed new hardware, open Control Panel and start the Add/Remove Hardware wizard.

9. Click Next. On the screens that follow, guide Windows through the process of searching for the drivers that are on the CD-ROM.

10. After Windows finds and installs the driver, reboot the computer.

11. If you haven't already installed the PC card along with the adapter card, insert the PC card wireless network adapter into the PCI or ISA adapter card as the computer restarts. Windows 95, Windows 98, Windows Me, and Windows 2000 are plug-and-play-compliant, so they should recognize that you have inserted a new device in the PC card slot and will automatically search the hard disk for the driver. If Windows finds the driver, it will enable the driver for the card. If Windows can't find the driver, it will start the Found New Hardware wizard.

12. Click Next. On the screens that follow, guide Windows through the process of searching for the drivers on the CD-ROM.

13. After Windows finds and installs the driver, you will need to reboot the computer.

Some manufacturers choose to mount the PC card more permanently on the PCI or ISA adapter. Some of the newest PCI adapters consist of a mini-PCI adapter mounted to a full-size PCI adapter. In either of these configurations, a "rubber duckie" type antenna or another type of range-extender antenna is attached to the back of the PCI or ISA adapter. Installing this type of PCI or ISA card is very similar to Steps 1 through 8 of the procedure just described.

USB Adapters

All new PCs and laptops come with at least one, usually two, USB ports. In addition to PC cards and PCI adapters, a number of wireless networking hardware manufacturers produce USB wireless networking adapters that connect to a USB port by a USB cable. Just as PCI wireless networking adapters often consist of a PC card mounted on a PCI adapter, if you were to open the plastic case of a USB wireless networking adapter, you would probably discover that it, too, contains a PC card.

NOTE

USB is supported by Windows 98 and later versions. Windows 95 does not support USB ports.

The installation procedure for a USB wireless networking adapter is very similar to that of a PC card. The general guidelines for installing a USB wireless NIC are as follows:

1. Insert the CD that accompanied the USB adapter into the CD-ROM drive. If the CD's auto run feature doesn't cause the setup program to start, use the Run command from the Start button (in Windows) or Windows Explorer to run the Setup.exe program on the CD.

2. Install the wireless station (client) software. During the installation of the wireless station software, you may be asked to indicate whether you want the USB wireless adapter to be set to infrastructure (Access Point) mode or to Ad Hoc (Peer-to-Peer) mode. You may also be asked for the SSID (network name), and to indicate whether you will use WEP encryption.

3. After the wireless station software is installed, restart the computer.

4. After the computer restarts, attach the USB adapter to one of the computer's USB ports. Windows will recognize that you have installed new hardware and will automatically search the hard disk for the driver. If Windows finds the driver, it will enable the driver for the adapter. If Windows can't find the driver, it will start the Found New Hardware wizard.

5. Click Next. On the screens that follow, guide Windows through the process of searching for the drivers on the CD-ROM. You may also be prompted for the disk that contains your original Windows setup files. If so, answer the prompts on the screen to specify the location of these files—usually a CD-ROM or the computer's hard drive in the Windows\options\cabs folder.

Windows XP Stations

Windows XP is the first version of Windows released since the widespread availability of wireless networking products. Consequently, Microsoft has integrated wireless networking support into the product for a select group of wireless adapters for which drivers were available for testing during the Windows XP beta process.

Wireless Zero Configuration

As we have observed before, one of the selling features of wireless networking is portability. Ease of roaming from room to room, building to building, and even town to town is an important capability for users of this technology. Windows XP promises to make connecting to new wireless networks easier than ever through a service Microsoft has dubbed *Wireless Zero Configuration.*

Although Microsoft's claim of "zero configuration" is a bit of an exaggeration, configuration is easier for supported adapters. When installing or configuring these adapters, you don't need to use software provided by the manufacturer. Instead, Windows XP recognizes the adapter and provides the necessary driver and configuration software.

Use the following procedure for installing and configuring a supported wireless network adapter:

1. Log on to Windows XP as Administrator.

2. Insert the PC card or attach the USB adapter. Windows XP displays a balloon message alerting you that it has found new hardware, as shown in Figure 8-4. Shortly thereafter, Windows XP displays a message that your new hardware is installed and ready to use.

Figure 8-4: Windows XP has found new hardware.

3. Next, Windows XP displays a message alerting you that it has detected the installation of a new networking device and suggesting that you click the Network Setup wizard, as shown in Figure 8-5. If you don't run the wizard at this point, you can do so later (see the next section in this chapter).

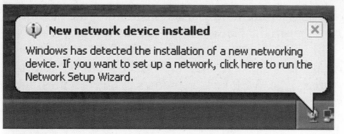

Figure 8-5: Windows XP has detected a new networking device.

4. If you also happen to be within range of a WLAN, Windows XP announces that one or more wireless networks are available and suggests that you click the Network icon to see a list of available networks. Click the Network icon. Windows XP displays the Connect to Wireless Network dialog, shown in Figure 8-6.

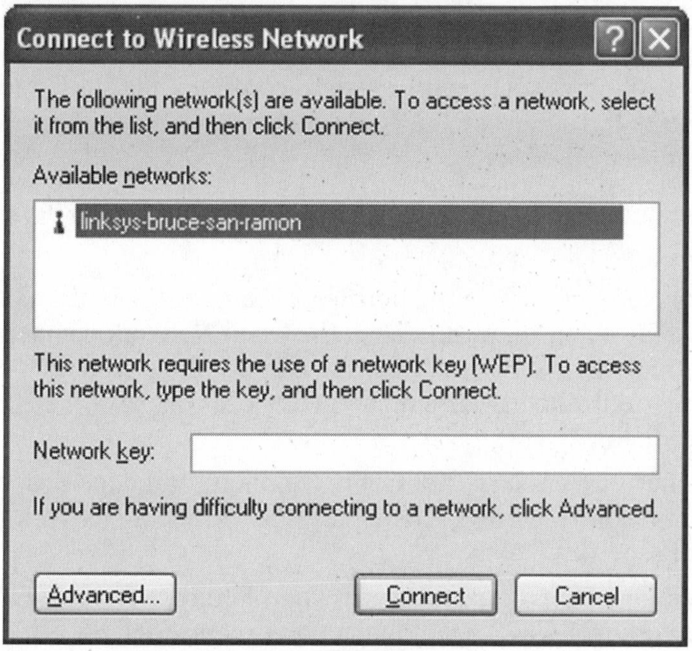

Connect to Wireless Network [?][X]

The following network(s) are available. To access a network, select it from the list, and then click Connect.

Available networks:

> linksys-bruce-san-ramon

This network requires the use of a network key (WEP). To access this network, type the key, and then click Connect.

Network key: [   ]

If you are having difficulty connecting to a network, click Advanced.

[Advanced...]   [Connect]   [Cancel]

Figure 8-6: The Connect to Wireless Network dialog box

5. If the WLAN is using WEP (and it should be), enter the key as a hexadecimal number in the Network key text box. (Note that if the AP provides for four keys, this key is equivalent to only the first key index.) After you have entered the key, click the Connect button. If you successfully entered the WEP key, Windows displays a message telling you that the computer is connected to the wireless network and indicating at what speed.

In a matter of minutes, you have installed and configured a wireless network connection. If you have trouble connecting, you can display more configuration information by clicking the Advanced button to display the Wireless Network Connection Properties dialog box.

Configuring Automatic Network Connections

Easy installation and configuration is only half of the Windows XP wireless networking story. If you know that a user will need to connect to several different WLANs, Windows XP enables you to configure the station to automatically detect and connect to each network on-the-fly, with no need for further configuration by the user.

To configure one or more wireless networks for automatic connection, follow these steps:

1. Right-click a Network icon in the notification area at the bottom of the screen to display a pop-up menu. Click the Open Network Connections option. Alternatively, you can display the Control Panel and then double-click the Network Connections icon. Windows XP displays the Network Connections dialog.

2. Right-click the Wireless Network Connection icon and click Properties in the pop-up menu. Windows XP displays the Wireless Network Connection Properties dialog.

3. Click the Wireless Networks tab, as shown in Figure 8-7. Notice that the wireless network that was present when you first inserted the wireless NIC is already listed.

4. To add another network to the list, click the Add button on the Wireless Networks tab to display the Wireless Network Properties dialog.

5. Type a network name (SSID) in the Network name text box.

6. If you have implemented a system for automatically providing users with network keys and/or WEP keys, click OK to save this network SSID and move on to the next network (if any) that you want to configure. If you don't have an automatic key distribution system in place, uncheck the check box near the bottom of the dialog and enter the WEP key and/or shared network key.

TIP

Entering WEP keys in the Wireless Network Properties dialog is a little different from the process used for other brands of networking equipment. First, specify whether you will be entering ASCII characters or hexadecimal characters and numbers. Then enter either a 5-digit key (a 40-bit key—64-bit WEP) or a 10-digit key (a 104-bit key—128-bit WEP). Notice the Key index scroll box. By default, the key index is set to 0. The first key you enter is key 0, which corresponds to key 1 on most other systems. Scroll the scroll box to 1, 2, or 3 in order to enter all four keys. Click OK when you are finished.

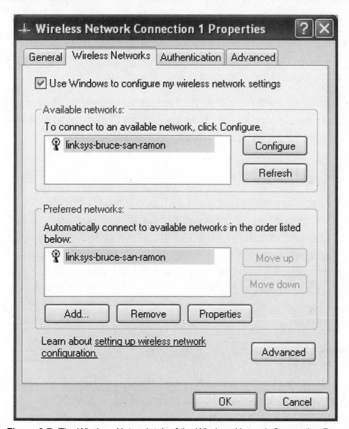

Figure 8-7: The Wireless Network tab of the Wireless Network Connection Properties dialog

7. If you are setting up an ad hoc mode wireless connection, click the last check box in the dialog. Otherwise, if you are configuring a connection to an AP, leave the check box unchecked and click OK. Windows XP adds the network to the list of preferred networks in the Wireless Network Connection Properties dialog box.

8. When you finish adding all wireless networks to which you expect this computer to need access, click the OK button in the Wireless Networks tab of the Wireless Network Connection Properties dialog. Windows XP returns to the Network Connections dialog. Windows XP now has the information it needs to automatically connect the computer to each wireless network whenever the wireless station comes into range.

XP includes support for the IEEE 802.1x standard for port-level authentication of stations on the network.

CROSS-REFERENCE

See Chapter 13 for more information about IEEE 802.1x port-level authentication. One ot the important features of IEEE 802.1x is support for automatic distribution of Wireless Equivalent Privacy (WEP) keys.

Windows XP also makes more networking technical data readily available than did earlier versions of Windows. You can quickly determine, for example, the IP address of a particular problem network adapter.

Macintosh Stations

Apple Macintosh computers were the first to have built-in wireless networking capability. All newer Macintosh iMacs, iBooks, and all G4 computers either come with built-in 802.11b wireless connectivity or with an Airport slot ready to receive an Airport card—which is not the same as a PC card slot. Some Mac laptops have both an Airport slot and a PC card slot. Apple computers that are equipped with an Airport slot also have built-in antennas; unlike wireless PC cards, nothing protrudes from the Mac when an Airport card is inserted.

The AirPort Card

Apple's AirPort wireless network adapter card was developed by Lucent and Apple, so it uses the Lucent chip set. It is similar in appearance and size to a PC card, but is mounted inside a special AirPort iMac Card adapter and cannot be used in a PC card slot. There is no antenna permanently attached to the card because the antenna for an AirPort card is built into the computer.

The Apple AirPort base station doesn't look much like the access points made by other manufacturers, but that's what it is. You should be able to use any Wi-Fi-compliant wireless NIC to communicate with an AirPort base station. Similarly, you should be able to use any Mac sporting an AirPort card to communicate with any Wi-Fi-compliant AP.

Apple designed the AirPort to be easy to install and configure. AirPort-compatible iMacs have an access door on top, just behind the handle. You can use a coin to unlock the compartment. Find the antenna cable inside the compartment and attach it to the AirPort card. Align the edges of the AirPort adapter with the guides inside the compartment and slide the card sideways into the slot. Close and latch the compartment door.

TIP

Before installing the AirPort card, write down the MAC address that is printed on the card's label, in case you need the number later.

G4 Macs have a slot inside the case intended for the AirPort card. To insert the AirPort into this slot, follow these steps:

1. First remove the card from the iMac AirPort Card adapter.

2. Open the G4's case; insert the AirPort card through the opening in the PCI card guide.

3. Attach the card to the connector on the main logic board.

4. You should be able to find the antenna cable tucked in on the side of the PCI card guide. Don't forget to attach the cable to the AirPort card before closing the case.

As with the G4, you need to remove the AirPort from the iMac adapter card in order to install the AirPort in an iBook. You can find the AirPort slot beneath iBook's keyboard. Follow the illustrated instructions that accompany the iBook to remove the keyboard and install the card. If you have misplaced the instructions, they are available on Apple's Web site.

The software for the AirPort card comes on a CD. Look for the AirPort Setup Assistant in the Assistants folder on the Mac's hard disk. If you can't find it there, you must install the software from the Mac OS CD-ROM before you can use the AirPort.

Power Macs

Older Power Macs, built before the introduction of the AirPort, have neither an AirPort slot nor a PC card slot. Some older Macs, however, do have PCI slots inside. Wireless networking hardware manufacturer, Proxim, offers both a Macintosh-compatible PC card and a Mac-compatible PCI adapter, under the SkyLine brand, that enables you to use the PC card in a PCI Mac. The SkyLine PC card is based on the Prism chip set. Because these older Macs don't have built-in antennas, the SkyLine card's antenna extends out the back of the Power Mac case.

Linux Stations

The Linux operating system is increasingly found on computers in all types of businesses. Although Linux is not commonly used for client workstations, you still may have a need or desire to create a connection between a wireless network and a workstation that is running Linux for use as a server or even as a high-end workstation.

Agere ORiNOCO PC cards and perhaps a few other Lucent-based PC cards can be used with Linux. The CD that accompanies ORiNOCO products contains an archive file that includes driver source files and a library of other related files that enable you to build and install an ORiNOCO PC card driver for the specific Linux kernel you are using. The drivers and source files that ORiNOCO provides support Linux kernel versions 2.0.*x*, 2.2.*x,* and 2.4.*x* for the Intel architecture. Supported Linux distributions from Red Hat include the following versions:

- ◆ 5.2
- ◆ 6.0
- ◆ 6.1
- ◆ 6.2
- ◆ 7.0
- ◆ 7.1

Linux distributions from Suse include the following versions:

- ◆ 6.1
- ◆ 6.3
- ◆ 6.4
- ◆ 7.0
- ◆ 7.1

To successfully compile the software, you will need to have the full set of Linux kernel source files installed, and you will require approximately 65MB of free disk space. After it's compiled, however, the driver will use only about 38KB of disk space.

Summary

This chapter examines the installation of PC cards, PCI and ISA wireless adapter cards, and USB adapters. It covers the basic steps for setting up wireless PCs running Windows, Windows XP, and Mac OS, and discusses the resources available to build a wireless PC card driver for Linux.

When the wireless access points are installed and the wireless stations are up and running, it is time to complete additional testing of your WLAN with the object of fine-tuning its performance. Turn now to Chapter 9 to get some pointers on how best to accomplish that testing.

Chapter 9

Analyzing the Network

In This Chapter

This chapter discusses the following topics:

- ◆ Signal strength testing
- ◆ Using protocol analyzers
- ◆ Testing network health

Every LAN is a living, changing organism—or at least you will begin to suspect that it is. Do you remember Colossus from the old Forbin Project movie, in which supercomputers took over the world? I'm not suggesting that the human race is about to be superseded by advanced technology; but it is important, nonetheless, to continually analyze any network to make sure all is working well and to identify trouble spots before they blow up in your face. This advice is particularly applicable to wireless LANs.

This chapter introduces you to the topic of testing and analyzing your network using the utility software that comes with commercial WLAN equipment. Because investing in a network analyzer is a good idea if you are responsible for a larger WLAN (more than two APs), this chapter also discusses the purpose and utility of this type of tool. The topic of network analysis and troubleshooting can fill several books (the book *Network Analysis and Troubleshooting*, J. Scott Haugdahl, 2000, Addison-Wesley, for example), so this chapter will just give you a few pointers.

Signal Strength Testing

By now, you have already performed the site survey prior to installing the WLAN, so you should be familiar with how to test signal strength. Every wireless networking device should ship with utility software that enables you to determine the signal strength to that device. Even if you are using Windows XP and it automatically detects your PC card wireless NIC, you should install the client configuration software from the manufacturer (after first obtaining the Windows XP version from the manufacturer's Web site, if it does not ship with the card). Figure 9-1 shows the Link Test window of the ORiNOCO Client Manager (Variant 1, Version 2.18) that ORiNOCO provides with the Windows XP version of its wireless NIC drivers.

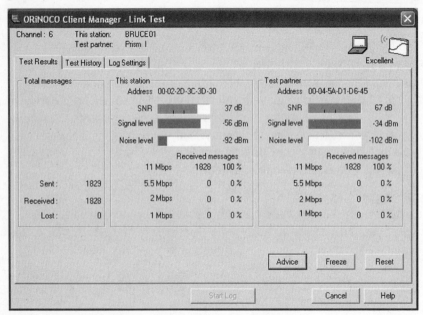

Figure 9-1: The Link Test window of the ORiNOCO Client Manager

You can display Windows XP's standard Wireless Network Connection Status dialog box, shown in Figure 9-2, by right-clicking the Networking icon in the Notification area of the Windows XP Taskbar and then clicking Status. Compare the link-related information shown in this dialog box to the information provided in the dialog in Figure 9-1.

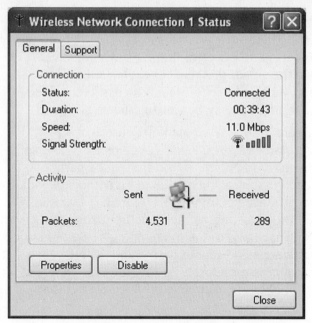

Figure 9-2: Windows XP's Wireless Network Connection Status dialog

Walk-Around Testing

When you performed the site survey, your primary concern was to ensure that a sufficient signal reached any location where a client station was likely to need it. After you install the WLAN, it is a good idea to run a post-installation site survey to confirm good signal coverage. The simplest way to perform such a test is to walk around the facility carrying a laptop computer with a wireless PC card and your original site-survey floor plan. Run a utility program that shows signal strength. Make a note of any areas that don't have a good signal, especially any area that utility software identifies as a poor or nonexistent signal.

You may find an area where users need a good signal but where, unfortunately, the signal is weak. The next step is to determine the cause of the weak signal:

♦ **Poor AP placement.** Your original testing may be faulty, which means the AP may simply be in the wrong place. If you are using external antennas, you may need to adjust their positioning. Otherwise, reposition the AP, if practical, to a location that gives a stronger signal.

Keep in mind that you may just be trading a better signal in this location for a poorer signal somewhere else.

♦ **Attenuation.** Many objects in an office or home environment can partially block or reduce the signal that reaches each station. For example, if an additional wall, cubicle, or bookcase has been added between the station and the AP, it may be causing the weak signal.

♦ **RF interference.** There are quite a few potential sources of RF signals—microwaves, portable phones, electrical generators, and so on—but many are momentary in nature. If you find that a particular location consistently receives a poor signal due to high "noise," look for a source that is likely to produce continuous RF output. It is unlikely that another WLAN cell broadcasting on the same frequency will cause continuous interference. The signal of the overlapping cell would not register in the utility software as noise, but momentary interference (when two PCs happen to transmit packets on the same frequency at exactly the same time) could cause excessive dropped packets and retransmissions.

The limitations of the simple wireless NIC utility software become apparent if you can't make a quick educated guess about the source of a weak signal. These utilities help you discover that you have a problem; however, they do nothing to identify either the cause or a solution.

Using Testing Equipment

If you are responsible for a business or institutional wireless LAN, you may quickly conclude that the standard-issue WLAN utility software doesn't adequately test and troubleshoot your WLAN. Although these utilities are free (which is, perhaps, the strongest argument for using them), their inability to diagnose your WLAN woes may end up costing you money. Fortunately, several products on today's market—although pricey—provide substantial help.

The most obvious tool for determining RF signal strength is a dedicated RF signal-strength meter device that accurately detects and displays signals in the 2.4 GHz ISM frequency range. Because these devices are standalone, they remove the wireless NIC—as well as the PC operating system and software configuration issues—from the troubleshooting equation. Some WLAN signal-device meters are handheld, which makes them even more portable than a laptop PC.

Berkeley Varitronics is a company that produces several wireless LAN testing products. One highly regarded tester from Berkeley is called the Grasshopper WLAN 2.4 GHz Scanner. The Grasshopper is a handheld, wireless radio receiver that measures and displays IEEE 802.11b RF power, and narrowband received signal strength (RSSI) total channel power. In addition, this device measures packet error rate, and tracks the amount of time that each 802.11b DSSS channel is used. It can detect and differentiate 802.11b signals from narrowband multipath interferences such as microwave ovens and Bluetooth signals.

Some such testing devices are installed as permanent devices to continually monitor the network. Not only can they diagnose known problems, they can also be configured to alert you to problems of which you aren't aware, such as excessive packet errors.

Dedicated signal analyzers are valuable tools, but they may cost as much as a nice laptop computer. Depending on the size of your WLAN budget, they may or may not be a luxury you can afford. On the other hand, if you are an administrator of a wireless network, you may not want to do without a protocol analyzer—the subject of the remainder of this chapter.

Protocol Analyzers

When you experience a problem with a network connection, it is often hard to know where you should start unraveling the knot. Dozens of protocols and algorithms may be involved in a wired network, and wireless LAN technology adds even more protocols. Thus, protocol analyzers are invaluable tools, not only for solving difficult networking puzzles, but also for nipping problems in the bud.

Sniffer, from Network Associates, is probably the best-known protocol analyzer product, but there are many other similar products for wired networks, including Microsoft Network Monitor and Novell LANalyzer. The choices for wireless LANs are more limited.

Network Associates has developed Sniffer Wireless for analyzing 802.11b wireless local area networks in particular. Sniffer Wireless is a software-based product that runs on Windows NT 4 or Windows 2000 — typically on a laptop equipped with a PCMCIA slot and either a Symbol Technologies Spectrum24 Model 4121 wireless NIC or a Cisco Systems Aironet 340 client wireless adapter card. However, the product is not limited to analyzing WLANs from Cisco and Symbol. You can use Sniffer Wireless to analyze and troubleshoot any brand of IEEE 802.11b wireless LAN. Nevertheless, the cost of this product is not for the faint-of-heart; you will spend approximately $18,000 for a lifetime license to run the software on up to two machines.

AiroPeek from WildPackets is a well-respected competitor to Sniffer Wireless. At around $2,000 for a single license, AiroPeek is pricey, but may be more within the budget of a small- to medium-sized business than the Network Associates product. AiroPeek is also a software-based wireless protocol analyzer. It runs on Windows 98, Windows Me, Windows NT 4.0 (service pack 3, or later), or Windows 2000. The host computer must have a PC card slot and a wireless NIC from any of the following:

♦ 3Comm AirConnect

♦ Cisco

♦ Intel

♦ Nortel

♦ Symbol

♦ Agere ORiNOCO

WildPackets even has a utility that enables you to convert data files between the Sniffer Wireless file format and its own.

> **NOTE**
>
> The examples shown in the remainder of this chapter are AiroPeek screen shots. The folks at WildPackets were kind enough to provide an evaluation copy of the software for my use while writing this book. AiroPeek is running on a Compaq Armada laptop with an Agere ORiNOCO Gold (Lucent) PC card wireless NIC. Release 1.1 of AiroPeek does not support the most current ORiNOCO firmware, but I was able to easily "downgrade" the firmware by running a utility obtained from ORiNOCO's Web site. By the time you read this, AiroPeek will probably support the most current firmware.

As products specifically designed for use with 802.11b wireless networks, both Sniffer Wireless and AiroPeek can be configured to decrypt packets that are encrypted with WEP. This feature is necessary because WEP encrypts all the data in a packet above the 802.11b level. The network analyzers need to be able to identify the protocols and network addresses that would otherwise be encrypted by WEP. You certainly don't want to turn encryption off, so each product supports WEP in its implementation.

How Protocol Analyzers Work

The user interface on a protocol analyzer may look intimidating because there are so many options. It turns out, however, that the fundamentals of this type of product are rather straightforward. The essential operation of a protocol analyzer is to *capture* the packets that are transmitted around the network. In 802.11b lingo, the packets that are broadcast on the wireless network are known as *frames,* but to be consistent with other networking discussion, I'll call them *packets.* The protocol analyzer puts the wireless PC card into a mode that views the packets of all Wi-Fi radios within range of the PC running the analyzer software, a mode often called *promiscuous* mode The protocol analyzer software then captures these packets.

For the purposes of diagnosing and preventing wireless networking problems, the application data that is carried by the packets is not relevant. Consequently, protocol analyzers immediately discard the data, holding on to the header and footer protocol-related information that encapsulates the data.

Time is an important aspect of diagnosing nearly any network problem related to data transmission. For the end user, the speed at which data is delivered from one device to another is often a priority. For the network administrator, the total throughput capability of the system—that is, the volume of data that the network can handle in a given period—is of primary interest. The protocol analyzer can only assist you in achieving optimum network speed and throughput if it keeps track of the time each packet is transmitted. Consequently, the analyzer timestamps each captured packet and stores the timestamp with the captured protocol information in a database for easy retrieval and analysis.

The amount of protocol-related information stored in a frame often exceeds the amount of information you actually need. Protocol analyzers, therefore, enable you to set up filters that discard protocol-related information that is irrelevant to your analysis.

Finally, so you don't have to do any heavy lifting, industrial-strength protocol analyzers such as Sniffer Wireless and AiroPeek provide a wide variety of reports that summarize and analyze the captured data, enabling you to see patterns and trends that help you determine whether the WLAN is up to snuff or not.

The protocol analyzer enables you to store all this information as packet *traces* for later retrieval and analysis. Figure 9-3 shows some captured data displayed in AiroPeek's Packets view. This screen shows the same data in three panes: the Packet List, Decode, and Hex view panes.

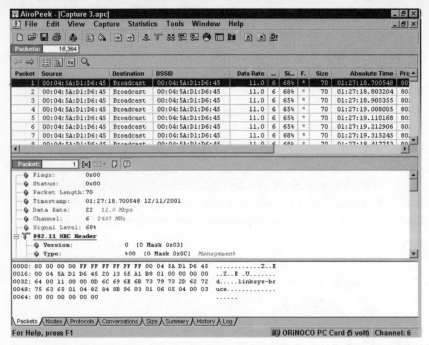

Figure 9-3: AiroPeek's Packets view, showing the same data in the Packet List, Decode, and Hex view panes

The real power of a network protocol analyzer derives from the incredible volume of information it collects in the packet traces and the flexibility with which you can filter and generate reports from this data.

Checking WLAN Health with a Protocol Analyzer

You can easily check the following basic WLAN vital signs using a protocol analyzer, either in real time or by analyzing a saved trace stream after-the-fact:

♦ **Transmission speed.** Wi-Fi wireless LANs can be configured to operate at speeds from 1 MBps to 11 MBps. If you set the AP and station cards to automatically pick the highest speed available, you can determine at what speed the WLAN is actually operating. Because the analyzer records the speed of every packet, you can easily tell whether the network is optimized for speed. If you see that one of the stations is operating at a slower transmission speed than the others, you will know that either the station is not configured correctly, or that it is not getting a good signal.

♦ **Signal strength.** The protocol analyzer records the signal strength of each packet sent, making it simple to identify trouble spots. Typically, low signal strength is coincident with slow transmission speed, but when that is not the case, you know to look for a different problem. The AiroPeek analyzer denotes signal strength as a percentage of the total allowable power.

♦ **Network traffic.** In addition to looking for problems at individual stations, protocol analyzers can show you overall network statistics. Figure 9-4 shows the Gauge view in the AiroPeeks Network Statistics window. These two analog dials with digital displays at their centers show network utilization (as a percentage of capacity) and traffic volume (in packets per second). If your wireless network begins to experience problems—slow connections, dropped connections, and so on—you can use this network traffic information to determine whether the problems are related to capacity issues.

♦ **Network throughput.** If you want to know precisely how much load the WLAN is handling, the best protocol analyzers provide network throughput. In Figure 9-4, for example, the network statistics show that the average utilization of the WLAN under analysis is 98.426 Kbps. The gauge at the bottom of the screen indicates that the average utilization is about one percent of the network's maximum capacity.

♦ **Average packet size.** Because of all the protocols involved in WLAN packets, a large amount of overhead information is included in each packet. As a result, data is transmitted most efficiently in the largest packets the WLAN will accept. The larger the packet, the higher the effective data transfer rate will be. Figure 9-5 shows a larger number of small packets, which could indicate the presence of interference, or could simply indicate that the type of packets transmitted most often are relatively small.

♦ **CRC Error frequency.** Each pair of radios that communicates over a WLAN automatically tests for transmission errors using a *cyclic redundency check* (CRC) algorithm. Protocol analyzers keep track of the total number of errors. Airopeek, for example, displays this type of information as an analog guage with digital readout.

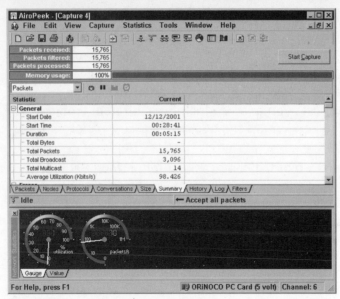

Figure 9-4: AiroPeeks Network Statistics window

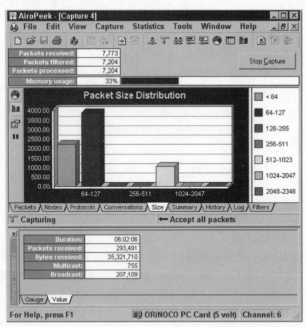

Figure 9-5: A protocol analyzer report showing packet-size distribution

Finding Rogue WLANs

Although unauthorized WLAN access by someone outside your company or institution may seem the most worrisome risk to network security, a much more common occurrence is unauthorized installation of a wireless access point by someone who is ,otherwise, a "friendly" user. In other words, an innocent, but impatient, user or group of users decide to "help themselves" by acquiring and installing a wireless LAN on their own. If they operate this so-called *rogue* WLAN as an independent basic service set (IBSS), not connected to any portion of the company/institutional LAN, the risk is not as acute. More typically, however, the rogue WLAN is attached to the LAN, often with no privacy security (WEP) activated.

In a small organization, you might be able to discover rogue WLANs by walking around the building; but in a larger, multifloor or multibuilding LAN environment, it's difficult. You can discover them more easily with a protocol analyzer. Then you can use a directional signal locater to track the rogues down in a matter of minutes. Even better, you can shut them out of your network by filtering their MAC addresses, and they will probably find you to get reinstated.

To detect rogue WLANs, take the following steps:

1. Make sure you have a current list of all the authorized SSIDs operating within range of the WLAN you are analyzing.

2. Using the protocol analyzer, examine a typical packet to determine the relative position of the SSID in the 802.11 frames.

3. Create a filter for the protocol analyzer that will filter out the authorized SSIDs.

4. Apply the filter. The only packets that remain will be those of the unauthorized, rogue WLAN.

If you are using Network Authentication, you can also use the protocol analyzer to detect failed authentications. Any failed authentication can potentially mean the existence of an attempted access by an unauthorized user.

Summary

This chapter describes some of the concepts and tools used to test and analyze your network, including a network signal-testing device. The chapter also discusses how a network analyzer can help you analyze your WLAN.

The next two chapters return to the topic of WLAN installation. Chapter 10 covers issues unique to installing home WLANs, and Chapter 11 covers installation of wireless networks on college campuses.

Installing a Home WLAN

In This Chapter

This chapter discusses the following topics:

- ◆ Implementing a home WLAN plan
- ◆ Network wiring issues
- ◆ Installing and configuring APs in your home
- ◆ Internet connection sharing

Assuming you have developed a plan for your home wireless local area network, as discussed in Chapter 6, this chapter helps you implement that plan—focusing on network wiring issues, installation and configuration of access point(s), and issues related to Internet connection sharing.

Network Wiring—Do You Need Any?

Unlike in office LANs that don't rely solely on a wireless network, in a home wireless LAN, you probably don't need to use network cable to reap the benefits of a local area network. A wireless LAN provides all the networking functionality you need, unless—here's the catch—you want to use the WLAN to share a high-speed Internet connection.

TIP

Access points that include a built-in modem are available from several manufacturers. If you don't intend to subscribe to DSL or a cable modem account but want to share a single dial-up Internet connection, consider purchasing one of these AP/modem bundles.

To share a cable modem or DSL Internet connection with other computers in your house, you need to connect a cable network from the high-speed modem (cable or DSL) to one of the computers in the WLAN or to the AP itself. (Refer to the discussion of cable modems and DSL later in this chapter). You may be able to get the technicians who install the cable or DSL modem to run the cable for you.

If you plan to set up Internet connection-sharing through the computer operating system (also discussed in more detail later in this chapter), you will need to run network cable from the cable or DSL modem to a wired network adapter installed in one of the computers that will also be a station on the WLAN. Ideally, you will install the wired PC card in the fastest computer that is also connected to the WLAN.

If the AP is an Internet gateway (that is, it provides DHCP and Internet routing services), then you should run the network cable directly from the high-speed modem to the AP/Internet gateway.

If you decide to run network cable in your house, you can always hire an electrician to do the work. However, if you decide to run the cable yourself, take a few minutes to review the "Network Wiring" section in Chapter 7 before you go shopping for the necessary parts and tools.

Because you rarely find dropped-ceilings in residential housing, it is difficult to run network cabling from one room in a house to another after the house is already built. If you are in the process of building your home, have the cable installed before the builders install the wallboard. The builders should use Category 5 UTP cable. They should also install an RJ-45 jack in every room that gets a phone jack. The cleanest installation is to use a modular wall plate with at least one phone jack and one network jack. Figure 10-1 shows a wall plate with one modular phone jack and two modular network jacks. Adding network cabling may increase the cost of your new house by hundreds of dollars, but it may also add thousands to its resale value (depending on the real estate market in your area).

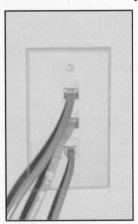

Figure 10-1: A wall plate with one phone (RJ-11) jack and two netowrk (RJ-45) jacks

Running network cabling on the outside of the house is the easiest way to run cable after the house is constructed. You can often tuck the cable under siding or overhangs to make it undetectable. You will, however, have to drill holes through the side of your house. You should be able to find supplies at stores such as Home Depot or Radio Shack for installing the cable through an outside wall. Make sure you purchase category-5 cable that is intended for outdoor use. Also, use a good silicon sealant to block moisture from permeating your walls.

The best location for an access point in a residence is usually the center of the house. Therefore, it may not be easy to run the network cable to the AP by simply running cable on the outside of the house. If you plan to install the WLAN in a one- or two-level home, the best location for the access point(s) is on the top level. Consequently, you can make use of your home's attic to run the cable. Keep in mind that no cable segment should be more than 100 meters in length.

Before you go to the trouble of running a network cable to a difficult-to-reach spot in your house, test the signal strength between the proposed AP location and the locations where wireless stations (computers) will be located. You may be able to find another location for the AP—one that is easier to reach with a network cable, but still provides an adequate signal to all stations.

Mounting the AP

The location in your house for the access point(s) should have been determined in the site survey; however, you still need to decide how to mount the AP. In most cases in a home installation, you won't need to go to great lengths to mount the access point(s) on the wall or the ceiling, but you should be aware of your options.

Any AP can be used in a home or small office environment and can be configured to sit easily on a tabletop, desk, bookshelf, dresser, or any other flat surface. The Linksys model, shown in Figure 10-2, has four rubber feet on the bottom, LEDs (light emitting diodes) on the front, and all network, antenna, and power connectors on the back—making it perfectly configured for placement on a flat surface.

Figure 10-2: A Linksys access point, configured for horizontal use on a flat surface

Some AP brands are designed to sit on a flat surface but are vertical in design. The modern-looking Residential Gateway line of APs from Agere ORiNOCO, for example, sits upright. The ORiNOCO Residential Gateways can also be mounted on the wall by attaching the removable back cover to the wall and then attaching the AP to the back cover.

Antennas

Antennas on access points vary from manufacturer to manufacturer. Several AP models do not have external antennas at all, using internal diversity patch antennas instead. Other APs have a single external dipole antenna, and still others have two external dipole antennas. Dual antenna external models should provide better signal coverage throughout the house, but only actual on-the-spot testing will determine whether your AP antenna configuration is adequate.

If you decide that the signal strength and coverage in your house is inadequate, most APs provide an option for adding one or two external antennas. Several manufacturers sell optional antennas that extend the range of the standard antennas—they attach to the AP to supplement or replace the existing antennas.

The standard AP antenna is always omnidirectional. The external variety is typically an omnidirectional dipole antenna attached to the AP with a connector that enables you to position the antenna at many different angles. Omnidirectional dipole radio antennas send and receive best in a vertical position. APs with two antennas may transmit from only one of the antennas, but receive through both antennas by sampling the signal and using whichever antenna is getting the strongest signal—this is called a *diversity antenna system*.

If your house has two or more levels and you have installed your AP on the second floor, you will have more difficulty getting a good signal on the first floor. The building materials in the floor, ceiling, and walls block some of the signal. In addition, you may get the weakest signal immediately above and below the AP. The signal from a dipole antenna radiates 360 degrees in the horizontal plane and 75 degrees in the vertical plane, creating a doughnut-shaped pattern. Consequently, the area directly above or below the antenna gets a very weak signal.

You can increase coverage in your house by adding an antenna with a higher *gain* than the antenna that comes standard with the AP. Manufacturers, such as Cisco and Agere (ORiNOCO), sell optional antennas that boost the signal. Compatible antennas are also available from third-party manufacturers, but make sure you use the correct connector to attach the antenna to the AP.

The Agere Range Extender add-on external antenna, for example, has a gain of 2.5 dBi. The FCC limits to 1 watt (30 dBm), the total power output from a radio transmitting in the 2.4 GHz ISM band plus an additional 6-dBi antenna gain. The FCC limits the maximum *effective isotropic radiated power* (EIRP) to 36 dBm. You arrive at the system's EIRP by adding the power of the radio (measured in dBm) to the gain of the antenna. To figure out the maximum gain antenna you can use, check the AP's specifications for total power output (in dBm) and subtract this value from 36. For example, if your AP puts out 20 dBm, you can use an antenna with up to a 16-dBi gain and remain "legal."

> **NOTE**
>
> AP manufacturers submit each AP model as a system to the FCC for testing and licensing. Each AP system includes an antenna. External add-on antennas from the same manufacturer have also been tested and licensed with the manufacturer's APs by the FCC, so you can be sure that when using these antennas you aren't exceeding FCC limits. If you decide to buy a third-party antenna, you are on your own to determine whether the maximum effective isotropic radiated power is within FCC limits.

Power Considerations

All wireless LAN access points are powered by electricity, so you have to install them near an electrical outlet. Ideally, each AP should be on a dedicated circuit, but that generally isn't practical in a home. Be sure, however, to use a good surge suppressor to protect your equipment.

Increasingly, AP models designed for the office can receive their electrical power over the network cable, eliminating the expense and inconvenience of running power to each AP. Manufacturers of APs intended for home or small-office use are following suit. Several home/small office APs will soon offer a *power-over-Ethernet* (PoE) option. If you want to install the AP in a hard-to-reach location, not close to an electrical outlet, you may find power-over-Ethernet a worthwhile option.

Configuration

Wireless access points designed for home use tend to come preconfigured with settings that enable you to plug in the system and use it with little or no user intervention. This is especially true if you purchase an AP and wireless NICs from the same manufacturer. Unfortunately, you don't want to use all these default settings. This section explains which settings you should change and why.

Each brand of access point has its own configuration software. Some products provide several methods of configuration. The most common types of configuration tools for home/small-office APs are as follows:

♦ **Software-based.** Some APs come with access point setup software that runs on a workstation and enables you to set up the AP over a wireless connection, a USB cable, or an Ethernet cable. Figure 10-3 shows the opening screen of ORiNOCO's RG Setup Utility software.

> **TIP**
>
> If you have a choice, it is better to make changes to an AP's configuration from a wired client computer rather than from a wireless station, because your changes may result in the wireless station's disconnection. If you don't have a wired connection to the AP, just be careful. For example, if you want to change the WEP key, change it on the AP first and save the change. When you lose the connection, change the WEP key in the station software to match the key you entered in the AP. The connection should be reestablished.

♦ **HTML-based.** Many of the newer lines of APs have a series of HTML forms stored in firmware that enable you to configure each AP. You can access these forms using a Web browser over a wireless connection or over an Ethernet cable if you know the AP's IP address. Figure 10-4 shows one of the HTML pages used to configure a Linksys AP.

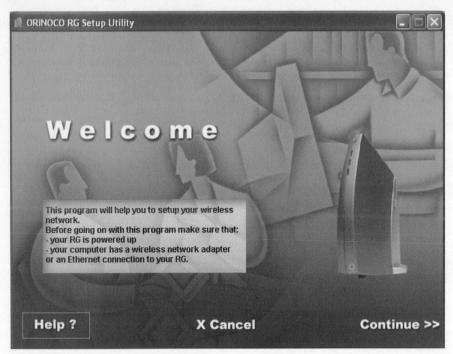

Figure 10-3: The Agere ORiNOCO Residential Gateway Setup Utility

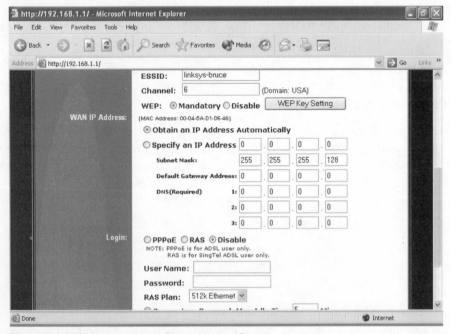

Figure 10-4: HTML page used to configure a Linksys AP

Regardless of the utility you use, you will need to record and/or set the following parameters in the access point (not necessarily in this order):

♦ **MAC address.** This is the physical address of the radio in the AP. You should find this number printed on a label attached to the device. You may need to know this value for troubleshooting, so write it down. If the AP uses a PC card as its radio, the MAC address for the AP is sometimes printed on the back of the PC card. The AP's Ethernet connection to the wired network also has a MAC address that is different from the AP's radio MAC address.

♦ **Local IP address.** In addition to a physical address (the MAC address), the AP will also have its own IP address. You need to know this IP address to access the configuration pages using a Web browser. Refer to the product documentation to determine this IP address. With several brands of APs, you can also use a utility program to scan the network for the IP address(es) of any AP(s) that are attached to the network.

If you have another device that is providing DHCP service, you may need to access the configuration software for the DHCP server to determine the IP address that the DHCP server has assigned to the AP.

♦ **Subnet Mask.** In most cases, this value, which is probably 255.255.255.0, is provided automatically by the DHCP server.

♦ **Service set identifier (SSID).** The SSID (sometimes called the *network name)* can be any alphanumeric string, including uppercase and lowercase letters, up to 32 characters in length. Sometimes the manufacturer "hard codes" a unique network name into each AP. In such cases, the network name is printed on a label that is attached to the AP. If you can change the setting, don't use the default setting. For most APs, changing the SSID doesn't really add much security; nonetheless, changing this identifier makes it a little more difficult for intruders to access your WLAN. When you configure wireless stations, you will need to use the same SSID/network name that is assigned to the AP.

♦ **Channel.** The DSSS channel over which the AP will communicate. If you plan to use more than one AP in your home, you should assign a different DSSS channel (over which the AP will communicate) for each AP to avoid signal interference. Eleven channels, set at 5 MHz intervals, are available in the U.S. However, because DSSS signals spread across a 22 MHz-wide spectrum, you can only use up to three channels (typically 1, 6, and 11) in a given WLAN. Some APs intended for home use refer to these three channels by letter names rather than numbers. The software for configuring ORiNOCO residential gateways, for example, provides only four possible channels: A, B, C, or D. These channels are equivalent to the DSSS channels 1, 4, 7, and 10.

◆ **WEP Keys.** You should always use 802.11b's built-in WEP encryption. Only a determined hacker with the proper equipment and software will be able to crack the key. However, if you don't use WEP, any nosy neighbor with a laptop, wireless PC card, and range-extender antenna may be able to see and access your WLAN. Whenever you use WEP, all wireless stations in your house attached to the WLAN must use the same key. Sometimes, the AP manufacturer will assign a default WEP key. Always assign a new key to avoid a security breach.

◆ **Password.** Configuration software, particularly the HTML variety, may require that you enter a password to make changes to the AP setup. The manufacturer will have provided a default password (see the user documentation). Use the default password when you first open the configuration pages, and then immediately change the password to avoid a security breach.

This list covers AP parameters that you will most often encounter and need to configure, but it is not comprehensive. Other settings that you probably don't need to change include the transmission rate—which normally adjusts automatically to give the best throughput—RTS/CTS protocol settings, the beacon interval, and the fragmentation threshold.

TIP

The *preamble type* setting can sometimes cause problems. This is particularly true when you are using a wireless NIC from one manufacturer and an AP from another. The majority of WLAN manufacturers set the *preamble type* to "Long" by default. If you are having trouble getting a particular PC card or other wireless station to work with the AP, check to see if the preamble type in the AP matches what the wireless station is expecting.

Sharing the Internet

The primary reason for installing a home network is often to share one Internet connection among all the computers in your household. Perhaps several members of the family are continually competing for the phone line to dial up your local *Internet service provider (ISP)*; or maybe you recently subscribed to a high-speed Internet service and you want to get your money's worth by connecting all the computers in your house. The following sections explain how to use a WLAN to share an Internet connection over dial-up lines or over a high-speed DSL or cable modem.

Using an Internet Gateway

The "cleanest" way to share an Internet connection is through a dedicated piece of hardware that combines an *Internet gateway* (Internet routing, and a NAT/firewall service) with a DHCP server. As discussed in Chapter 5, the DHCP service assigns the local IP addresses for all the devices on your LAN, which usually include the computers in your house, but can also include printers with network connections and any wireless station devices connected to your wireless LAN. The Internet gateway function enables all computers connected to the Internet through the Internet gateway device to share the same IP address on the Internet. Figure 10-5 depicts a home network with both wired PCs and wireless PCs.

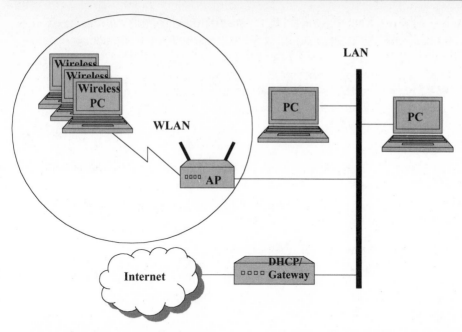

Figure 10-5: A network that uses a combination DHCP server/Internet gateway to enable all computers in the network to share a single IP address

Several of the leading wireless networking equipment manufacturers offer access points that can also perform the functions of a DHCP server and an Internet gateway. Some models can even be used as switched hubs for wired workstations on the LAN. If you are not planning to have any wired workstations on your network, the design of your network looks more like the one depicted in Figure 10-6.

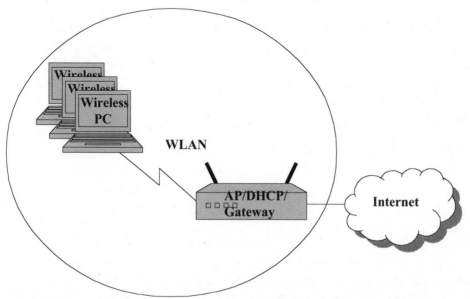

Figure 10-6: A wireless-only network that uses a combination AP, DHCP, NAT-firewall—*Residential Gateway*—to enable all computers on the network to communicate with the Internet using a single IP address.

Configuring a device on the LAN to use a DHCP server/Internet gateway device is very easy. To configure a network device to use DHCP, follow one of the procedures outlined below:

If the computer is running the Windows 9x operating system, perform the following steps:

1. Click the Start button and select Settings then Control Panel from the Start menu to display the Control Panel.

2. Double-click the Network icon in the Control Panel to display the Network dialog box.

3. In the Configuration tab, highlight the TCP/IP item for the device you want to configure.

4. Click Properties to display the TCP/IP Properties dialog box.

5. On the IP Address tab, click the "Obtain an IP address automatically" option button.

6. Click OK to return to the Network dialog box.

7. Click OK again to return to the Control Panel.

8. Close the Control Panel.

If the computer is running the Windows 2000 operating system, perform the following steps:

1. On the Start menu, click the Start button and select Settings. Then click the Network and Dial-up Connections to display the Network and Dial-up Connections window.

2. Highlight the Local Area Connection item for the device you want to configure.

3. Click File to display the File menu, and click Properties to display the Local Area Connection Properties dialog box.

4. Highlight the Internet Protocol (TCP/IP) option and click the Properties button to display the Internet Protocol (TCP/IP) Properties dialog box.

5. On the General tab, click the "Obtain an IP address automatically" option button, as well as the "Obtain DNS server address automatically" option button.

6. Click OK to return to the Local Area Connections dialog box.

7. Click OK to return to the Network and Dial-up Connections window.

8. Close the Network and Dial-up Connections window.

If the computer is running the Widows XP operating system, perform the following steps:

1. From the Start menu, click the Start button and select Control Panel.

2. Double-click the Network Connections icon in the Control Panel to display the Network Connections window.

3. Highlight the Network Connection item for the device you want to configure in the LAN or High-Speed Internet section of the Network Connections window.

4. Click File to display the File menu, and click Properties to display the Network Connection Properties dialog box.

5. On the General tab, highlight the Internet Protocol (TCP/IP) option and click the Properties button to display the Internet Protocol (TCP/IP) Properties dialog box.

6. On the General tab, click the "Obtain an IP address automatically" option button, as well as the "Obtain DNS server address automatically" button.

7. Click OK to return to the Local Area Connections dialog box.

8. Click OK to return to the Network and Dial-up Connections window.

9. Close the Network and Dial-up Connections window.

If the computer is running the Mac OS 9.*x* operating system, perform the following steps:

1. From the Apple menu, display the Control Panels list and select TCP/IP to display the TCP/IP window.

2. Using the Connect Via pop-up menu, select the network device you want to configure.

3. Using the Configure pop-up menu, select the Using DHCP Server option.

4. Close the TCP/IP window, saving changes when prompted.

If the computer is running the Mac OS X operating system, perform the following steps:

1. From the Apple menu, choose System Preferences and click Network to display the Network pane.

2. Choose the network interface that you want to configure from the Configure pop-up menu.

3. Click the TCP/IP tab.

4. Using the Configure pop-up menu, select the Using DHCP Server option.

After completing one of these procedures, the DHCP server will *lease* a local IP address to the device you are configuring, enabling it to communicate with other IP devices on the network. (Sometimes you will have to restart your computer to successfully achieve the desired result.) The DHCP server will renew the lease each time you restart your computer; or if you leave your computer on all the time, the DHCP server will renew the lease on a periodic basis.

When the DHCP server assigns an IP address, it also assigns DNS servers and a default gateway. If the DHCP server device is also an Internet router, the gateway address will be the same IP address as the DHCP server. The DNS server addresses will be supplied by your ISP's DHCP server and will be passed on by your LAN's DHCP server to each workstation.

Using Windows Internet Connection Sharing

Windows 98 Second Edition and later versions of Windows provide a software solution for sharing an Internet connection over a local area network. This option is available whether you are using a wired network, a wireless network, or a combination of the two. When you set up a shared Internet connection using this method, you must select one computer as the *Internet connection host*. This computer must be turned on, running Windows 98 or later, and connected to the Internet to enable any other computer on the LAN (or WLAN) to access the Internet. This Internet connection host computer must also have two network adapters—one that connects to the Internet and another that communicates with the local area network. (The connection to the Internet could be through a dial-up modem.) After you complete the setup, Windows will turn the Internet connection server computer into both a DHCP server and a NAT Internet Router.

To set up Windows Internet connection sharing in Windows 98 Second Edition or Windows Me, perform the following steps:

1. On the Start menu, click the Start button and select Settings. Select the Control Panel button to display the Control Panel.

2. Double-click the Add/Remove Programs icon in the Control Panel.

3. Highlight the Internet Tools option, but don't change the check box.

4. Click Details and click the Connection Sharing check box.

5. Next, click OK twice. Insert the Windows CD when prompted.

6. When Windows displays the Internet Sharing Setup Wizard, click Next.

7. The next screen will ask "What type of connection do you use to access the Internet?" If you will be connecting to the Internet by modem, select the Dial-up Connection option button. If you have DSL or a cable modem, select the High-Speed Connection option button.

8. Click Next. The screen shows a list of network adapters—all the adapters ever installed on this computer.

9. Select the network adapter that you will be using to connect to the Internet. If you are using DSL or a cable modem, select the adapter that is connected to the DSL/cable modem. Click Next.

10. The next screen will look almost the same as the previous screen, but will no longer list the adapter that you selected in the previous step. This time, select the adapter that will communicate with your LAN or WLAN. Click Next.

11. When the wizard prompts you to create disks for the client computers, click Cancel. Click Finish to complete the Wizard.

To set up Internet connection sharing in Windows 2000, perform the following steps:

1. On the Start menu, click the Start button and select Settings. Then click the Network and Dial-up Connections menu item to display the Network and Dial-up Connections window.

2. Highlight the Local Area Connection item for the network connection device that will be connected to the Internet.

3. Click File to display the File menu, and then click Properties to display the Local Area Connection Properties dialog box.

4. Click the Sharing tab and click the Enable Internet Connection Sharing for this connection.

5. Click OK to return to the Network and Dial-up Connections window.

6. Close the Network and Dial-up Connections window.

To set up Internet connection sharing in Windows XP, perform the following steps:

1. From the Start menu, click the Start button and select Control Panel.

2. Double-click the Network Connections icon in the Control Panel to display the Network Connections window.

3. Highlight the Network Connection item for the network device you want to use to connect to the Internet.

4. Click File to display the File menu, and click Properties to display the Network Connection Properties dialog box.

5. On the Advanced tab, click the "Allow other network users to connect through this computer's Internet connection" check box.

6. Click OK to return to the Network and Dial-up Connections window.

7. Close the Network and Dial-up Connections window.

The other computers in the LAN or WLAN can only access the Internet if the host computer is on, with Windows running, and connected to the Internet through the adapter specified in the Wizard. In addition, each of the other computers (the *clients*) must be set up to obtain an IP address automatically, as described earlier in the chapter.

Summary

This chapter describes how to implement the home WLAN plan that you developed in your site survey in Chapter 6. It explores network wiring issues, installing and configuring APs in your home, and adding range-extender antennas. Finally, it covers Internet connection sharing using both a router and Windows' Internet Connection Sharing feature. Chapter 11 also covers special installation issues, but instead of focusing on home installation, it describes the installation of a WLAN on a college campus.

Chapter 11

<u>Planning and Installing</u>
<u>a Campus WLAN</u>

In This Chapter
This chapter discusses the following:

♦ Planning a campus wireless network

♦ Implementing the campus WLAN plan that you developed in your site survey

♦ Network wiring issues

♦ Installing and configuring APs around the campus

This chapter supplements the more general chapters in this book on planning and implementing a wireless network by discussing the unique issues regarding WLANs on the college campus. The chapter covers planning issues, supplementing the material provided in Chapters 4 and 5. It also supplements the general discussions found in Chapters 7, 8, and 9 on installing, configuring, and testing APs and wireless stations.

The Appeal of Wireless LANs on Campus

Standards bodies, such as the one that developed IEEE 802.11b, routinely focus their attention on *use cases*—hypothetical scenarios that describe how technology is likely to be used. The idea is to develop technology standards that will actually fill the needs of intended users. Apparently, a typical college campus is the ideal use case for taking full advantage of the benefits of wireless networking. A number of college campuses have already installed full-scale wireless networks, and those that haven't are making plans to. In case you are ever involved in such an effort, this chapter helps you consider the most important issues related to installing and configuring a WLAN on a college campus.

Colleges and universities have long recognized the benefits of wired networks. A list of the top 200 wired schools of 2001 has been published, with Carnegie Mellon University sitting atop the rankings for the second year in a row (see "America's 200 Most Wired Colleges " in Yahoo! Internet Life's features section at `www.yil.com/features`). Quite a few schools are adding wireless networking capabilities. Drexel University, in Philadelphia, PA, topped the wireless networking portion of the Yahoo! Internet Life survey with an A+ rating; nevertheless, most of the top 200 "wired" schools received a rating of C or below in the wireless category.

The Benefits of College WLANs

College campuses are especially suited to hosting IEEE 802.11b WLANs for the following reasons:

♦ **Highly mobile user base.** The mobility of WLAN devices matches the mobility of the primary users of a campus local area network—students and faculty. The students and faculty on a college campus rarely stay in one room during the day for more than an hour at a time. Student dorm rooms are now almost universally wired with network and Internet connectivity, but during the day, students move from classroom to classroom and building to building. Students may study in their rooms, but are just as likely to study in the library, student union, or some other common area on campus. Faculty members usually have an on-campus office, but may be physically present in the office only a couple hours a week.

♦ **Strong need for frequent network and Internet connectivity.** Faculty and students need frequent access to the university LAN for intra-university communication, and to the Internet for external communication and online research. Providing either students or faculty continuous connectivity using a wired network would be difficult, if not impossible, but a wireless network can be configured to reach every nook and cranny on campus.

♦ **Wide variety of hardware.** Although some private universities require students to purchase a particular laptop computer when they register, most student bodies use a wide variety of brands and types of computers. The 802.11b standard and the Wi-Fi certification program increase the likelihood that the majority of students with portable computers will be able to purchase wireless networking cards that will work with their computers and be compatible with the wireless network.

♦ **Early adopters.** Faculty and students in a university setting are more likely to embrace new technology than the populace as a whole. In fact, the availability of a wireless network may be one of the deciding factors for students in the process of choosing a college.

♦ **Saves time and money.** By some estimates, the cost of installing a wireless network is about 20 percent (or less) of the cost of installing a wired network in older buildings to the same number of users. One university recently estimated that it will save over $7 million if it installs a WLAN, rather than rewiring the more than 100 buildings on its campus. Projects that take months to implement with standard network wiring can be completed in a few weeks using wireless networking technology. Furthermore, upgrading to faster and more secure wireless networks at a future time will be much faster and easier than upgrading a wired network. Several universities have even been able to work out special business relationships with wireless network hardware manufacturers to greatly reduce the cost of wireless equipment.

The Risks of College WLANs

Of course, using a wireless network on a college campus is not without its problems. Some administrators are concerned about unauthorized individuals accessing the campus network to snoop, or worse, to cause trouble. In addition, IS personnel are already finding that so-called *rogue WLANs* can be a significant problem on a college campus. Setting up a simple wireless LAN is affordable for many students because the cost of equipment is so low. A student could have a wireless network up and running in the dorm in a matter of hours, or even minutes, with no guidance, control, or consent from the university. Although students may consider this a harmless activity, rogue WLANs can wreak havoc for the IS department, which won't be able to actively manage the network traffic these rogue WLANs create. At least one college IS department has "banned" the use of Apple AirPort base stations on campus.

The Yeas Have It

In weighing both sides, wireless networks clearly are a relative bargain for colleges that have yet to wire their campuses, and are enormously valuable to students and faculty. Consequently, it is only a matter of time before every college installs (or should install) a wireless network.

In my research for this book, I spoke with individuals involved in implementing IEEE 802.11b wireless networks at two small private universities: Pepperdine University in Malibu, CA, and Saint Francis University in Loretto, PA. Both Pepperdine University and Saint Francis University have embraced the use of wireless networks. According to Jack Putterflam of the Pepperdine Information Technology department, Pepperdine uses a combination of Lucent and Cisco IEEE 802.11b technology. They started with Avaya APs, but switched to Cisco equipment. Students and faculty use either Lucent or Cisco PC cards. I also spoke with Robert Griffin, Assistant Director for Distance Learning, and Mike Shanafelt, Information Technology Specialist, both with the Center of Excellence for Remote and Medically Under Served Areas (CERMUSA) project on the Saint Francis University campus. CERMUSA developed a wireless campus prototype that has recently been rolled out to the entire Saint Francis University campus. All freshmen in 2001 were issued an IBM Thinkpad laptop, including a built-in wireless NIC. All APs are based on Lucent technology.

NOTE

For more information about CERMUSA, go to www.cermusa.francis.edu. For information about other universities that have implemented wireless networks, visit www.educase.edu/issues/wireless.html.

Planning and Implementing the Campus WLAN

In some ways, planning a campus wireless network is similar to planning a WLAN for a large business campus. As described in Chapter 4, you should perform a detailed site survey, or hire a consultant to do so, before purchasing equipment and attempting to install the WLAN. Wiring and installing access points on a college campus also involve the same types of issues and challenges as in most business environments (although significant differences exist as well). The following sections address issues that are specific to college IEEE 802.11 networks.

Access Point Location

A core mission of any college or university is to provide an environment that is conducive to learning. Personal computers, local area networks, and the Internet can all be powerful learning tools. On a modern college campus, personal computers have moved from the category of "luxury appliance" to that of "necessity"—at least from the perspective of the college student.

Any computer network that you install, especially any wireless network, should be designed to support effective use of computers by students and faculty. To that end, colleges and universities are installing wireless access points in the following types of locations:

- **Administration Buildings.** The administrative offices on most campuses already have wired networks, but the flexibility of wireless networks makes it worthwhile to add APs even where wired jacks exist. Many administrative buildings serve different functions; in addition to being a place of work, these buildings may include common areas where students and faculty can relax or study. Wireless networking is an attractive option because it enables so-called "ubiquitous computing" or "computing from anywhere." Administrators want to give students the ability to sit and study or do research with their laptops anywhere on campus, including the administration building.

- **Libraries.** For years, libraries have made good use of computers, first to catalog and manage thousands of books, and more recently, to provide convenient access to the Internet's vast electronic research capabilities. It is only natural, therefore, to facilitate students' study and research facilities by adding wireless networking. Students can bring their laptop computers to the library and access the Internet without having to wait in line to access one of the library's computers. The library's collection management system can even be configured to permit students to search the card catalog from their laptops, helping them determine whether a book is checked in or out.

- **Classrooms.** Students and faculty spend a great deal of time in the classroom, so allowing them to access the network wirelessly *within* the classroom seems worthwhile. Consequently, many college WLANs have concentrated initial AP installations in classroom buildings. Some early-adopter schools have discovered, however, that students are more likely to use a wireless network connection outside of class. Most students bring their laptops to class in order to take notes, not to access the school network or the Internet. As faculty gets used to the idea of students being "wired" during class, they will certainly take better advantage of the technology to provide a richer multimedia experience. For example, with screen synchronizaton programs such as NetMeeting, and similar capabilities now built into Windows XP, lecturers can broadcast a presentation to students' laptops, either supplementing or replacing *liquid crystal display* (LCD) projectors. If all students come to class with a wired laptop, they can take in-class quizzes and exams on "electronic paper," making the correction and grading process more accurate and efficient—more accurate because there is less chance for misreading a student's handwriting, and more efficient because all grading can be done electronically.

The Pepperdine crew installed Lucent Avaya and Cisco APs in classroom buildings, high on the wall just outside the door of each classroom. They found that this placement gave the best overall coverage and made for a clean installation. Other universities report success using a similar approach.

At Saint Francis University, the team who installed the WLAN in the classroom buildings chose to install dual-card Lucent ORiNOCO APs attached to support beams above the dropped ceiling. They used power-over-Ethernet (PoE) to avoid the need for running additional power lines. They experimented with range-extender antennas, but determined that these external antennas improved the signal only in limited circumstances.

♦ **Dorms.** Many students do their studying and schoolwork in the dorm. For that reason, wiring student dormitories is typically one of the first stages of any campus network initiative. There's an irony here, however. Because dorm rooms are typically wired by the time a wireless network initiative is formulated, this initiative reaches the dormitories only after other areas on campus are covered. Both Pepperdine University and Saint Francis University have completed phase I of their programs without installing any APs in the undergraduate dorms. Several schools that have installed wireless connectivity in their dorms have discovered that students are much more likely to use a WLAN in the dorm than anywhere else on campus. In all likelihood, most campuses will eventually decide that getting "wired" is great, but that getting "unplugged" is even better, motivating them to move to wireless connectivity everywhere on campus, including the dorms. If you are still planning a campus WLAN, I suggest you consider covering the dorms in phase I, along with the rest of the campus. (Of course, I don't have to justify the budget—that's your job!)

♦ **Common Areas.** Wireless networks really shine when you can connect to the Internet sitting on a comfortable couch, lounging by the pool, or sitting in a quiet carrel in the library. The point is, you choose where to connect to the network—you're no longer tethered by cable to a wall jack. On a college campus, students can study in a variety of places. The ideal wireless network will cover all those areas. At Saint Francis and Pepperdine, all campus buildings, except the dorms, are fully covered (see Figure 11-1). Similarly, two of the top "wired" campuses in the country, Carnegie Mellon University in Pittsburgh, PA and Drexel University in Philadelphia, have outfitted their entire campuses, except the dorms, with 802.11b wireless network connections (including Internet access). These two schools are among the first universities in the country to cover every (non-dorm) square inch on campus. Both Pepperdine and Saint Francis have covered most of the non-dorm areas of their respective campuses, but not every square inch.

As you can see, every spot on campus benefits from wireless coverage. Positioning access points to achieve this blanket coverage may seem challenging at first, but when you start mapping the project out, piecing together AP cells so that no portion of the campus is missed is not as large a problem as finding enough DSSS channels (the radio frequency (RF) channels used by Wi-Fi systems to communicate) to get complete coverage without interference.

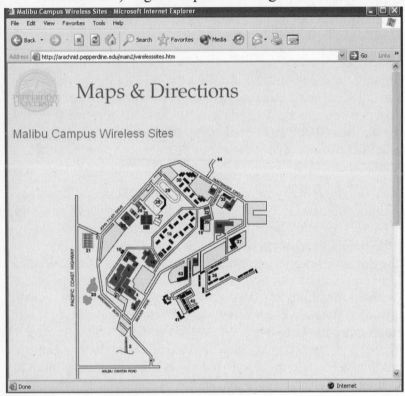

Figure 11-1: The Pepperdine Malibu campus wireless sites

AP manufacturers recommend using channels 1, 6, and 11, leaving four channels between any two channels that are used. Some installations successfully use four channels—1, 4, 7, and 10 or 11. This setup should work if you avoid overlapping cells that have channels with less than 25 MHz of separation. Whenever possible, you should not overlap two cells using the same channel. Overlapping cells on the same channel can result in dropped packets and excessive retransmission in both cells, slowing network traffic and reducing network capacity. Figure 11-2 shows how to achieve maximum coverage when overlapping cells and using only three channels. When you want to cover a large area completely, you may occasionally be forced to create adjoining cells that use the same channel. The negative impact of overlapping cells that are transmitting on the same channel can be minimized by ensuring that the overlap occurs at or near the limit of each cell's coverage.

Figure 11-2 shows five cells defined by the area that receives at least a –83 dBm signal (the sensitivity of an ORiNOCO wireless NIC at 11 Mbps—assuming that the WLAN is configured to connect at 11 Mbps). Notice the overlapping areas between each pair of cells. The area where any two cells overlap in an 802.11b WLAN is a *hand-off area*. If someone uses a wireless station in a hand-off area, the station maintains a connection with the cell that has the strongest signal between AP and station. As soon as the signal drops below –83 dBm, the station radio "looks" for another AP. The new AP will take over and establish an association with the station. In a hand-off area between two cells using the same channel, enough interference could cause packets to be dropped. Consequently, you should design the system to minimize the size of or eliminate these potentially contentious hand-off areas.

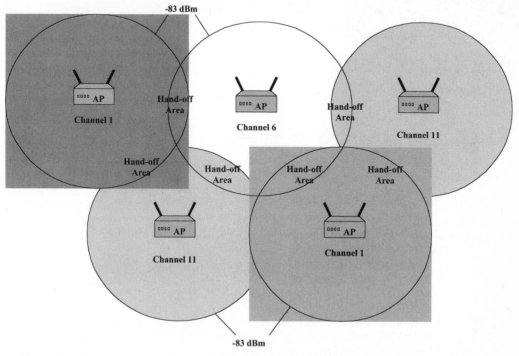

Figure 11-2: How to maximize coverage and avoid overlapping two cells using the same channel

The typical maximum number of users per cell for most 802.11b WANs is about 30, depending on the actual throughput capability of the network and the type of work the users are doing. At large universities, however, classes with more than 30 students are common. When you need coverage in a lecture hall or large classroom where more than 30 students are using the WLAN at one time, you could overburden the WLAN. If you reach network capacity, everyone may be denied service.

CROSS-REFERENCE

Refer to Chapter 9 for tools that help you determine network throughput and also determine whether you are reaching network capacity.

One way to solve this problem is to use an AP with more than one radio, or to use multiple APs to create concentric cells using two or even three channels at the same time. Figure 11-3 shows three cells covering the same physical area but using different channels—in this case, channels 1, 6, and 11. Because each cell can handle 30 students, this configuration increases the capacity to at least 90.

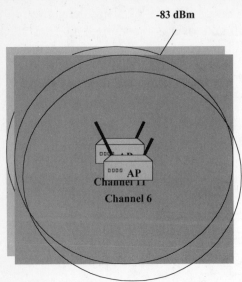

-83 dBm

Figure 11-3: Three concentric cells using channels 1, 6, and 11

Wiring

In my conversations with the technicians from Pepperdine and Saint Francis, I learned that an important factor in their selection of a hardware vendor was the capability to provide power to the APs over the Ethernet cable. It just so happened that Pepperdine was building a new science building at the same time it was installing its wireless network, so electrical wiring could easily be run wherever needed. However, in the other campus buildings, and in all the buildings on the Saint Francis campus, new electrical circuits were needed if power couldn't be provided over the network cable, more than doubling the cost of installing each AP.

On most college campuses, rewiring buildings is neither easy nor inexpensive. Category 5 UTP cable is easier and cheaper to install than new electrical circuits. Whenever possible, plan to use wireless equipment that can be powered over the network cable.

If you have already purchased equipment that doesn't have the power-over-Ethernet (PoE) option, you may be able to purchase this option from a third-party manufacturer. In addition, it is relatively straightforward to build your own power injector using parts that can be purchased at any Radio Shack. Only four of the eight wires in the Ethernet cable—1, 2, 3, and 6—are used for the network signal. You can use the other four wires—4,5, 7, and 8—to send electricity to the AP. You will need to build an adapter to install near the network hub, as shown in the schematic in Figure 11-4.

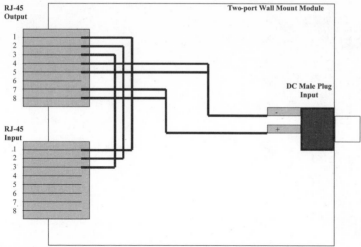

Figure 11-4: A schematic for the network-hub end of a do-it-yourself power injector for providing power over Ethernet to an 802.11b access point

In this schematic, a category 5 UTP Ethernet cable runs from the network hub to the RJ-45 input jack. You plug the AC to DC power adapter that came with the AP into the DC input. You run Cat 5 Ethernet from the RJ-45 output jack to the AP location. This PoE cable carries data on pins 1, 2, 3, and 6, and DC power on pins 4, 5, 7, and 8.

Figure 11-5 depicts a schematic for the adapter that you would install near the access point. You plug the end of the PoE Cat 5 Ethernet cable, originating from the network hub, into the RJ-45 input. The purpose of this adapter is to split-out the DC power from the Ethernet cable. You run a standard Cat 5 Ethernet patch cable from the RJ-45 output jack to the AP. You will need to use a voltmeter to determine whether the electrical signal that reaches the AP reaches the voltage required to operate the device. Long cable runs can cause enough signal drop to require you to purchase a stronger power source.

NOTE

Refer to the article by Terry Schmidt at `www.nycwireless.net/poe/` for step-by-step instructions on building these adapters.

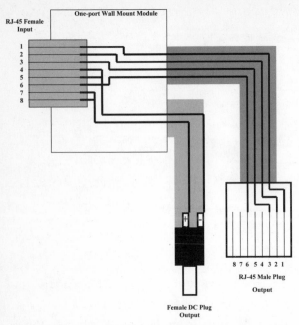

Figure 11-5: A schematic for the access-point end of a do-it-yourself power injector for providing power over Ethernet to an 802.11b access point

Security Considerations

Data security issues on college campuses differ greatly from those that pertain to the typical business environment. Although portions of the network are highly confidential—student records, tests, and ongoing academic research, for example—the overall process of educating is public in nature. In addition, the sheer number of students and the variety of equipment and experience levels that they bring to one environment make it difficult to establish complex security rules and regulations. Consequently, wireless LANs are often operated on college campuses with minimal privacy and authentication.

Typically, students must have user identifications and passwords to access e-mail accounts and other personal information. Little to no identification is required, however, to access the network and the Internet through a wireless connection. The university administration normally intends the system to be wide open for students and faculty. Many university WLANs require only that the user enter a specific service set identifier (SSID) in the configuration for each wireless device that will connect to the wireless network.

With current technology, virtual private networks are the best way to provide a wide open system for students and faculty and also provide security for portions of the network that should not be wide open. Students should have to provide a student ID number for authentication, but further screening is unnecessary. Individuals who need to access administrative records, faculty information and projects, and other information of that nature will need to log into the private portion of the network through a virtual private network (VPN).

Interoperability with Student Equipment

One of the greatest sources of frustration for a college IT department is the variety of hardware and software that students expect the department to support. The widespread availability of 802.11b equipment will inevitably lead many students to buy brands and models of wireless network equipment that you have never before seen.

Fortunately, the existence of the WECA organization and the Wi-Fi certification tests helps ensure interoperability between student-owned equipment and university-installed and university-owned/leased WLAN equipment. If your school has a mandatory computer acquisition program—similar to one recently started at Saint Francis—then you can at least control the configuration that comes with those machines. Otherwise, you should publish a set of guidelines to help both students and faculty select equipment that works well with the school's WLAN. You may even decide to go as far as Carnegie Mellon did and ban certain wireless equipment (the Apple AirPort base station, for example) that you know will cause problems for your system.

Summary

This chapter supplements the more general chapters in this book on planning and implementing a wireless network by discussing the unique WLAN-related issues of concern on a college campus. It covers the pros and cons of adding wireless LANs to college campuses, presents ways to provide adequate campus-wide coverage, and discusses the merits of power over Ethernet (PoE).

College campuses are ideally suited to the use of wireless networks. Increasingly, students and faculty at any leading university will come to expect wireless network access to be available anywhere on campus. It is up to technicians like you to see that they aren't disappointed.

Part III

Managing a Wireless Network

Chapter 12

Ensuring Basic Wireless Security

In This Chapter

This chapter discusses the following topics:

♦ The most common security risks for wireless LANs

♦ The strengths and weaknesses of Wired Equivalent Privacy (WEP)

If you have read anything in the computer trade press about 802.11 wireless networking, you may have the impression that 802.11b WLANs are deficient in terms of security features. This chapter explains both the strengths and weaknesses in 802.11b security, and describes what you should do, minimally, to ensure adequate security for your WLAN. Chapter 13 goes into more detail about enhanced WLAN security options.

The Risks

The security risks to your wireless networks fall into two categories:

♦ Accidental, casual, or other benign breaches that might coincidentally expose confidential information

♦ Intentional malicious breaches designed to steal information or damage your system

The security options built into the 802.11b standard will adequately protect against the first category of security breach, but not the second. If used at all, these standard features come close to providing the security that the name *Wired Equivalent Privacy* implies—that is, the same level of security provided by a wired network. Wireless networks, however, are meant to broadcast information, including confidential information, into the ether, where it can be retrieved by anyone with the right equipment. Wired networks have finite physical boundaries that provide more of a built-in barrier to intruders than is possible with wireless networks. Nonetheless, WEP successfully protects against snooping by the merely curious.

The real mystery is why so many WLAN administrators choose not to turn on the WEP feature. In some cases, WLANs use other security systems, such as virtual private networks (VPNs) that don't use WEP. In other cases, the wireless networks are fee-based services intended for public use, such as MobileStar, which is installed in many Starbucks coffee shops. Encryption is not offered on public wireless networks. The remaining unprotected WLANs are, however, hard to explain. I suspect that the person who installs a WLAN that doesn't use WEP either is not aware of WEP, or just never gets around to implementing it.

CROSS-REFERENCE

See Chapter 18 for a discussion on how to use public wireless networks such as MobileStar.

Protecting your network and the data it contains against an attack by a determined hacker requires the addition of disciplined security policies, supplemental user authentication, and better encryption. This chapter addresses the best way to use the standard 802.11b security features and how to implement sound network security policies.

CROSS-REFERENCE

Refer to Chapter 13 for additional information about enhanced security.

Remembering to Pull the Blinds—Always Use WEP

Protecting one's privacy starts with personal diligence. Just as you would pull the blinds before getting undressed, make it a habit to activate security features in a wireless LAN before transmitting any data.

Most users and even some technicians assume that the standard safeguards built into a typical local area network are adequate to protect data on a wireless segment of the network. It is important, however, to think of the WLAN as a public network that can be accessed by anyone who has a desire to do so—even with security features activated.

If your LAN has a firewall, you may be tempted to think that the WLAN is protected as well. Unfortunately, the reverse is true. In most cases, the WLAN is set up *inside* the firewall. As a result, the WLAN can actually defeat the purpose of the firewall, not only for the wireless section, but for the entire LAN. If an unauthorized person is able to connect to the WLAN, he or she will have bypassed the firewall unless the WLAN is set up *outside* the firewall.

CROSS-REFERENCE

Refer to Chapter 13 for a discussion of ways to set up your WLAN as a separate section of the network that is "walled off" from the rest of the LAN.

At the very least, require every computer accessing your wireless network to use WEP because every Wi-Fi-compliant AP and wireless NIC is required to support WEP. The only requirement is that all stations must use the same shared-key.

"Net Stumbling"

If you have already set up your WLAN, you may wonder how an unauthorized person would even know that your wireless network exists. Furthermore, how would he know the SSID that all stations must enter to access the network? As always, where there's a will, there's a way; and, in this case, the way is easy. Wireless access points and stations are, after all, radios that broadcast their signals in many directions. The signal almost certainly gets broadcast beyond the boundaries of the building that houses the WLAN, unless you go to great lengths to block the signal. Although the signal at the edges of your physical property may be too weak to be used by a standard wireless NIC with its built-in patch antenna, the signal may be strong enough to be picked up a block away by someone with a better antenna.

Radio technology has always been the playground for the technically adventurous, and wireless network technology is no exception. A popular activity for today's WLAN radio hound is known as *net stumbling*. The name is taken from the software that is used—a shareware program called Network Stumbler (www.netstumbler.com). The goal of net stumbling is to discover and log as many wireless networks as possible—not necessarily for gaining unauthorized access to the discovered WLANs. The *net stumbler* uses Network Stumbler on a Windows-based laptop that is equipped with the following:

- ◆ A Lucent chipset-based wireless NIC
- ◆ A range-extender antenna
- ◆ A GPS peripheral device

As long as the antenna-enhanced NIC can receive a minimal signal, Network Stumbler retrieves and displays the following information from each WLAN's broadcast (refer to Figure 12-1:

- ◆ MAC address
- ◆ SSID—Also sometimes called the *network name*
- ◆ AP name—This may be permanently set by the manufacturer, although in some cases, it may be set in the AP configuration software
- ◆ The channel over which the AP is broadcasting
- ◆ AP vendor
- ◆ Type-AP (infrastructure) or Ad Hoc
- ◆ WEP—Is it turned on?
- ◆ SNR—Signal-to-Noise Ratio
- ◆ Signal strength
- ◆ Noise strength
- ◆ Time first seen
- ◆ Time last seen

If the net stumbler has a GPS attached, Network Stumbler also specifies the following:

- ◆ Latitude
- ◆ Longtitude

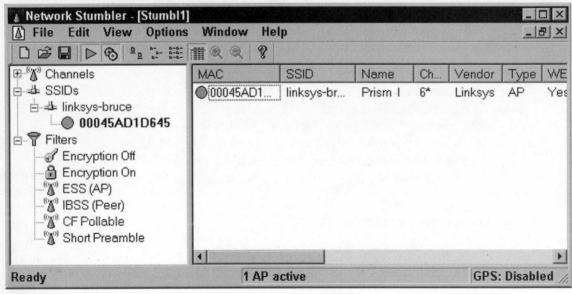

Figure 12-1: The Net

Net stumblers have identified literally hundreds of WLANs all over the country by simply driving around with their net-stumbling laptop, antenna, and GPS. What's more, as many as 60 percent of these WLANs did not have WEP enabled. The point of this section, of course, is to emphasize that you shouldn't be caught with your WEP down. Nosey "ears" are everywhere. The better AP management software enables you to use WEP to encrypt the SSID, and every 802.11b AP will enable you to encrypt the data transmitted over the WLAN. The next section explains how WEP works.

Wi-Fi Standard Security—Wireless Equivalent Privacy (WEP)

The original IEEE 802.11 1997 edition included a specification for an optional privacy algorithm called *Wireless Equivalent Privacy (WEP)*—the same WEP used in 802.11b wireless LANs. The stated intent of this algorithm is to protect authorized users of a wireless LAN from casual eavesdropping by providing a functional level of security equivalent to the physical security inherent to a wired LAN. WEP encrypts data transmitted over a WLAN using a private key. The same key is used to encrypt and decrypt the data—a system generically called *symmetric cryptography*. The IEEE 802.11 committee also strongly recommended that WEP shouldn't be considered adequate security without first implementing an authentication service and external key management service.

CROSS-REFERENCE

For more information on symmetric cryptography, refer to Chapter 14, and for a detailed discussion of authentication, refer to Chapter 13.

How WEP Works

WEP protects the privacy of the data transmitted over the WLAN. WEP can also be used to prevent unauthorized users from accessing the WLAN. WEP uses a shared key that has to be distributed to and configured in each wireless station ahead of time. The shared key is never transmitted in the clear over the network. However, unless you change the shared key on a regular basis, you run the risk that an unauthorized person will obtain the key and eavesdrop on the WLAN. Consequently, the WEP algorithm uses an additional key-like value called an *initialization vector (IV)* that can be changed frequently (as often as for every new packet sent). WEP uses the shared key and the IV together to accomplish the encryption. The packet that is sent to the recipient includes the *ciphertext* (encrypted) data, as well as the *cleartext (*unencrypted) IV. The recipient, in turn, uses the shared key and the IV together to decrypt the ciphertext data.

The entire WEP process is summarized in the following steps (Figure 12-2 depicts steps 1 through 5, and Figure 12-3 depicts steps 6 through 10):

1. The originating station uses an integrity algorithm to generate a 32-bit *cyclic redundancy check (CRC)* value called the *integrity check value (ICV)*. This value is sent along with the *MAC protocol data unit (MPDU—*the data provided by the upper-level protocols to be sent over the network by the MAC layer) in ciphertext form so the recipient can use it to ensure that the data has not been altered during transmission.

2. The originator generates a 24-bit value called the *initialization vector (IV)* and concatenates the IV with the shared key to form a *seed*. Wi-Fi-compliant wireless NICs must be able to handle a shared key of 40 bits in length. When the 40-bit key is combined with the 24-bit IV, the resulting seed value is 64 bits long. Most vendors also provide for a stronger 104-bit shared key, which results in a 128-bit seed.

3. The originator inputs the 64-bit or 128-bit seed into a *pseudorandom number generator (PRNG)* that uses the RC4 algorithm (a stream cipher design by Rivest for RSA Data Security, now RSA Security). The WEP PRNG produces a bit sequence that is equal in length (that is, number of bits) to the MPDU plus the ICV.

4. The originator uses a bitwise *exclusive OR (XOR)* boolean operation to combine the key sequence with the cleartext MPDU+ICV string of bits. The resulting *message* is a bit string that is a ciphertext version of the MPDU+ICV string.

5. The originator sends the ciphertext message, along with the cleartext IV, to the recipient over the wireless LAN.

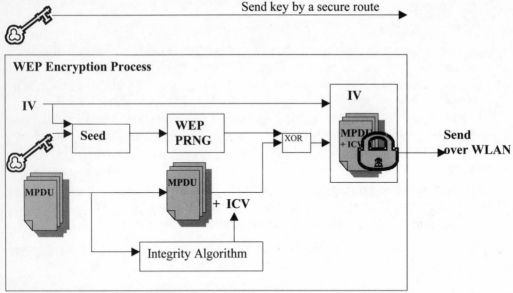

Figure 12-2: The WEP encryption process

6. The recipient, also using 802.11b-compliant WEP software, combines the shared key with the IV that arrived in the packet from the originator to form the same seed that was used to encrypt the MPDU+ICV string.

7. The recipient inputs the seed into the WEP PRNG to generate the bit sequence for deciphering the message.

8. The recipient uses a bitwise XOR operation to combine the bit sequence with the ciphertext message to produce the original cleartext MPDU+ICV.

9. The recipient uses the same integrity algorithm used by the originator to generate a 32-bit ICV from the plaintext MPDU.

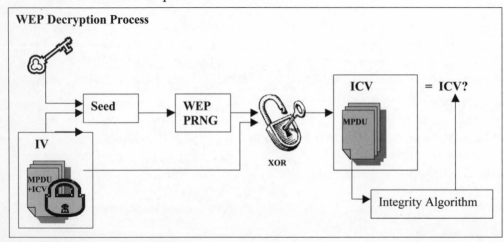

Figure 12-3: The WEP decryption process

10. The recipient compares the ICV included in the decrypted message with the ICV produced by the integrity algorithm. If the values match, the data arrived unaltered.

Entering WEP Keys

Sometimes the procedure for entering the key varies from one manufacturer to another, but if the same key is entered on two Wi-Fi-compliant devices, they will be able to communicate.

Several of the Intersil chipset-based products, both APs and wireless NICs, have a feature that enables you to generate a key (actually, four separate keys) from a *passphrase,* rather than enter a key directly (see Figure 12-4). This feature is easier to use than configuration utilities, in which you must type a long string of letters and numbers.

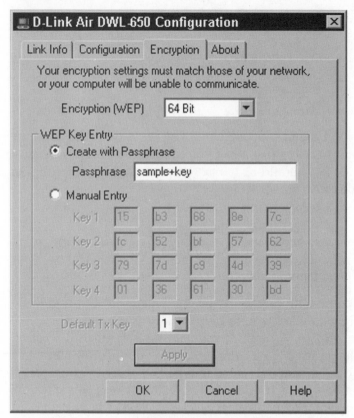

Figure 12-4: Entering a passphrase in an Intersil-style configuration utility

If you choose to use a wireless NIC that is based on the Lucent chipset, you will have to enter the key manually, as shown in Figure 12-5. To use a Lucent-based card with an Intersil-based passphrase-generated key, make sure you select the Use Hexadecimal option button in the Lucent client configuration utility and type the same sequence of numbers (0 through 9) and letters (a through f) as was generated by the passphrase key generator.

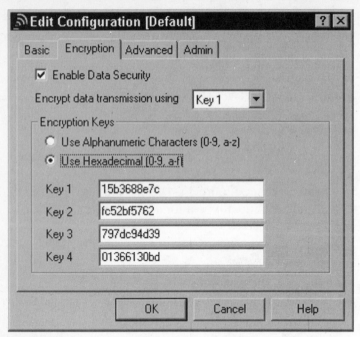

Figure 12-5: Entering an encryption key in a Lucent-style configuration utility

Each character or number that you type in a hexadecimal key is stored in the computer as a sequence of four bits. For a 40-bit key (usually referred to as a 64-bit key because of the addition of a 24-bit IV), the key should be ten hexadecimal digits in length. For example, the following sequence represents a 40-bit key:

```
15B3688E7C
```

You may sometimes see all uppercase letters used (A through F) and sometimes all lowercase letters (a through f). In other words, it doesn't matter whether you use upper- or lowercase letters to type the hexadecimal key.

The configuration utilities that come with Lucent-based equipment do not provide a passphrase key generator, but they do allow you to type the key as a series of alphanumeric characters (a through z, A through Z, and 0 through 9) rather than as a hexadecimal number. Each alphanumeric letter or number that you type for a key represents an eight-bit ASCII code, so you only need to type five letters or numbers for a 40-bit key, or 13 letters or numbers for a 104-bit (that is, 128-bit) key. However, typing the key as a string of alphanumeric characters produces weaker keys than generating the key as a truly random string of hexadecimal numbers because there are fewer keys possible, making it statistically easier for a hacker to use hacking software to "guess" the key. In addition, unlike typing a hexadecimal key, it does matter whether you use upper- or lowercase. If your WLAN has computers with wireless NICs that accept only hexadecimal keys, refer to an ASCII/hex translation table to determine the hexadecimal equivalent to the alphanumeric key. (The help file that accompanies Lucent-based wireless NICs contains an ASCII/hex translation table.)

You have probably asked yourself, "Why are there four keys in Figure 12-4 and four in Figure 12-5?" IEEE 802.11 provides for entering up to four WEP keys, so most wireless NIC and AP configuration software provides for entering all four keys in the same screen. The Intersil passphrase key generator supplies all four keys at once. Nonetheless, when data is transmitted, only one key is used to encrypt the data. The receiving AP or station can only decrypt the data if the same four keys are entered in the same order. For example, if the sending station indicates that it used the third key to encrypt the data, the receiving station will use the third of the four keys that are stored in its configuration. The intent of providing four keys is to enable use of the four keys in a rotation, using different keys at set intervals without needing to enter new keys until all four keys have been used. For such a system to be usable, however, the process of selecting which of the four keys is used and in what order needs to be automated. Several of the enterprise-quality wireless LAN manufacturers include key-distribution software with their APs.

> **TIP**
>
> 802.1x is the new IEEE standard, ratified in June 2001, and supported by Windows XP and several of the leading enterprise-level wireless LAN equipment manufacturers. This new standard enables the network to authenticate and to determine the identity of an entity, as well as the entity's access rights at the time that the entity attempts to connect to a LAN port, without depending on the MAC address. Using this standard and well-established key derivation algorithms, such as Transport Layer Security (TLS—equivalent to SSL discussed in Chapter 14), Secure Remote Password (SRP) protocol, or Kerberos, per-session WEP keys can be dynamically derived and assigned. See Chapter 13 for a more complete discussion of 802.1x.

WEP Vulnerabilities

Computer scientists from the University of California and Zero Knowledge Systems (Nikita Borisov, Ian Goldberg, and David Wagner) published a paper in February 2001 that posited that, with the right approach, it is only an exercise in patience before any WEP key is discovered. In August 2001, leading cryptographers Adi Shamir, Istik Mantin (both of Israel's Weizmann Institute of Science), and Scott Fluhrer (of Cisco Systems) published another paper describing additional vulnerabilities. Since that time, several teams of cryptographers have successfully attacked the WEP system, including 128-bit implementations, using the approach described in the Shamir-Mantin-Fluhrer paper. What's more, a software toolkit called Airsnort has been published that makes the process easier. The attack implemented in Airsnort is possible because certain initialization vectors (IVs) are "weaker" than others—in other words, they produce keys that are very similar to one another for encrypting different data packets. Using Airsnort, or some other similar tool, hackers can build a list of likely key values that greatly narrows the number of key values that are candidates for "guesses," conversely increasing the likelihood that the key will be guessed. This vulnerability has been confirmed by numerous researchers. To exploit this WEP weakness, hackers probably need access to a large amount of data, but if the target is a busy WLAN, they may not have to wait long.

WEP Fixes

WEP's weakness lies in key generation, not in the encryption algorithm. As discussed earlier in this chapter, the key used for encryption is generated by combining the WEP key with an IV. One could take either of the following two approaches to reduce WEPs vulnerabilities:

♦ Fix the tendency to generate weak IVs, thus closing off the known method of attack.

♦ Generate WEP keys more often, ideally by session, thereby narrowing the window for existing relevant attacks.

The first "work around" for the WEP vulnerability is to frequently change WEP keys manually, but this is not a practical solution for any but the smallest of WLANs. Fortunately, several commercial methods of producing stronger IVs are already available:

♦ **Agere.** Agere Systems has released an enhanced version of WEP, dubbed WEPplus, that remains compatible with existing WEP but avoids the use of initialization vectors that can create weak keys. This solution is fully compatible with existing WEP implementations, but greatly reduces the likelihood of a successful attack. WEPplus drivers for all current Agere ORiNOCO products are included in a free Internet download as part of its Winter 2002 Software release. Agere's Winter 2002 Software release also includes updates to AP management software that adds support for 802.1x, including dynamic per-session WEP key distribution.

♦ **Cisco.** Cisco has implemented *Extensible Authentication Protocol (EAP)*, an extension to Remote Access Dial-In User Service (RADIUS) that enables use of RADIUS servers to authenticate WLAN users. Cisco has also implemented support for IEEE 802.1x, which provides controlled port access, mutual authentication, and automatic distribution of WEP keys on a per-session basis.

♦ **RSA.** The encryption algorithm used in WEP is RC4, a technology licensed from RSA. In December 2001, RSA announced that it had developed a "fix" for WEP that will rapidly generate a unique RC4 key for each packet sent over the WLAN. The new solution ensures that an initialization vector will not be used more than once with each WEP key. This solution has been presented to the IEEE 802.11 working group, who will include it in an information section of the 802.11i document currently under development. Task group I of the IEEE 802.11 committee is working toward a fix for WEP. This solution can be implemented as a software patch/upgrade for use by existing Wi-Fi WLAN users and administrators.

Summary

This chapter covers the most common security risks for wireless LANs, as well as the strengths and weaknesses of Wired Equivalent Privacy (WEP)—IEEE 802.11's standard encryption feature. At this point, you should be aware of the existing problems with securing 802.11b WLANs and know the best way to deal with these problems.

You should also keep in mind that the basic security provided by WEP is just one tool of several that are intended to secure WLANs. Be sure to take a look at both Chapters 13 and 14 for coverage of other security tools such as user authentication and public key encryption.

Chapter 13

Implementing Enhanced Wireless Security

In This Chapter

This chapter discusses ways to implement security in a wireless LAN beyond the basic security discussed in Chapter 12. The following security methods are covered:

♦ Wireless Demilitarized Zones (WDMZ)

♦ IPsec

♦ Automatic key updates

♦ 802.1x network port authentication

♦ The Kerberos Authentication Service

Have you ever pushed back from the table after eating a meal at your favorite restaurant, feeling like you're about to burst? I have, and I usually decide that the only way for me to lose weight is to start frequenting restaurants where the food tastes bad. In a way, wireless LANs are analogous to good food. They're so easy to hook up that the users of your network may be tempted to "overindulge" to the detriment of network security. This chapter explores a few ways to enjoy the benefits of WLANs without jeopardizing the security of your network.

The Risks

Most network administrators, and even many home users, would never think of connecting a personal computer directly to the Internet. Instead, individual computers are hidden behind Internet *firewalls* that render the computers invisible to other computers on the Internet. However, any time a wireless station is connected directly to your network inside the firewall using an 802.11b wireless device, your network's firewall has effectively been neutralized. This can potentially be as dangerous as removing the firewall between your wired LAN and the rest of the Internet.

Rogue WLANs

Gartner, Inc., a research and advisory firm based in Stamford, Connecticut, released a report in August 2001 estimating that more than 50 percent of enterprises plan to install WLAN systems. Gartner further stated that at least 20 percent of enterprises already have rogue WLANs attached to their corporate networks. These wireless networks have been installed by end users getting out ahead of IS organizations.

No Security at All!

As discussed in Chapter 14, the Wired Equivalent Protection (WEP) encryption that comes standard with Wi-Fi networks is easily hacked. Even worse, Gartner estimates that most WLANs don't even bother to use WEP. In a September 7, 2001 white paper on wireless LAN security, the Wireless Ethernet Compatibility Alliance (WECA) stated, "By far, the biggest threat to the security of a wireless LAN is the failure to use any form of security." Consequently, any hacker with a notebook computer and a Wi-Fi PC card can drive by one of these unprotected WLANs and "jump" right over the corporate firewall as if it weren't there. In fact, the April 27, 2001 *Wall Street Journal* reported that as a test, two hackers drove around Silicon Valley while operating laptops outfitted with 802.11b wireless network interface cards (NICs) and were able to gain *unauthorized* access to multiple corporate networks.

In August 2001, Craig Ellison and several associates conducted a similar experiment for the online magazine ExtremeTech.com in various locations in New York, New Jersey, Boston, New Hampshire, and the Silicon Valley area of California. They used laptops, ORiNOCO-brand wireless PC cards, a 14 dB yagi antenna, a 3 dB magnetic mount omnidirectional antenna, and a nifty shareware program called NetStumbler (www.netstumbler.com). The ExtremeTech.com crew successfully located nearly 500 access points, with less than half of those sites protected even by WEP. They were able to gain access to many of those networks with no effort at all. (See the complete article titled "Exploiting and Protecting 802.11b Wireless Networks," by Craig Ellison, dated September 4, 2001, at www.ExtremeTech.com.)

The Response

You may recall that WEP was originally intended to provide the same level of protection as a wired network infrastructure. The only protections against hackers afforded to the typical wired LAN are physical isolation, password-level protection, and firewalls between the LAN and the Internet. By design, it is much easier to connect a new machine to a Wi-Fi network. This convenience greatly increases the risk that an unauthorized entity will be able to attach to the LAN To provide the level of protection that you can expect from a wired LAN, you need to change your way of thinking about the wireless LAN, adding several levels of protection in addition to WEP.

Think of Your WLAN as a Public Medium

Instead of thinking of a WLAN as an extension of your wired LAN, you should treat it as you would a public medium. To protect the wired portion of your network, you could take steps to ensure that all wireless stations are "walled" off from wired stations, with no direct access to enterprise resources. If your wireless stations didn't need to communicate with the rest of the LAN, adding a firewall or two would solve the problem. Of course, the primary reason for adding wireless stations is to facilitate connecting people to your LAN. Sticking them behind a firewall seems to defeat the purpose of even having a WLAN.

Follow Best Practices

Rather than quarantining all your wireless users behind firewalls, you should implement the following "best practices":

- Use WEP, at least, to encrypt all network traffic.
- Use IP Security (IPSec) to create virtual private network (VPN) connections for each wireless connection.
- Make sure you can detect "rogue" WLANs and then ensure that they follow your security policies.
- In your published security policies, include guidelines on using WLANs both in the office and at home.
- Make sure that everyone who uses a wireless station to connect to your LAN understands the security policies and the risks involved with not following them.

Employ one or more of the following measures to supplement WEP:

- Turn WEP on and manage your WEP key by changing the default key and, subsequently, changing the WEP key daily-to-weekly.
- Password protect drives and folders.
- Change the default SSID (Wireless Network Name) and use an SSID other than your company's main names, divisions, products, or street address.
- If your access point supports it, create a "closed" wireles LAN by disabling "broadcast SSID." You must also configure each client workstation with an SSID that matches the AP's SSID.
- Use session keys, if available, in your product.
- Use MAC address filtering, if available, in your product.
- Use a VPN system. Although doing so requires a VPN server, the VPN client is already included in many operating systems, such as Windows 98 Second Edition, Windows 2000, and Windows XP.

♦ Change the default password on your access point or wireless router.

♦ Locate access points toward the center of your building rather than near windows.

♦ Periodically survey your site using a tool such as NetStumbler to see if any rogue access points pop up.

♦ Take a notebook equipped with NetStumbler and an external antenna outside your office building and survey what someone parked in your parking lot might detect.

♦ Consider using MAC address tables, if your access point supports them.

♦ Consider using an additional level of authentication, such as RADIUS, before you permit an association with your access points.

♦ If you're deploying a wireless router, think about assigning static IP addresses for your wireless NICs and turn off DHCP.

♦ If you're using a wireless router and have decided to turn off DHCP, also consider changing the IP subnet.

♦ Buy only access points or NICs that support 128-bit WEP.

♦ Only purchase access points that have flashable firmware.

♦ If your access point supports it, consider deploying a closed network.

♦ Put your wireless access points into a DMZ and have your wireless users tunnel into your network using a VPN.

The remainder of this chapter takes a more detailed look at several of these recommendations. It reviews segregation of all wireless devices into a separate network, sometimes called a Wireless Demilitarized Zone (WDMZ), including creation of a virtual private network (VPN) using IP Security Protocol (IPSec); automatic encryption key management; using an IEEE 802.1x-compliant network access system; and using the Kerberos Authentication Service. It is up to you to decide which of these approaches best fits the needs of your WLAN users.

Implementing a Wireless Demilitarized Zone

In the "real" world, a *demilitarized zone* (DMZ) is a physical area—usually a strip of land—that provides a buffer between two hostile countries. For example, the cease-fire agreement at the end of the Korean War established a DMZ between North Korea and South Korea that exists to this day.

In a LAN, a *DMZ* is usually a network added between an internal network, such as a company intranet, and an external network, such as the Internet. This type of DMZ may contain an HTTP/FTP proxy server, an HTTP/FTP Web server, and a News proxy server. Like the real-world DMZ, a DMZ in a LAN provides an added layer of security between the internal (*trusted*) network and the external (*not trusted*) network. DMZ networks are also sometimes called *perimeter networks*.

In the context of protecting your LAN from outside intruders that might be able to slip in through a wireless station, it is often useful to think of all the wireless stations together as a separate network that should play the role of a *wireless DMZ* (WDMZ). To play such a role, the WLAN must provide strong security between the wired portion of your WAN and the rest of the world. The next few sections discuss the functions of a good WDMZ. Ideally, you will find a single software solution that will integrate with your wireless hardware (AP(s) and wireless NICs), as well as with the operating system of each station in the WLAN. A couple of example software solutions are examined later in the chapter.

Segregating the Wireless Stations

Whenever you plan to create a LAN that mixes wireless stations with wired stations on a LAN, you should improve security by first *compartmentalizing* the network. In other words, segregate wireless stations into one or more separate network segments that are not able to communicate directly with other stations and resources on the wired portion of the LAN—that is, without going through a network access authorization system first. This compartmentalization enables you to isolate the risks and apply a common set of security measures to all wireless stations uniformly.

The easiest way to start building a WDMZ is to connect all the access points together and then place a network authorization server (NAS) between the WDMZ(s) and the rest of your LAN (see Figure 13-1). Each WDMZ should have its own DHCP server to assign IP addresses when users connect. If you have many wireless stations, you can create several WDMZs.

If you think of critical data as the center of a large onion, your WLAN, in its role as WDMZ, should build many layers of security—many layers of onion—around your data. WEP provides one layer; the next several sections of this chapter describe other layers that you can add.

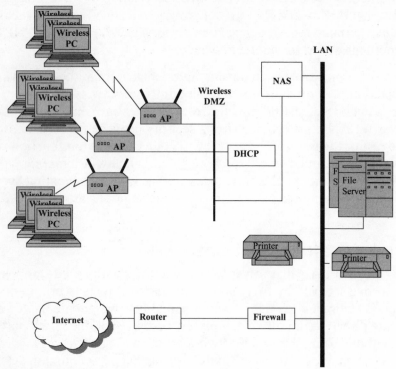

Figure 13-1: To compartmentalize your network, connect all wireless access points into one or more wireless DMZ(s), each with a dedicated DHCP server.

Controlling LAN Access

To fulfill its role of protecting the LAN from intruders, the WDMZ should require that all access go through a *network access server (NAS)*. The NAS server authenticates users and authorizes their access to the LAN. If your network has remote access capability, such as a dial-in port for remote users to connect by modem, you may have already addressed the issue of controlling access to the LAN by these remote users. System administrators commonly use a Remote Authentication Dial-In User Service (RADIUS) server to control LAN access by remote users who dial in to the network. RADIUS is discussed later in this chapter.

Whether you already use RADIUS or some other type of network access server, you should be able to use the same NAS server to control access to the LAN by wireless stations. The IEEE international standards organization has recently approved 802.1x as the standard protocol for authenticating stations connecting to a LAN. Built into this standard is the capability to make use of legacy NAS servers (such as RADIUS), as well as new NAS technologies that are bound to emerge.

For example, the most promising technology in the NAS space is the use of *Smart Cards*—credit-card-sized identification cards that contain a microchip—as authentication devices. The chip in each Smart Card contains a public-key certificate identifying the card's owner. Using *public key infrastructure* (PKI) technology, NAS servers will be able to limit access to a pre-approved list of authorized users who will use Smart Cards to identify themselves each time they access the LAN. When Smart Cards become widely available and less expensive to roll out, everyone needing access to your WLAN will be able to use their personal Smart Card to prove their identity and gain access to the network.

CROSS-REFERENCE
Refer to Chapter 15 for a discussion of public-key cryptography, including public-key certificates.

Windows XP is the first operating system to implement support for the new 802.1x standard. Undoubtedly, leading manufacturers of wireless access points will quickly update their products to support this implementation. Windows XP's implementation is briefly discussed later in this chapter.

If you can't implement 802.1x network access services on your LAN—perhaps because your operating system or the access points in your WLAN won't support 802.1x—you should implement a VPN and use it to provide network authentication.

Keeping Data Confidential

In a WLAN with WEP enabled, only users who have entered the shared key into the configuration software for their wireless network adapter can gain access to data on the network. Thus, WEP should always be enabled in your WLAN.

WHY DOES 802.11B USE THE RC4 ENCRYPTION ALGORITHM IN WEP?

According to people who are familiar with the work that led to the current 802.11b standard, several good reasons exist to use RC4, the encryption algorithm employed in WEP:

The algorithm itself, especially using 128-bit keys, is normally strong enough to provide good protection. (However, as implemented in 802.11b with only a 24-bit initialization vector (IV), the algorithm has proven to be breakable by clever hackers.)

RSA, the intellectual property owner, charges only a small royalty for using RC4.

RC4 has, until now, withstood traditional attacks well over a significant amount of time.

In terms of computer resource use (memory usage, and CPU usage—often called *clock cycles*), RC4 is cost-effective to implement compared to alternatives.

The next version of WEP will reportedly use the Advanced Encryption Standard (AES) encryption algorithm and will implement a 128-bit IV, resulting in a much more difficult nut to crack.

WEP conveniently provides security that doesn't require any user intervention—no passwords to remember. However, even if the cryptology were harder to break, WEP's reliance on a shared key makes it inherently insecure. Keep in mind that, at its best, WEP provides confidentiality only between stations. When enabled, WEP only encrypts during transmission from station to station. As soon as the confidential information arrives at the intended recipient's station, it is available in plain text. WEP doesn't provide any more confidentiality than you currently have on a wired network before doing encryption.

To supplement the data security provided by WEP, require users to implement at least password-level security on truly confidential data. Most operating systems provide the capability to password-protect individual files, as well as entire folders (directories). You should also encourage/require WLAN users to employ application-specific password protection on the files that they produce, store, and transmit on the network.

Controlling Resource Access

As a network administrator, you have other tools at your disposal that can enhance network security. You can apply more stringent criteria to wireless users before granting them access to network resources. In other words, you can set different user privileges for users that access the network via a wireless connection. For example, you can restrict users from changing their passwords and any other aspect of their user profile from a wireless station—that is, from a station in the WDMZ. If an intruder gains access to the network through a wireless connection, your WDMZ must ensure that the intruder cannot open a permanent hole in your security.

In addition to limiting wireless users' rights to change user profiles, you can typically limit other network resources, such as the following:

♦ Access to enterprise archive folders

♦ Permission to make changes to a station's network connection configuration

♦ Access to company-confidential data that may be published on the company intranet

♦ Network file and folder creation and deletion rights

♦ Access to portions of the network that don't relate directly to the user's job

You can implement a metered approach that grants access to these resources based both on the "need-to-know" and on the number of other layers of the security "onion" you have added to the standard 802.11b implementation. If a user's job doesn't require her to access files in the enterprise archives, you don't need to grant that access. If you implement a VPN, users of the VPN could be given less restricted access to sensitive network resources than those who don't access the network through the VPN.

Managing Bandwidth

Wireless bandwidth is a more limited commodity than wired bandwidth, largely because it tends to lag behind the transmission speed of comparable wired systems by at least one order of magnitude. Some WLAN equipment based on 802.11a, which transmits at 54 Mbps, is already available; but the predominant wireless transmission speed for WLANs is currently 11 Mbps (802.11b's top speed), and the typical Fast Ethernet wired LAN transmits at 100 Mbps.

At any moment in time, only one wireless NIC on a WLAN segment can transmit its data. Therefore, the more stations trying to transmit, the longer it takes each one to send out its data. To conserve valuable bandwidth, design your LAN so that network traffic does not use the wireless LAN unnecessarily. One of the side benefits of segregating all wireless stations into a separate network segment is to minimize the network traffic originating outside the WLAN. If you place a DHCP server and router between the wireless network and the rest of the LAN, only traffic originating within the WLAN or addressed to a wireless station needs to use the WLAN's bandwidth.

It would also be beneficial to the entire network if the WDMZ actively manages the bandwidth by enforcing rules that you have set up for ensuring that wireless bandwidth is not used unnecessarily. For example, many APs enable you to establish a finite list of MAC addresses that are permitted to access the WLAN. Network traffic from devices not on the approved list is not transmitted to the stations on the WLAN.

Using IPSec to Create a VPN

You may recall that one of the "best practices" listed at the beginning of the chapter is to create a *Virtual Private Network (VPN)* to improve security in a wireless network. Internet Protocol Security (IPSec—RFC 2401-2409) defines an architecture, protocol, and related Internet Key Exchange protocol that together enable secure data sessions over a network's IP layer (at the Network layer in the ISO/OSI model). IPSec was designed to provide high quality security for Internet traffic. Most typically, IPSec is used to create a secure session between two computers that may be connected to the same LAN/WLAN or may be communicating over the Internet. IPSec security services can include the following:

♦ Access control

♦ Connectionless integrity

♦ Authentication of the originator of data

♦ Rejection of replayed packets

♦ Confidentiality

♦ Limited data flow confidentiality

Because IPSec is a suite of services, specific implementations may or may not provide all these security services.

AH and ESP

IPSec adds two extensions to the Internet protocol (IP)—the Authentication Header (AH) protocol and the Encapsulating Security Payload (ESP) protocol—that together provide authentication, integrity, and confidentiality services.

To ensure the integrity of the data transmitted over the connection, AH and ESP use digital signatures. AH authenticates each packet's IP header and *payload* (packet content). ESP encrypts the payload and uses a *digital envelope* process (see the discussion of digital envelopes in Chapter 15) to encapsulate the data that will be transmitted over the network. AH signs the complete IP packet. The hashed method authentication code (HMAC) algorithm that is used to sign the packets depends on the specific implementation of IPSec, but is typically either MD5 or SHA-1. As part of its message integrity services, IPSec ensures that packets are not being replayed. This prevents a hacker from hijacking packets, changing their content, and resending the packets containing bogus content.

Internet Key Exchange

IPSec uses a companion key management protocol, Internet Key Exchange (IKE—RFC 2409), to control access and to handle keys. The two computer systems on either end of an IPSec session can only exchange data if they are using the same set of security parameters, known as a Security Association (SA). The parameters in an SA include shared session key, identity authentication method, and data authentication and encryption algorithm. Successful communication between two stations over IPSec can only take place if they first agree on SAs. IKE uses the Internet Security Association and Key Management Protocol (ISAKMP)/Oakley to negotiate and manage SAs at the initiation of an IPSec session. Oakley (named after Annie Oakley) is the name of the keying protocol used to derive the keys used in ISAKMP.

IP Security Policy

In order to negotiate an IPSec session, IKE must be able to refer to a published IP security policy to determine which security parameters to use for the particular users and machines attempting the handshake. The following parameters are typically included in an IP security policy:

- **IP filter list**—Lists IP addresses that are eligible to participate in a connection.
- **Filter action**—Defines security methods that will be used during a session.
- **Authentication methods**—Specifies the authentication method to use, such as Kerberos, certificate, or shared key.
- **Tunnel setting**—Specifies whether a computer is required to connect to the network through an IPSec tunnel server. In your WLAN, you would specify that all wireless machines are required to use a tunneled connection.
- **Connection type**—Specifies the type of connection—for example, LAN or remote access—through which a machine is permitted to connect to the network.

Your policy choices should balance the need for security against practicalities such as time and money. For example, the IPSec ESP protocol provides data confidentiality by encrypting the payload data using a symmetric encryption algorithm such as DES or 3DES. 3DES is stronger encryption, but requires more time and computing power to execute. Your enterprise security policy should state which algorithm to use depending on the sensitivity of the data that is transmitted during a session.

Examples of criteria that you may use to set IP security policies include the following:

- Group membership
- LAN access to the network versus dial-in access
- Wired LAN access versus wireless LAN access
- Time of day that connection is attempted

Tunnel Mode or Transport Mode

IPSec can operate in two different modes: *tunnel mode* and *transport mode.* In tunnel mode, IPSec encrypts the entire original IP packet inside a packet envelope and adds a new IP header, protecting the network address information stored in the original header as well. In transport mode, IPSec encrypts only the original payload. To implement a VPN through which wireless stations access the wired portion of your network, you will need to use IPSec's tunnel mode.

Windows 2000's L2TP/IPSec Support

IPSec is one of several VPN implementations supported by Windows 2000. Microsoft recommends using IPSec to secure Layer Two Tunneling Protocol (L2TP/IPSec), rather than pure IPSec tunnel mode. L2TP/IPSec addresses remote access VPN requirements better than pure IPSec, which was designed more for gateway-to-gateway tunneling.

L2TP is a combination of PPTP and Cisco's Layer 2 Forwarding protocol. It has evolved, along with IPSec, through the IETF standards process and garners broad vendor support. L2TP uses PPP as the method of negotiating user authentication; therefore, it supports legacy password-based user authentication systems such as the following:

- Password Authentication Protocol (PAP)
- Challenge Handshake Authentication Protocol (CHAP)
- Shiva Password Authentication Protocol (SPAP)
- Microsoft Challenge Authentication Protocol (MS-CHAP)

It also supports EAP-based authentication services, such as $802.1x$, that integrate with RADIUS and LDAP-based directories.

When L2TP and IPSec are used together, the L2TP packet becomes the payload in an IPSec packet. This combination delivers the encryption, integrity, and replay protection of IPSec while still benefiting from the user authentication, tunnel address assignment and configuration, and multiprotocol support of PPP-based tunneling.

Another advantage that L2TP/IPSec has over pure IPSec tunnel mode is support for DHCP. Because it uses PPP, L2TP/IPSec is already compatible with existing DHCP technology and can take advantage of any advances in that technology.

Both Windows 2000 Professional and Windows XP support L2TP/IPSec on the client side. Configuration of the client in Windows 2000 Professional can be a little tricky for an end user, but Windows XP includes a handy wizard to help accomplish the task.

Probably the most complicated task in configuring IPSec on a Windows 2000 Server domain controller is using the Microsoft Management Console (MMC) to set up IP security policies. Fortunately, Windows 2000 Server ships with several preconfigured IP security policies that you can plug in and use as a starting point. You can also use MMC snap-ins to automate policy distribution to a large number of workstations.

For detailed instructions on how to set up IPSec on Windows 2000 Server, refer to the excellent guidelines found at this Web address:

```
www.microsoft.com/windows2000/techinfo/planning/security/ipsecsteps.asp
```

> **WINDOWS 2000 POINT-TO-POINT TUNNELING PROTOCOL**
>
> The easiest way to implement a VPN in Windows 2000 is to use Point-to-Point Tunneling Protocol (PPTP)—a VPN protocol developed by the PPTP Industry Forum before the existence of IPSec and PKI. It is easier to set up, not requiring complicated security policy configuration, and is generally the lowest-cost solution. It provides encryption of all data during a session, but the security is based on passwords only, not on public-key infrastructure technology.
>
> PPTP may be the only option if a VPN connection needs to pass through Network Address Translators (NATs). It is possible, in such cases, to implement IPSec within a PPTP tunnel, to get the benefits of IPSec's strong security while maintaining the capability to pass through NATs. Several popular AP vendors market products that combine access point and NAT services in the same device. L2TP/IPSec won't work through this device unless the NAT service is disabled. Microsoft recommends, however, that its customers implement L2TP/IPSec whenever possible.

Select a machine authentication method

Because IPSec is implemented in the Network (IP) layer, you can't use it to authenticate users. However, you still need to choose a machine authentication method. Most implementations, such as Windows 2000, provide several alternatives. In Windows 2000, you can choose to use Kerberos, certificate, or shared key.

Windows 2000 uses Kerberos 5 as the default machine authentication method. In this type of system, the Kerberos server keeps track of a database of secret keys that identify each computer and user in the domain. Whenever two machines are negotiating a VPN connection, they use the Kerberos server to obtain authentication credentials. Kerberos works well in a closed network and may be more than adequate for your WLAN, especially if you also implement 802.1x authentication. However, if you need to provide remote access to machines outside your Windows 2000 domain, you will need to implement a certificate-based authentication method. Windows 2000 Server also comes with a Certificate Authority that you can use to issue certificates to the client stations in your WLAN.

> **NOTE**
>
> Single sign-on is the "Holy Grail" that Microsoft is promising through use of Passport, its proprietary security software. Microsoft has been oft-criticized because Passport is not yet compatible with other single sign-on technologies. In response to this criticism, Microsoft stated recently that it would open up this user authentication system by basing it on Kerberos.

Securing Against Intrusion Detection

The primary risk a WLAN represents to your enterprise LAN, as described at the beginning of this chapter, is penetration of the LAN by an unauthorized intruder. In order to effectively protect the LAN, a WDMZ must be able to detect and stop intruders. The intrusion detection software should also immediately notify the network administrator with enough specificity to prevent future attacks from the same source.

Facilitating Roaming

One of the top reasons for implementing a wireless network is to provide end users with *roaming* capability. In other words, end users will be able to connect to the network from several different locations within the enterprise—in the office and the boardroom, or in the dormitory and the library.

If you are installing multiple access points, avoid a WDMZ software solution that ties a user to a particular access point. Instead, look for a solution that permits a user to connect through any access point in the enterprise.

Maintaining Multisite Consistency

Wireless users frequently carry their laptop computers with them when traveling to other offices in the enterprise. If you plan to implement WLANs at more than one company site, keep in mind that users may not only roam within a particular site but also between sites. When it is practical to implement a wireless bridge between locations, you may be able to implement a single NAS and administer the bridged WLANs as a single WDMZ. Otherwise, if you operate WLANs at two or more remote locations, you may need to implement multiple WDMZs (one or more at each site).

When you set up multiple WDMZs, whether at the same site or at remote sites, keep in mind that a single user may need to access each WDMZ as he or she roams around your enterprise.

Managing Access Points and Access Point Security

Each access point in your network serves as both a hub and a gateway for the wireless stations connecting through it. To ensure good workload balance and enforcement of wireless security rules, the WDMZ software should monitor access point performance, evaluate access point loads, and manage access point configurations.

The configuration software resident in each AP should be capable of enforcing wireless security policies. For example, the AP software should be able to require that each wireless station use WEP and the appropriate ESSID. You should also be able to configure the AP so that it does not broadcast—or *beacon*—the SSID.

For a large WLAN, you should probably use a RADIUS-based authentication database server to manage access of users by registering their MAC addresses. A less flexible alternative available in some systems is a static MAC access control list.

WDMZ Weaknesses

Although control of unauthorized access to your WLAN is significantly improved by implementing a WDMZ, a few weaknesses remain that hackers may try to exploit:

◆ **Gateway discovery.** If your enterprise is large, you may need to set up several WDMZs, each with its own DHCP and DNS server, for example. This scenario leaves your WDMZ vulnerable to attack by a "rogue" server that offers itself as a

DHCP or DNS server to a workstation attempting to connect to the network. Special DNS security services may be necessary to protect against this risk.

♦ **IP Security.** IPSec can be susceptible to a man-in-the-middle attack in which a rogue VPN server successfully negotiates Challenge Handshake Authentication Protocol (CHAP) authentication and tricks workstations into providing their passwords.

♦ **Mobility.** IPSec tunnels are typically established through a specific access point. If either party to the connection roams out of range of the first AP and into the range of another, the tunnel will probably be lost and will have to be reestablished through the second AP.

♦ **Interoperability.** Very few vendors yet support IETF VPN standards, such as L2TP/IPSec, so the promise of seamless interoperability is a myth if VPNs are widely deployed.

Secure the WLAN with Network Access Authentication

A *network access authentication* system restricts network access to authorized entities. Whenever you sign in to a LAN, you are making use of a network access authentication system. After the system authenticates the entity, it should also *authorize* the particular session—at least if it is to be really useful in securing a network. After the entity is authenticated and the session authorized, the system should ideally authenticate each packet to prevent the session from being "hijacked" midstream.

Network access authentication can be accomplished at every layer of the wireless networking model—PHY, MAC, IP, and UDP/TCP. As noted earlier in the chapter, WEP encrypts data in the MAC (Medium Access Control) or Data Link layer of the wireless networking model. WEP provides authentication to a degree—in other words, only entities with the shared key are permitted "physical" access to the network. However, you have already learned that WEP has its flaws. For example, WEP's all-or-nothing approach means that a wireless station either has access or it doesn't, without regard to actual user, session, or packet.

The recently adopted IEEE 802.1*x* standard as well as Point-to-Point Protocol (PPP—the standard method for dialing in by modem to Internet Service Providers) are implemented in the MAC layer. Implementing network access authentication at the MAC level has several important advantages over implementations in higher levels of the OSI model including that it is inexpensive and faster to implement. Furthermore, MAC-level network access authentication doesn't require network access to perform authentication. MAC-level authentication also works with multiple network-level protocols, such as the following:

♦ IPv4

♦ IPv6

♦ AppleTalk

♦ IPX

♦ SNA

♦ NetBEUI

For the purposes of your WLAN, MAC-level authentication should also be very extensible. For example, you can use any of several implementations of RADIUS, or one of several other already-developed network access server products, to manage your authorized user database.

IEEE 802.1x: Network Port Authentication

Within the 802.11b standard, each station that connects to the network is identified by its MAC address. Even though each station is supposed to have a unique 48-bit MAC address, a hacker can easily "clone" the MAC address of an authorized station. As far as the network is concerned, the imposter and the real station are the same entity. If the true MAC address owner has network access, so does the undetected hacker.

What's more, a hacker can fool the network into substituting a bogus IP address— perhaps the hacker's own IP address—in the Address Resolution Protocol (ARP) cache in place of the IP address of a legitimate station on the LAN. The ARP cache is a MAC-address to IP-address mapping of the stations that have recently attached to the network. Theoretically, this type of attack—called *ARP cache poisoning*—can be perpetrated on any LAN. However, WLANs are more susceptible because a hacker doesn't need a physical connection to the LAN's infrastructure to communicate with the network.

802.1x is a new IEEE standard, ratified in June 2001. IEEE 802.1x enables the network to authenticate and determine the identity of an entity, as well as the entity's access rights at the time the entity attempts to connect to a LAN port, without depending on the MAC address. In the context of a wireless LAN, network switch software that complies with the 802.1x standard would be able to require that a wireless station be authenticated against a list of authorized entities before permitting the station access to the network.

IEEE 802.1x is based on Extensible Authentication Protocol (RFC 2284). It is not a wireless standard per se, because it also applies to all IEEE 802 technologies, including Ethernet. It is not a substitute for tunneling or encapsulation protocols such as PPP over Ethernet (PPPOE). Although it can be used to derive keys for any encryption algorithm, 802.1x is not an encryption algorithm. It is not a protocol per se, but a framework for managing authentication and keys. Using this standard, and well-established key derivation algorithms such as Transport Layer Security (TLS), Secure Remote Password (SRP) protocol, or Kerberos, per-session keys are derived that can, in turn, be used to provide per-packet authentication, integrity, and confidentiality.

CROSS-REFERENCE

See Chapter 14 fpr a discussion of Secure Socket Layer (SSL), the most widely used public key infrastructure-based protocol for establishing a secure channel between two parties communicating over the Internet or over an intranet.

The Extensible Authentication Protocol (EAP) is a relatively simple encapsulation protocol that is implemented in the link layer of the network architecture. EAP employs IETF standard key derivation methods such as Transport Level Security (TLS), Secure Remote Password (SRP), and Kerberos. When EAP is implemented over a LAN, it is called EAPOL. When implemented over a WLAN, EAP is called EAPOW.

Figure 13-2 depicts the topology of a WDMZ using an 802.1x-based and Ethernet-based network access server (EtherNAS) for network port authentication, and a RADIUS-based authentication server. Windows XP is the first operating system to support this type of network access security. Using such a system, users, sessions, and packets are authenticated throughout the session.

Notice that in the 802.1x lingo, the station requesting access to the network is called the *supplicant,* and the EtherNAS server that eventually either grants or denies access is called the *authenticator.* Workstations running Windows XP are equipped to handle the supplicant role. Assuming you install Windows XP on each of the wireless stations in your WLAN, you will also need access points with updated firmware that can handle the Authenticator/EtherNAS function. Fortunately, the access points should be reasonably priced (about $300 or less) because much of the work—most of the EAP and the authentication server functions—will be performed by either the wireless supplicant or the authentication server (the RADIUS server in Figure 13-2).

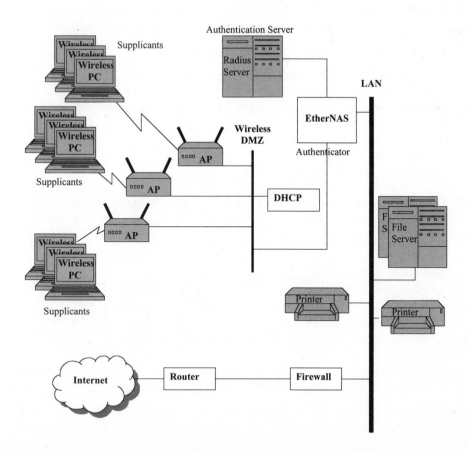

Figure 13-2: WDMZ topology using an 802.1x-based EtherNAS and a RADIUS-based authentication server

In addition to Windows XP, Cisco APs provide support for 802.1x over Windows 9x, Windows NT4, Windows 2000, Mac OS, and Linux.

Setting up Windows XP Workstations for 802.1x Authentication

Windows XP is the first operating system to include drivers for most popular wireless network adapters out-of-the-box, making wireless NIC configuration much easier. XP also features what Microsoft calls "enhanced media sense," which means that XP enables users to automatically reconfigure their computers to connect to a new wireless network. This sounds very convenient—perhaps a bit too convenient if your network contains sensitive information.

Fortunately, Windows XP is also the first operating system to implement native support for 802.1x authentication. For each workstation (desktop or laptop) running Windows XP, you simply need to activate the 802.1x-compliant features. To activate 802.1x authentication in Windows XP, first open Network Connections:

1. Click the Start button to display the Start menu.
2. In the Start menu, select Control Panel.
3. In the Control Panel, click Network and Internet Connections.
4. Click Network Connections to display the Network Connections dialog box.

In the Network Connections dialog box, perform the following steps:

1. Right-click the connection for which you want to activate support for 802.1x authentication. A pop-up menu will appear.
2. Click Properties to display the Connection Properties dialog box.
3. Click the Authentication tab and then select the Network access control using the IEEE 802.1x check box. This is the default selection.
4. Click the EAP type tab and select the Extensible Authentication Protocol type to be used with this connection.

The remaining configuration depends on the EAP type that you intend to use. For example, if you are going to use Smart Cards, you need to specify that you want Windows to use the certificate embedded in the Smart Card. Similarly, you need to specify if you plan to use a certificate that has been provided by a certificate authority in an electronic file.

RADIUS—Remote Authentication Dial-In User Service

Because this book is about wireless networking, not dial-in networking, you may wonder why Remote Access Dial-In User Service (RADIUS) is relevant. The answer is that RADIUS has broader application than either dial-in or wireless. It supports authentication, authorization, and accounting for network access from any port—physical ports such as access over Ethernet or ISDN, or virtual ports such as access over tunneled (VPN) or wireless connections. Any time an entity connects to the LAN, the system can employ a RADIUS server for authentication, authorization, and accounting.

Figure 13-3 depicts the 802.1x-based "conversation" that takes place between the wireless station and the network access server (NAS) from the moment a connection is initially attempted and blocked to the moment the connection is permitted.

Until the supplicant (the wireless station) is authenticated and authorized, the access point will deny the supplicant all access to the LAN. At the end of the successful conversation, the AP removes the filter and passes a WEP key to the supplicant. Now, under 802.1x, the WEP key is a single session key, rather than a multisession key that must be shared by all wireless stations using a common AP. Even if a hacker discovers the WEP key, it is good for the current session only.

The 802.1x authentication process provides strong authentication, integrity, and confidentiality for the following reasons:

♦ 802.1x authentication uses EAP-compliant, public-key dynamic key derivation methods, such as EAP-TLS, EAP-SRP, Kerberos, and Tunneled TLS.

♦ Keys are automatically derived on both the wireless station and the authentication server.

♦ All transmissions are encrypted using single-session keys.

RADIUS servers that support EAP and 802.1x include the following:

♦ Microsoft Windows 2000 Server

♦ Windows .Net Server

♦ Cisco ACS

♦ Funk RADIUS

♦ Interlink Networks RADIUS servers

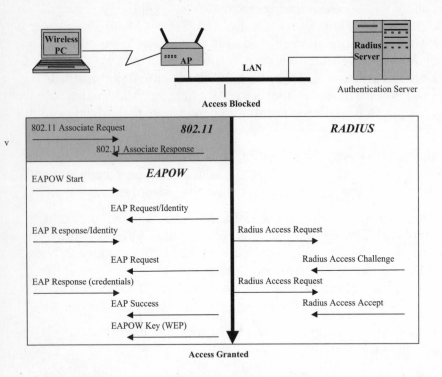

Figure 13-3: The IEEE 802.1x-based conversation between wireless station, EtherNAS, and RADIUS server

Summary

This chapter explores some of the security risks that result from the convenience that makes wireless networks attractive in the first place. Various methods of dealing with these risks—such as virtual private networks, establishing a wireless DMZ, and using IEEE 802.1x port-based authentication—are discussed. By now, you should be well educated about the best practices to follow when implementing security in a wireless LAN. The next chapter explores issues that arise when you decide to upgrade a wireless network.

Chapter 14

A Short Course in Public Key Infrastructure

In This Chapter

If the previously discussed WEP-based security is not sufficient protection for the data that will be transmitted over your network, consider using a Public Key Infrastructure-based security scheme. This chapter gives you a thorough overview of Public Key Infrastructure (PKI), covering the following topics:

♦ PKI terminology

♦ How PKI works

♦ How PKI protects your data

♦ Certificates and Certificate Authorities

♦ PKI-based security protocols

Public Key Infrastructure Terminology

If you intend to implement a home or small-office WLAN, using Public Key Infrastructure (PKI) to protect your network is almost certainly overkill. The basic security measures described in Chapter 12 should be sufficient. On the other hand, if you use the Internet, you probably already use PKI. For example, the *Secure Sockets Layer (SSL)* protocol used in Web browsers for secure information access uses a form of PKI. Even if you don't use the Internet, chances are that sometime in the near future, you'll carry a *Smart Card* credit card that contains a chip that uses PKI. In short, having a better understanding of PKI is useful.

When you use the term "security system" in connection with your WLAN, you probably think first of a hacker breaking into your confidential files. Public Key Infrastructure is intended to prevent

that sort of unauthorized access. It also ensures that information sent to authorized individuals over the network is kept confidential—recipients can be confident that they know who sent the message and that the message and its content have not been altered.

Webster's *New World College Dictionary* defines *cryptography* as "the art of writing or deciphering messages in code." When used in computers, cryptography is the science of writing and deciphering computer data in secret code for the purpose of protecting the data from unauthorized access. PKI makes use of a combination of two very sophisticated types of cryptography—private key cryptography and private/public key cryptography. The workings of PKI are described in more detail later in this chapter, but the following list introduces you to the players involved in the PKI process:

♦ End users

♦ The digital certificate

♦ Certification authorities

♦ Registration authorities

End Users

PKI is applied to messages and files transmitted over computer networks, but the computer data to be protected originates and ends with people—that is, *end users*. The security system you implement in your WLAN has to be "user-friendly," or no one will use it. In the world of PKI, an end user is either sending or receiving data. The sender wants to make sure the data arrives accurately and uncompromised. The recipient has the same goal, but also needs to be confident of the sender's identity.

The Digital Certificate

In the "days of yore," one of the king's musketeers could prove he carried a message from the king by showing any challenger the king's seal. In a similar fashion, PKI uses a *digital certificate* in a process that proves that a message or file originated with its purported author. If you have ever permitted a plug-in such as Macromedia Flash or Adobe Acrobat to download and enhance your Web browser , you have received an electronic PKI certificate vouching for the authenticity of the files that you permitted your computer to install.

Certification Authorities

For PKI to work, an entity known as a *Certification Authority (CA)* creates the certificate that accompanies the computer data. End users can obtain certificates from a directory or database called the *certificate repository*. Sometimes, a certificate is distributed directly between the certificate owner, who originated the data, and the recipient of the data.

Registration Authorities

A *Registration Authority* (RA) issues the certificates generated by a CA to end users, or *subscribers,* who will be sending PKI-protected data. The RA is responsible for verifying the identity of the subscribers.

Public Key Infrastructure Concepts

Before delving into the workings of PKI, you should understand the problems Public Key Infrastructure is intended to solve.

Electronic Threats

Although the need for confidential correspondence has been around for a long time, the scope of the need has exploded with the advent of electronic communication—especially so with the growing popularity of electronic commerce.

When information is communicated electronically, an electronic security system protects it by ensuring the following four things:

- Confidentiality
- Integrity
- Authenticity
- Non-repudiation

The security system can be fully successful—that is, commercially acceptable—only if it takes each of these goals into account. Stated in a positive way, the security system should ensure *confidentiality, integrity, authenticity* and *non-repudiation*

Confidentiality

Just as individuals can eavesdrop on your conversations, malicious parties can intercept your e-mail or other electronic correspondence. The need to protect the privacy of your communication is perhaps the most obvious goal of any electronic security system. The ideal security system should provide a way to ensure that only the intended recipient can read confidential information, even if a snoop successfully obtains the electronic file that contains the information.

Authenticity

What if you bought a Rolex watch from a street vendor and found out later that it was a fake? You wouldn't be very happy. The convenience and ubiquity of e-commerce results in countless transactions between strangers who never have the opportunity to meet face-to-face. When monetary transactions occur electronically, the authenticity of the parties in each transaction is of utmost importance. The security system should prevent miscreants from impersonating a legitimate party in a transaction—sometimes called *spoofing*—by providing a method for positively identifying the originator of information protected by the system.

Integrity

In the last couple of years, attacks by computer viruses have been much in the news. A typical computer virus performs a very visible trick, or inflicts obvious damage, on the target computer. But what if a virus were designed to make only small but significant changes to files that contain important information or data? It may be worse to have damaged data that goes unnoticed than to have data damaged in a way that can be seen and repaired.

The possibility that someone could intercept and make unauthorized changes to important files as they move through your network is another cause for worry. Even accidental, undetected changes in financial data can be devastating. Intended recipients need a way to verify the integrity of the data.

Non-repudiation

When transmitting information electronically, the least obvious security risk is that the originator of the information will claim, truthfully or not, that he didn't send the information—a situation called *repudiation*. The fourth goal of an ideal security system is to ensure *non-repudiation* by making sure that the information arrives intact, and providing proof of the sender to the recipient.

Electronic Solutions

Accomplishing the multiple goals of confidentiality, authenticity, integrity, and non-repudiation is challenging. Electronic solutions exist for each of these problems, but PKI uses a combination of several approaches—a "best of all worlds" approach—to accomplish all four goals within one system. Before you examine the PKI approach, however, the electronic solutions will be discussed.

Confidentiality—Data Encryption

When you send printed correspondence, you keep the information confidential by sealing it in an envelope. If the seal on a letter is broken, you suspect that someone has read its contents. The envelope doesn't effectively prevent disclosure to someone willing to tamper with your mail, but it provides adequate protection for most correspondence, especially when coupled with the way mail is transferred and the federal laws that provide steep penalties for mail tampering.

Electronic data can be wrapped, figuratively, in an electronic envelope through encryption. You can encrypt data in many different ways, but the most effective methods involve the use of *cryptographic keys* that are mathematically encoded in the data to be transmitted. Using a type of cryptography known as *symmetric encryption*, the data is encrypted using a key; the recipient must use the same key in order to read and use the data. The same key—sometimes called a *shared key*—is used to encrypt and decrypt the information.

As discussed in Chapter 13, WLAN hardware that complies with the Wi-Fi (802.11b) standard provides a method for automatically encrypting all data using either a 64-bit or 128-bit shared key. To use the feature, all client workstations connecting to the WLAN must use the same key that has been entered into the access point (AP). Because the key must be entered at every workstation, it is not very "secret." In addition, every workstation on the WLAN automatically decrypts the data as it arrives, so the data isn't protected from the "prying eyes" of anyone who has physical access to these workstations.

Electronic data would be more fully protected if the key used for encryption were kept secret between the sender and the recipient. Of course, that raises several practical problems. How do you communicate the key in a secure manner so that you can then communicate the data securely? If you exchange confidential information with more than a handful of people and want to use a different key for each person, you may have difficulty keeping up with multiple keys.

Unfortunately, even if you could devise a way to communicate the key securely and keep track of all your secret keys, a determined hacker could still use high-powered software tools to break into data that uses symmetric encryption. Later in this chapter, you will learn how PKI combines symmetric encryption with *asymmetric encryption* to ensure greater confidentiality.

Authenticity—Digital Signatures

For hundreds, if not thousands of years, a written signature has been used to indicate the authenticity of important documents. A signature on a check, contract, will, written correspondence, or other types of documents verifies that the person signing the document has read and approved it. Therefore, to prove the authenticity of electronic documents, computer scientists have developed the idea of *digital signatures*.

A *digital signature* is not an electronic facsimile of someone's written signature. It is a process that uses a portion of an electronic file to help the recipient of the file verify the identity of the person who sent it. Credit card transactions are based on the same concept. As soon as you receive a new credit card from your bank, you are supposed to sign the back. A vendor compares this signature to the one on the credit card receipt; if the two signatures match, the vendor can feel reasonably secure that you are the card's owner. Similarly, a recipient of a file that includes a digital signature can compare the electronic signature to the electronic equivalent of the signature on the back of a credit card to determine the authenticity of the file.

The following steps describe the digital signature process (see Figure 14-1):

1. The originator uses a hash algorithm to create a message digest from the original message.

2. The originator encrypts the message digest to create an encrypted version (often called *cipher-text*).

3. The originator sends a copy of the unencrypted message (usually called the *clear-text* version), along with a copy of the encrypted digest, to the recipient.

4. The recipient decrypts the cipher-text digest.

5. The recipient uses the hash algorithm to create a message digest from the clear-text message.

6. By comparing the message digest that the recipient created with the unencrypted version, the recipient can determine whether the file is authentic.

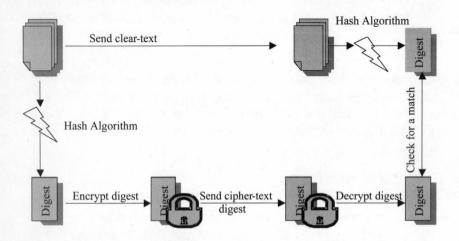

Figure 14-1: The digital signature process

For this digital signature process to work, one or more cryptographic keys need to be transmitted between end users, which again leaves the problem of authenticating and transmitting the keys securely. Much of the remainder of this chapter explains how PKI deals with these authentication and key transmission issues.

Integrity—Hash Algorithms and Message Digests

Data integrity has always been a primary concern of computer scientists. One of their favorite expressions is "garbage in, garbage out." In fact, computer programmers long ago came up with ways to check for changes to transmitted data.

The most common method to determine data integrity is to use a *hash algorithm*, which performs a mathematical computation on the data to be transmitted. The result of this algorithm is typically a smaller amount of data than the original file, often referred to as a *message digest* or simply a *digest* of the original file—a sort of *digital fingerprint*.

A simple hash algorithm for creating a digest of a plain-text message assigns a number from 1 to 26 to each letter in the alphabet. Add up the values of all the letters in the text message. The answer you get is a digest of the message. The idea is to perform this computation on the original message, and later, on the message that the recipient receives. These two digests should match.

Computer scientists use more complex hash algorithms to verify data integrity. When data is transmitted electronically over a modem, for example, blocks of data are accompanied by a number known as a *cyclic redundancy check (CRC) value*. The software of the sending computer creates this number using a hash algorithm. The receiving computer applies the same algorithm to compute the CRC. If the two CRCs don't match, the data has been corrupted in transmission and must be retransmitted.

The digital signature process uses a hash algorithm, along with encryption techniques, to confirm the identity of the originator of data. At the same time, this process ensures the data's integrity.

Non-Repudiation—Digital Signatures, Audit Logs

As explained earlier in this chapter, a commercially acceptable electronic security system enables originators and recipients of electronic correspondence to prove that the intended correspondence took place. The proof may need to be substantial enough to withstand legal challenge. Although a digital signature may be strong evidence, it may not be sufficient evidence, by itself, to avoid the possibility of repudiation.

If you want to prove you purchased something from Wal-Mart, you save the receipt. Similarly, parties to electronic transactions should—at the very least—keep a record of each transaction. Even better, the security software should put a tamper-proof time stamp on the original data and keep a detailed log of all transactions.

NOTE

Security systems based on PKI provide for digital signatures, time stamping, and logging of transactions, but this technology may or may not hold up in court. Consequently, third-party services known as *non-repudiation services* are available, for a fee, to gather and maintain sufficient evidence to prove that each transaction occurred.

Ensuring Confidentiality

Once again, the main reason to create a security system for your WLAN is to ensure that confidential data transmitted over the network cannot be successfully "attacked" (accessed) by an unauthorized user. Cryptography is the obvious solution, but which form of encryption is safe enough? The Nazi German government during World War II relied on a cryptographic solution that they considered foolproof, a system known as the *Enigma*. However, early in the war, the British Secret Service was able to break the system's code. For the remainder of the war, the Allies easily decrypted every Enigma-encrypted message sent by the Germans.

PKI uses a cryptographic scheme known as *public key cryptography,* a combination of *symmetric* and *asymmetric cryptography*. The following sections explain how each of these schemes works.

Symmetric Cryptography—Single Key

Symmetric cryptography is the simplest form of cryptography (see Figure 14-2). It works like this:

1. The originator starts with a clear-text (that is, not yet encrypted) message and encrypts it using a secret key.

2. The originator transmits the cipher-text over the network to the recipient.

3. The originator uses a secure method to send the key to the recipient.

4. The recipient uses the key to decrypt the cipher-text, resulting in the original clear-text message.

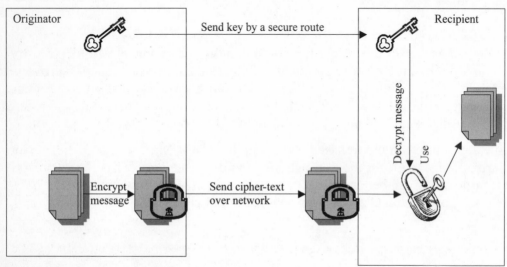

Figure 14-2: Symmetric cryptography

Symmetric cryptography is thus named because the originator and the recipient use the same key to both encrypt and decrypt the message. (Note: In this description, and others in this chapter, the so-called "message" can be any electronic data.) Sometimes this method is described as using a "shared secret," but even if the key is not secret, this method always uses the same key for both encryption and decryption; in other words, it uses symmetrical keys.

Strengths of Symmetric Cryptography

Cryptologists have developed highly sophisticated symmetric encryption algorithms. Even a supercomputer, using mathematics, would require an inordinate amount of time to discover the key. However, with the advent of incredibly powerful—yet inexpensive—personal computers, it is both easy and cheap to implement symmetric cryptography, and the encryption process itself is fast.

It is technically possible to guess a key, but as the key gets longer (that is, in bits), the likelihood of doing so is greatly diminished. The WEP encryption built into the Wi-Fi (802.11b) wireless networking standard includes the option to use either 64- or 128-bit keys. There are about 3.4E38 possible key values that are 128 bits in length.

TIP

Keep in mind that to take advantage of the full length of a key, you should choose each bit in the key in a truly random fashion. If you use this method, guessing the key could take a very long time. But if your key uses only a subset of the values that are available, and if a hacker can determine the sort of values that you tend to choose, his job gets much easier and your system is less secure.

Weaknesses of Symmetric Cryptography

The most obvious weakness of symmetric cryptography is that both the originator and the recipient must know the key. If you need to encrypt data to begin with to protect it from prying eyes, how do you protect the key when you need to transmit it to the recipient? Do you encrypt it with another key? If an unintended recipient intercepts the key, the confidential contents of the message will be compromised.

Another weakness surfaces in situations where the originator wants to make the message available to a large number of recipients. Before the transaction can take place, the originator must have a relationship with each recipient. Furthermore, he must provide each recipient with the key. If the originator uses the same key to encrypt all copies of the message, he has to provide that key to many people, increasing the likelihood that an unauthorized party will obtain the key. Alternatively, if the originator uses a different key for each recipient, the number of keys grows rapidly if the number of recipients is large. This lack of scalability is even more acute if many individuals want to execute confidential transaction with a large number of other individuals. Each unique pair of individuals will need a unique key. For example, ten individuals who want to share information will need 90 keys (10 times 9); 20 people will need 380 keys (20 times 19); 100 people will need 9,900 keys (100 times 99); 1,000 people will need 999,000 keys (1,000 times 999); and so on. As you can see, management of keys in a symmetric encryption scheme can become a real headache.

Symmetric cryptography also does not enable the originator to sign the message. Because originator and recipient both know the key, the use of the key does not prove the identity of either party. Neither authentication nor non-repudiation can be achieved using symmetric encryption alone.

Finally, no matter how good the algorithm, using symmetric encryption makes the security system more susceptible to "brute force" attacks. Essentially, hackers use a very fast computer, or perhaps several fast computers working in tandem, to continually "guess" the key until it's broken. Once hackers have the key, all data encrypted using that key is wide open. Three computer scientists from the University of California and Zero Knowledge Systems (Nikita Borisov, Ian Goldberg, and David Wagner) wrote a paper in February 2001 positing that it is only a matter of time before any WEP key is discovered. In August 2001, leading cryptographers Adi Shamir, Istik Mantin (both of Israel's Weizmann Institute of Science), and Scott Fluhrer (of Cisco Systems) published another paper describing additional vulnerabilities. Since then, several teams of cryptographers have successfully attacked the WEP system using the approach described in the Shamir-Mantin-Fluhrer paper. What's more, a software toolkit called Airsnort has been published, which makes the process easier. This attack on WEP is possible because the encrypted data is transmitted over a network that sends data in blocks in a predictable way. Through some ingenious analysis of the data blocks flying around the network, these scientists have proven that hackers can build a list of likely key values that greatly narrows the number of key values that are candidates for "guesses," conversely increasing the likelihood that the key will be guessed.

TIP

Until a better version of WEP or a viable alternative is developed, change the WEP key in your WLAN as often as possible. Although changing the key doesn't make WEP harder to attack, it reduces the damage that will be done if a hacker successfully retrieves a WEP key.

Asymmetric Cryptography

Asymmetric cryptography makes use of two keys in the encryption process and two keys in the decryption process. A *private* key and a *public* key are used in every encrypted transaction. The owner of a private key keeps it secret, but the owner of a public key intentionally stores the public key in a public directory maintained for that purpose.

At first, this may sound odd. Of course a key should be private. And if a key is public, how can you use it to encrypt confidential data? You will see, however, that using two keys has significant advantages over using a single key. In effect, both keys are used together, but not at the same time. That is, if one key is used to encrypt data, the other key must be used to decrypt the data. Both keys must be created at the same time using a complex mathematical algorithm for this type of cryptography to work.

In an asymmetric cryptographic scheme, if a corresponding private key is used to encrypt a message, a public key must be used to decrypt the message. Conversely, if a public key is used to encrypt a message, a corresponding private key must be used to decrypt the message (see Figure 14-3).

Figure 14-3: Asymmetric cryptography

In each of the two cases depicted in Figure 14-3, the same user owned the encryption and decryption keys.

Suppose your bank wants to send your bank statement to you via e-mail, using asymmetric cryptography to ensure confidentiality. Assume also that you have a public key and a private key. The bank can use your public key to encrypt the statement, and then transmit the encrypted statement to you. When you receive the encrypted statement, you can decrypt it using your private key. In short, anyone who has access to your public key can use it to encrypt a message, but only someone with access to your private key can decrypt the message.

In a second example, suppose you want to electronically place a purchase order for a large quantity of supplies for your company, and the supplier wants to verify the authenticity of your message. Using asymmetric cryptography, you can use your private key to encrypt the purchase order message. The supplier then uses your public key to decrypt the purchase order message. Because your public key cannot be used to decrypt a message that was encrypted with a key other than your private key, the supplier knows that you sent the purchase order.

A BRIEF HISTORY OF ASYMMETRIC CRYPTOGRAPHY

Symmetric cryptography has been around for a long time, but asymmetric cryptography has been around for fewer than 30 years. In 1976, Whittfield Diffie and Martin Hellman conceived asymetric cryptography in an effort to address the weaknesses of symmetric cryptography.They proposed an asymmetric algorithm based on the mathematics of discrete logarithms that is still in use today.

In 1978, MIT scientists Rivest, Shamir, and Adleman developed the widely used asymmetric algorithm that is known as *RSA* (named for its inventors, ***Rivest, Shamir, and Adleman***). The patent for this technology expired in the year 2000, so this algorithm is a strong candidate for mandatory inclusion in protocols that require asymmetric cryptography.

Strengths of Asymmetric Cryptography

Asymmetric cryptography algorithms always use two keys in any transaction, but the recipient only needs one of the keys to successfully decrypt a message. The use of two keys—a private key and a public key—solves the problems of symmetric cryptography.

With asymmetric cryptography, you don't need to provide the recipient with a key before he receives the cipher-text. If the originator used his private key to encrypt the message, the recipient need only look up the originator's public key in the public key directory. Alternatively, if the originator used the recipient's public key to encrypt the message, the recipient uses his own private key to decrypt the cipher-text message. In neither case is it necessary to transmit a private key; therefore, the risk of interception is eliminated.

Because each party in an asymmetric cryptographic scheme needs only one private key, this type of system is much more scalable than a symmetric system. In cases where the originator wants to supply different confidential information to many people, as in the case of bank statements, the originator can use the public key of each respective recipient to encrypt the confidential message intended only for that recipient; the originator is never required to transmit a private key electronically. Each recipient uses his own private key for decryption.

If an originator wants to supply a single message to multiple recipients, the originator can encrypt the message with his private key and the recipients can then use the originator's public key to decrypt the message. The recipients can feel confident that the message is authentic because the originator's private key was used to encrypt the message.

Cryptographic algorithms that use two keys at a time require longer keys, which makes the encryption more difficult, time-consuming, and much harder to attack. Many implementations of RSA, for example, use 1,024-bit keys that would, according to cryptography experts, take a supercomputer millions of years to crack.

> **NOTE**
> The fact that it is impractical to successfully attack asymmetric cryptography using a computer should not lure you into a false sense of security. As long as any human knows a private key, or can find it stored on paper or in an electronic database somewhere, there is a possibility that an unauthorized person will come into possession of the key. As part of your security procedure, you should require that private keys be changed as often as is practical.

Weaknesses of Asymmetric Cryptography

The primary weakness of asymmetric cryptography is its complexity. Although it is easy to select a key for use in symmetric cryptography—just use a random number generator—it takes a complex algorithm to select a matching set of private and public keys. Asymmetric encryption algorithms are also much slower than comparable symmetric algorithms—10 to 100 times slower, to be specific. For short messages, this sluggishness isn't a problem, but if the message is large, creating the cipher-text can be very time-consuming.

Another bothersome aspect of asymmetric cryptography is that the cipher-text is larger than the clear-text from which it originated. If you decide to put the cipher-text through another round of encryption (to increase the level of protection), the file size will continue to grow.

Asymmetric cryptography doesn't provide a convenient method of authentication and non-repudiation. The originator can use his own private key to encrypt the message, which would prove that the message originated from him, but the contents of the message would no longer be confidential because anyone can use the originator's public key to decrypt the cipher-text message.

Public Key Cryptography

Although asymmetric cryptography presents clear advantages over symmetric cryptography, its complexity and resulting slowness renders it impractical in many circumstances. Fortunately, clever computer scientists realized that the two systems could be combined to create a cryptographic system with all the advantages of asymmetric cryptography and the relative speed of symmetric cryptography. Because this hybrid system still uses the public-key aspect of asymmetric cryptography, it is known as *public key cryptography*.

Public key cryptography (see Figure 14-4) works very much like asymmetric cryptography, except that the clear-text message is encrypted using a symmetric cryptographic algorithm. However, to avoid the necessity of transmitting the symmetric key, with its corresponding risk of interception, public key cryptography uses an asymmetric cryptographic algorithm to encrypt the symmetric key. The whole system works like this:

1. The originator uses a random symmetric key to encrypt the message.
2. The originator uses the recipient's public key to encrypt the symmetric key. This is sometimes called *wrapping the key*.
3. The originator combines the cipher-text message and the wrapped key into a package that is sometimes called a *digital envelope*.
4. The originator sends the digital envelope to the recipient.
5. The recipient separates the wrapped key from the cipher-text.
6. The recipient uses his private key to decrypt the symmetric key.
7. The recipient uses the symmetric key and the cipher-text to generate the original clear-text message.

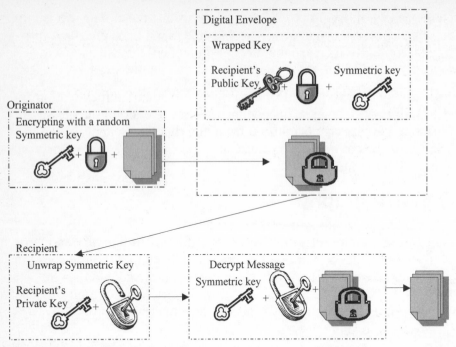

Figure 14-4: Public-key cryptography

By combining symmetric and asymmetric cryptography, the strengths of both systems are tapped and the weaknesses cancelled out, leaving the "best of both worlds." As an added benefit, because the wrapped random (symmetric) key is transmitted with the message, it can be a one-time-use key. In fact, the key can be used to encrypt an entire session between two computer systems and then discarded because a new random key can be quickly generated for the next session. This technique is used in the Secure Sockets Layer (SSL) system, which is used in Web browsers such as Netscape and Internet Explorer.

Dealing with Authentication and Non-Repudiation

When confidentiality is the primary goal, the public key cryptography system described in the preceding section works well. Similarly, if the goal is authentication, the same system works—with one minor change. The originator should use his private key to encrypt the symmetric key. The recipient should then use the originator's public key to decrypt the symmetric key. Keep in mind that anyone who intercepts the message can also use the recipient's public key to read the message, so the message is no longer confidential.

Consider the bank statement scenario again. You want to be sure not only that the bank maintains the confidentiality of your information, but also that the bank statement is really from your bank. To provide confidentiality, as well as authentication and non-repudiation, PKI uses *digital signatures*, a concept described earlier in this chapter.

Adding Digital Signatures

The digital signature process is applied to the public key process in the following way:

1. The originator uses a random symmetric key to encrypt the message.

2. The originator uses a hash algorithm to create a message digest version of the cipher-text message.

3. The originator uses the symmetric key to encrypt the message digest.

4. The originator uses the recipient's public key to create a *wrapped key*.

5. The originator combines the cipher-text, the encrypted message digest, and the wrapped key into a *digital envelope*.

6. The originator sends the digital envelope to the recipient.

7. The recipient separates the wrapped key from the cipher-text and encrypted message digest.

8. The recipient uses his private key to decrypt the symmetric key.

9. The recipient uses the symmetric key to decrypt the cipher-text and the encrypted message digest to generate the original clear-text message and the message digest.

10. The recipient uses the hash algorithm to create a message digest from the clear-text message.

11. By comparing the message digest that the recipient created with the unencrypted version, the recipient can determine whether the file is authentic.

Adding Digital Certificates

The system depicted in Figure 14-4 will only work if the originator uses the recipient's public key. But how can the originator be sure that a hacker hasn't substituted a bogus public key for his in the public key directory? The hacker could then intercept the message and use a matching private key to read it. What's worse, the intended recipient would not be able to read the message. You wouldn't want someone to hijack your bank statement in that fashion. You need a way to *certify* that the public key is authentic.

A related problem occurs when the originator wants to send a file to many recipients—say, for example, when a software company makes a free plug-in program for use with Web browsers available for download on the Internet. Confidentiality is not the issue in this case, but authentication certainly is. The software company could use the following digital signature process:

1. The originator (in this case, the software company) uses a hash algorithm to create a message digest from the original message (the plug-in software).

2. The originator then encrypts the message digest to create an encrypted version.

3. The originator sends a copy of the clear-text message, along with a copy of the cipher-text digest, to the recipient (the Internet user who downloads the plug-in for use in his Web browser).

4. The recipient looks up the originator's public key and uses it to decrypt the cipher-text digest.

5. The recipient uses the hash algorithm to create a message digest from the clear-text message.

6. By comparing the message digest that the recipient created with the decrypted cipher-text digest, the recipient can determine whether the file is authentic.

In this scenario, the weakness is still the public key (the software company's public key). If a hacker substitutes a bogus public key for the software company's public key, you might be tricked into permitting the hacker's software into your computer, rather than the plug-in you thought you were getting.

As I mentioned at the beginning of the chapter, *digital certificates* solve the problem of authenticating electronic files, such as software. To be accurate, a digital certificate authenticates a public key. However, authenticating the public key results in de facto authentication of the file the public key is used to decrypt.

Authentication—Certification Authorities

So far, this chapter has taken a "behind the scenes" look at PKI. Digital certificates and Certification Authorities (CAs) are the more visible aspects of the system. If you use the Internet frequently, you have probably already encountered certificates and Certification Authorities.

For example, to use Internet Explorer to see a list of certificates that have already been installed on your computer system, follow these steps:

1. Open Internet Explorer.

2. Click the Tools menu and select Internet Options.

3. In the Content tab of the Internet Options dialog box, click Certificates to display the Certificates dialog box, as shown in Figure 14-5.

4. Click the Intermediate Certification Authorities tab and scroll through the list of *intermediate certification authorities* that have already been added to your system.

5. Click the Trusted Root Certificates tab and scroll through that list, too.

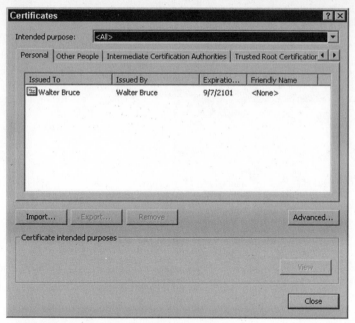

Figure 14-5: Internet Explorer's Certificates dialog box

6. Click an item in one of the lists and then click the View button to view the details of that certificate.

7. Click the Close button to close the Certificates dialog box.

NOTE

At least one certificate is listed in the Personal certificates list—yours. Internet Explorer creates this certificate automatically.

Each line in these certification authority lists represents a digital certificate that is installed on your computer. Either these certificates came preconfigured in your Web browser, or you accumulated them by visiting Web sites and downloading software and/or by visiting Web sites secured by a public key software system such as SSL. When you encounter a certificate that has not yet been installed on your system, you will see a Certificates dialog box similar to that shown in Figure 14-6. This dialog requires you to decide whether to *trust* the CA and install the certificate on your computer.

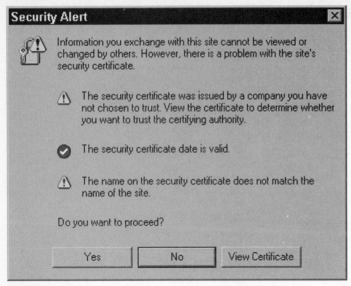

Figure 14-6: Internet Explorer's Security Alert dialog box

A Sample Certificate

As shown in Figure 14-7, a digital certificate typically includes the following information:

- ♦ The name of the entity to whom the certificate was issued (called the *subject*—the certificate's owner) and its public key
- ♦ The name of the CA that issued the certificate, and its digital signature
- ♦ A version number
- ♦ A serial number
- ♦ The type of encryption algorithm used in the digital signature
- ♦ Dates that establish the period in which the certificate is valid (the *valid from* and *valid to* dates)
- ♦ Various other types of information about the certificate's subject

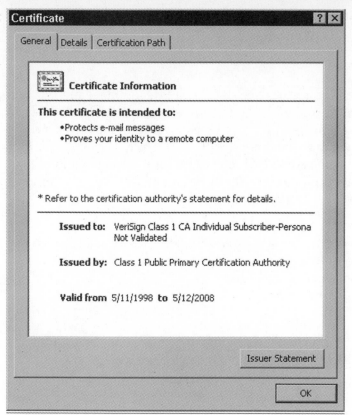

Certificate   ? ×

General | Details | Certification Path |

Certificate Information

This certificate is intended to:
- Protects e-mail messages
- Proves your identity to a remote computer

* Refer to the certification authority's statement for details.

Issued to: VeriSign Class 1 CA Individual Subscriber-Persona Not Validated

Issued by: Class 1 Public Primary Certification Authority

Valid from 5/11/1998 **to** 5/12/2008

Issuer Statement

OK

Figure 14-7: A sample digital certificate

Root Certification Authorities

As you have learned, a security system can only provide authentication and/or non-repudiation if a certificate is used to assert the validity of each public key. The integrity of each transaction, therefore, depends on the trustworthiness of the Certification Authority that issued the certificate for the public key.

As you can imagine, it would be impractical for every end user to establish an actual relationship with every Certification Authority in order to make an independent judgment about his or her trustworthiness. Instead, each CA is permitted to certify other Certification Authorities. The certificate lists the entire chain of Certification Authorities up to the top-level CA, which is known as the *root certification authority*. A relatively small number of root certification authorities have established themselves as so trustworthy that they are permitted to sign their own certificates. You can see the list of root CAs recognized by your system by clicking the Trusted Root Certification Authorities tab in the Certificate dialog box.

To see a long list of CAs, including lists of CAs that have been licensed by various state digital signature acts, take a look at the Web page www.pki-page.org/#CA.

X.509 Certificates

The ITU's Telecommunication Standardization Sector (ITU-T) Recommendation X.509 defines a framework for implementing authentication services at two different levels: first, by using a simple password scheme; and second, by using cryptography. This recommendation has been developed in collaboration with the Internet Society (ISOC)/Internet Engineering Task Force (IETF) which has, in turn, formed the Public-Key Infrastructure X.509 (PKIX) working group with the intent of developing Internet standards that will support an X.509-based public-key infrastructure.

For the purposes of this chapter, you need only understand that PKIX is a de facto standard that is very flexible but sometimes not clearly defined. As a consequence, several types of PKI certificates comply with X.509 but are not compatible. The form and content of a certificate will vary depending on its purpose.

PKI Protocols

PKI is a framework that can be used in many ways to make the electronic transmission of data more secure. You can use PKI to enhance the security of your WLAN.

SSL Certificates

The most widely used PKI-based protocol is the Secure Sockets Layer (SSL) protocol. Version 1.0 of this protocol was implemented only in the Netscape Web browser. Now, in Version 3.0, it has become a de facto standard for establishing a secure channel between two parties communicating over the Internet or over an intranet. It may be the best candidate of all the public key-based protocols for use in your WLAN to enhance the built-in WEP protocol.

SSL uses PKI in two ways:

♦ SSL uses public key cryptography to establish a confidential stream of data between two parties. A wrapped single-session key is passed between the parties. This symmetric key is used to ensure confidentiality.

♦ Through the use of public key cryptography and *message authentication codes (MACs),* SSL ensures that the messages between the parties are not modified in transit.

Most popular Web servers, such as Internet Information Server and Apache, can support SSL (although Apache requires configuration of supplementary API modules and the OpenSSL toolkit). Web pages with SSL support have the *https* URL prefix, rather than the *http* prefix, to indicate they are secure pages. You should consider adding SSL support to your WLAN's intranet.

Support for SSL is a standard feature in the current versions of most popular Web browsers, such as Netscape and Internet Explorer. When a Web browser connects to an SSL-enabled Web page, the browser and server perform a *handshake* to negotiate the security parameters that establish the secure connection. The handshake protocol uses PKI-based digital signatures and certificates to establish the identity of each party, to establish a secure connection, and to ensure the integrity of the data that is transferred during the session. The Netscape Web browser informs the user that the session is secure by displaying a key icon in the status bar at the bottom of the Netscape window. Internet Explorer places a closed lock in the status bar for the same purpose.

If you choose to secure your Web or intranet site with SSL, any Web-based application that can be run within the SSL session will automatically be protected by this PKI-based security system.

IPsec

Whereas SSL works at the transport level to establish confidentiality and authentication, IP Security Protocol (IPsec), a recommendation of IETF, works at the network level in one of two modes: tunnel mode or transport mode. IPsec is supplemental to IPv4 (the current version of IP), but it is a part of IPv6.

In tunnel mode, IPsec is used by gateways and proxies, not by the computers that are communicating on either end of the transaction. However, in transport mode, the endpoints must both implement IPsec. You can permit IPsec to operate through your WLAN's firewall by opening UDP port 500 (for IKE), IP type 50 (for ESP), and/or IP type 51 (for AH).

The most common use of IPsec is to establish secure, virtual private networks (VPNs) where one or more nodes on the network are connected from a remote location. Through IPsec, the remote computer is provided most, if not all, of the same network services that it would have if physically on-site with the WLAN.

S/MIME

The most commonly used Internet application is e-mail, and the Multipurpose Internet Mail Extension (MIME) protocol is widely used to encode e-mail messages sent over the LANs and the Internet. A special secure version of this protocol, Secure/Multipurpose Internet Mail Extension (S/MIME) uses a public key technique to provide confidentiality, integrity, and authentication to network e-mail.

Summary

This chapter teaches you the fundamentals of public key cryptography and Public Key Infrastructure (PKI). If the WEP-based security described in Chapter 13 doesn't adequately protect the data that is being transmitted over your network, you may want to consider using SSL, IPsec, and/or S/MIME—all Public Key Infrastructure-based security schemes—to enhance network security.

Chapter 15

Upgrading a Wireless Network

In This Chapter

This chapter discusses the following topics:

♦ Keeping up with changes in wireless LAN technology

♦ Implementing updates

♦ Planning upgrades

As the old newsreels used to say, "Time marches on." Even while this book was being written, several new products have started shipping—products that may eventually replace the 802.11b products discussed in this book. Most WLAN equipment manufacturers continually make updated drivers and firmware available for download at no charge as they make improvements and/or fixes to their products. This chapter presents strategies for keeping up with wireless LAN technological improvements and for planning and implementing updates and upgrades.

Keeping Up with IEEE 802.11 Updates

IEEE 802.11 is, and will probably always be, a work in progress. The group of people who formulate and maintain the IEEE standards are organized into committees, working groups, and task groups. The naming convention for the various updates reflects this structure. IEEE 802.11b, for example, was developed by Task Group B of the IEEE 802.11 Working Group for WLAN Standards. Similarly, the update to 802.11 known as IEEE 802.11a was developed by Task Group A of the 802.11 Working Group. At least seven 802.11 task groups are still hard at work developing standards that will become a part of IEEE 802.11 (for more information, visit `http://grouper.ieee.org/groups/802/11/`).

Keeping up with the IEEE 802.11 standards alone is not sufficient to keep you well informed. The IEEE approved and adopted the work of Task Group A and Task Group B at the same time in 1999 as amendments to IEEE 802.11. Even though the 802.11a specification defines products that are, in terms of speed, superior to 802.11b, it happens that 802.11b-compliant products became both widely available and widely adopted before the first 802.11a products became available. The 802.11a-based products that are currently shipping are as much as ten times faster than the 802.11b products on the market, but only time will tell whether and how quickly they will dominate the market for wireless network equipment.

Whether you are responsible for making IS purchasing decisions, for keeping a wireless network running smoothly, or for advising others on wireless LAN technology, you need to stay informed about the standards that are approved and under development, the products that are available on the market, and the relative market share of the various technologies and products.

To stay abreast of technological changes, you should periodically browse both the IEEE Web site (`http://www.ieee.org`) and the Web site of the Working Group for WLAN Standards (`http://grouper.ieee.org/groups/802/11`). By reviewing the agendas for working group and task group sessions, as well as timelines and other attached documents, you can get a sense of the status of the various ongoing tasks. The sites also provide information about how to participate in the working groups and task groups.

Discussion groups or mailing lists on wireless networking are a good source of current information. The *wirelesslan* discussion group at `http://groups.yahoo.com/`, for example, is active and often receives press releases from vendors announcing major new WLAN products. Also, special interest groups, such as the Bay Area Wireless Users Group (BAWUG), maintain mailing lists and online discussion areas that are excellent sources of information on current trends, providing expert advice and feedback.

The text of the IEEE 802 standards themselves is available for purchase from IEEE at `http://www.ieee.org`. Six months after initial publication, the text of each specification (in PDF format) can be downloaded at no charge from `http://standards.ieee.org/getieee802/`.

The following sections briefly describe the 802.11 technologies that you should track.

High-Speed Wireless WLANs in the 5 GHz Band—IEEE 802.11a

IEEE 802.11a-1999 sets out specifications for the *coded orthogonal frequency division multiplexing (COFDM)* protocol in the 5 GHz Band. By operating at higher frequencies than HR/DSSS, and by using of a variety of modulation techniques, this COFDM layer is able to provide data transmission rates up to 54 Mbps.

During the writing of this book, Proxim became the first manufacturer to release 802.11a-compliant products. Proxim is now shipping access points and wireless NICs under its Harmony brand. Not only do these products offer all 802.11a-compliant speeds up to 54 Mbps, but they also offer speeds up to 108 Mbps in Proxim's proprietary 2X™ mode. According to testing by Proxim and by Altheros, the manufacturer of the 802.11a chipset used in the Proxim product line, these products deliver higher throughput rates than any other available wireless LAN technology—at all ranges. This finding seems to contradict the predictions that 802.11a 5 GHz radios would have a shorter range than 802.11b 2.4 GHz radios because higher frequency signals don't travel as far at the same power output level. Nonetheless, the much higher data rate of the 5 GHz radios more than makes up for the theoretical reduction in range. Even at distances where the transmission rate has to drop back, it still exceeds the fastest rate that can be achieved by 802.11b equipment at the same distance from the AP. In addition, the wider available bandwidth in the 5 GHz ISM band, with eight non-overlapping channels compared to 802.11b's three, supports more users and higher network density. The 5 GHz band also experiences much less "traffic" than the 2.4 GHz band, with a lower probability for interference by nonnetwork devices such as microwave ovens and portable phones.

You may be asking yourself whether you have been wasting your time (and money) on 802.11b technology. The answer is no. Although other 802.11a products are sure to follow the Proxim offering, 802.11b still offers many more vendors, products, and price ranges from which you can choose. The main benefit of 802.11a is speed and total throughput—about four times higher at 54 Mbps, and up to ten times higher at 108 Mbps, as measured in recent tests. If you are implementing a WLAN where you already know that 11 Mbps is not going to be fast enough, you should consider the Proxim products—either that, or hold off for a wider variety of 802.11a (or 802.11g, discussed later in this chapter) products. Otherwise, you might as well take advantage of the many benefits of wireless networking offered by 802.11b and consider upgrading later.

TIP

If your users need wireless connectivity primarily to access e-mail or the Web, 802.11b's 11 Mbps is more than adequate. Typical Internet connections are 1.5 Mbps or less. However, if you expect users to attempt large intranetwork file transfers, or to use real-time streaming video, 11 Mbps may seem a bit pokey. 802.11a then becomes a more attractive option.

The lack of direct compatibility between 802.11b and 802.11a equipment is an important consideration when deciding whether to stick with 802.11b or immediately move to 802.11a. In fact, Microsoft has been reluctant to certify 802.11a technology with its Windows Hardware Quality Labs certification unless it can demonstrate backward-compatibility with 802.11b, which Windows XP supports. Proxim addresses this issue, to a degree, with its Harmony AP controller; this controller enables you to use one product to manage 802.11b access points and 802.11a access points on the same LAN, including support for roaming across IP subnets. Even without this controller, you can have 802.11a access points and 802.11b access points on the LAN together, but you would need to use different software to manage the different types of WLANs. Even with Proxim's products, however, a user cannot roam from an 802.11a cell to an 802.11b cell. It is only a matter of time before products come to market that support both standards, transparently. At least one company has announced a chipset that contains a radio that can connect to either type of AP.

Currently, the cost of implementing an 802.11a WLAN is about double that of an 802.11b WLAN, for the same number of APs and wireless NICs. However, if you need to support a large number of users and a high density of APs, the 802.11a vendors claim that because of increased network capacity, the real cost of buying APs may be less than the cost of implementing 802.11b.

WECA has already developed a test suite to test interoperability between 802.11a products from different vendors. Products that pass these tests will be authorized to carry the Wi-Fi5 logo.

If you have already invested in 802.11b, however, 802.11a's lack of backward-compatibility may be a major hurdle. Although you can selectively add new 802.11a access points and PC cards, replacing all APs and all wireless NICs at once may be prohibitively expensive. Other than Proxim's AP controller, products that support both 802.11a and 802.11b are not yet available. Several vendors have announced AP products that support both 802.11b and 802.11a by providing slots for two radio cards. The AP shown in Figure 15-1 has two slots for PC card wireless network adapters. The network administrator can install one wireless networking PC card, two cards of the same type, or one of each type. This two-card AP solution doesn't require that you upgrade all clients to the faster standard before you can provide a faster connection to clients who need it.

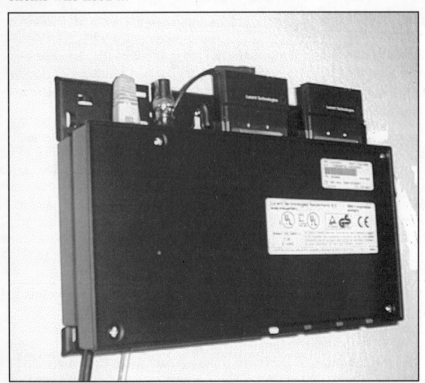

Figure 15-1: An access point that takes two PC cards can potentially support both 802.11a and 802.11b stations at the same time.

In short, the jury is still out on whether you should wait for 802.11a or take the plunge with 802.11b. As with most computer technology, something new and better is always just around the corner. For my money, I like to get the most out of what is available today, and then upgrade when the time and price is right.

Higher-Rate Extensions in the 2.4 GHz Band—802.11g

By the time you read this book, the IEEE will almost certainly have adopted IEEE 802.11g which, as a supplement to 802.11, will set the specifications for protocols that can transmit data up to 54 Mbps over the 2.4 GHz frequency ISM band. Two different protocols were originally proposed—Intersil's *Orthogonal Frequency Division*

Multiplexing (OFDM) modulation protocol and Texas Instrument's *Packet Binary Convolutional Coding (PBCC)* technology. In November 2001, the IEEE 802.11 Task Group G approved the first draft of 802.11g. According to an IEEE press release, this draft is based on *Complementary Code Keying (CCK)*, OFDM, and PBCC. However, the mandatory modulation schemes of this protocol are CCK, used in 802.11b, and OFDM, used in 802.11a. Two optional modulations—CCK-PBCC and CCK-OFDM—are permitted if manufacturers choose to include them. Texas Instrument's (TI) technology, which includes a 22 Mbps speed (PBCC-22), may in fact be used by some vendors as an enhanced 802.11b technology. Linksys, for example, has announced that it will ship an 802.11b product line with a 22 Mbps mode that uses PBCC-22. TI is already shipping PBCC-22-enabled devices.

Many companies have already announced that they will produce products that comply with 802.11g, even before it is formally approved. The reason for strong vendor support is the promise of backward-compatibility, the main obstacle for 802.11a. Interestingly, it may be relatively easy for vendors to create products that support all three standards—802.11a, 802.11b, and 802.11g — in the same chipset because 802.11b and 802.11g share the same ISM band, whereas 802.11a and 802.11g share the same modulation protocol.

Although no product shipment dates have been announced, products based on 802.11g will very likely be available before the end of calendar year 2002—assuming the final draft of the standard is adopted in time. Again, you are faced with the question of when to invest in WLAN technology. Fortunately, in this case, the decision is easier. The 802.11g standard will require backward-compatibility with 802.11b network equipment. You will be able to upgrade one AP at a time without losing any functionality. Both 802.11b and 802.11g stations will be able to roam from AP to AP. For instance, if an 802.11b station connects to an 802.11g AP, the maximum transmission speed will still be 11 Mbps. Conversely, 802.11g stations will get no better than 11 Mbps from an 802.11b AP, but wherever you install an 802.11g AP, any new 802.11g station will be able to get up to 54 Mbps.

Choosing Between 802.11a, 802.11b, and 802.11g

When 802.11g products become available, you will have to choose between a wide variety of products that comply with 802.11b, a growing list of products that comply with 802.11a, a short list of products that comply with 802.11g, and possibly a very short list of products that comply with all three standards. You may have to make a choice before a dominant product emerges (if you are as old as I am, you probably remember the Beta/VHS videotape wars). Here are a few criteria you can use to make your decision:

♦ **Speed.** By the end of 2002, both 802.11a (Wi-Fi5) products and 802.11g products will provide 54 Mbps transmission speeds. 802.11b (Wi-Fi) products will still deliver a maximum speed of 11 Mbps. If the primary reason for installing a wireless LAN is to enable users to access the Internet, 802.11b WLANs will be fast enough. Frequent large file transfers, streaming multimedia, and/or heavy network traffic will be best served by 802.11a or 802.11g systems. MPEG2, for example, requires 6 Mbps for video streaming, but 802.11b devices typically deliver no better than 4.5 Mbps. Both 802.11a and 802.11g should be able to deliver 54 Mbps, a speed that is more than adequate for streaming video. However, it may be necessary, with either of the high-rate standards, to dedicate a channel to streaming video.

♦ **Network capacity.** With eight non-overlapping channels, 802.11a products should provide higher network capacity compared to either 802.11b or 802.11g. When network capacity is your primary criteria, go for 802.11a, because 802.11a and 802.11g can achieve the same speeds. You will be able to pack APs more tightly together due to the increased number of non-overlapping channels.

♦ **Range.** Tests have shown that 802.11a products, which transmit in the 5 GHz band, have more problems with signal attenuation from solid objects than products that transmit in the 2.4 GHz band. Even glass doors, for example, have a signficant attenuation effect on the signal from 802.11a devices. When comparing 802.11a devices to 802.11b devices, 802.11a still wins because of its increased transmission rate. However, 802.11g devices should have an advantage over 802.11a devices when transmitting at the same rate because 802.11g devices use the 2.4GHz band that has a superior capability to penetrate solid objects.

♦ **Interference.** One continual criticism of 802.11b products is the overuse of the relatively crowded 2.4 GHz ISM band. Microwave ovens, 2.4 GHz portable phones, and BlueTooth devices all transmit in this frequency band. Although 802.11b's modulation protocol avoids most of this potential interference, the noise level is certainly higher in this band than in 5 GHz, the band used by 802.11a devices. Because 802.11g will also use the 2.4-GHz band, it would seem that 802.11a again has the advantage. The high-rate modulation schemes used in both 802.11a and 802.11g are more robust in avoiding interference than 802.11b's standard protocol, however, so interference may not be a real problem for 802.11g.

♦ **Backward-compatibility.** 802.11g products will provide the most straightforward backward-compatibility. If your WLAN is already up and running with 802.11b equipment, 802.11g may be the best choice for an upgrade. You will be able to add 802.11g APs and stations at your own pace, or as you notice that certain groups of users need faster WLAN access.

Unless you can buy wireless NICs that seamlessly support both 802.11a and 802.11b, making the decision to switch from 802.11b to 802.11a requires a larger initial investment than a staged switch to 802.11g because you need to add enough new APs to cover your entire site.

If you can upgrade your existing APs to 802.11a while still supporting your existing 802.11b stations, you may have the best of all worlds. Upgrading the APs should be less expensive than replacing them.

♦ **Price.** The first wave of 802.11b products has already started coming down dramatically in price, although the newest lines of enterprise-level Wi-Fi products are still several times more expensive than 802.11b access points designed for the home or small office. At their introduction, however, you will pay a premium to get the enhanced speed and throughput of 802.11a or 802.11g. If you can "make do" with 11 Mbps for a year or so, prices for 54 Mbps should drop significantly. 802.11g products should be cheaper to build than 802.11a products because they are based on repurposed existing technology.

♦ **Market share.** Choosing a product line that is successful in the marketplace is to your advantage because high demand tends to result in strong competition, lower prices, and better support options. At the beginning of 2002, 802.11b products will certainly account for close to 100 percent of the sales of 802.11-based products, simply because only one 802.11a product line is currently available.

According to a study sponsored by Microsoft and released in October 2001 (available at `http://www.wi-fi.org`), about 40 percent of companies with at least 500 employees have deployed wireless networks, with another 31 percent intending to do so in the next 18 months. One of the top reasons that companies have cited for not deploying WLANs was transmission speed. A significant number of companies are just now purchasing WLANs for the first time, and many are looking for faster speeds.By the end of 2002 or the middle of 2003, the market share of 802.11a and 802.11g will certainly account for a significant portion of installed WLAN sites.

Only time and the marketplace will determine whether 802.11a or 802.11g becomes the dominant high-speed standard. 802.11g-based products are backward-compatible with 802.11b-based products—a distinct advantage. On the other hand, 802.11a-based products enjoy first-to-market status.

Quality of Service—802.11e

Quality of Service (QoS) is a buzzword that I never noticed until I started studying WLAN technology. Now I see it everywhere. QoS is a networking term that means "guaranteed throughput level," a feature needed to support transmission of streaming video and high-quality voice. IEEE 802.11e is an unratified extension to 802.11, intended to add support for multimedia and QoS to wireless LANs. The standards being considered for 802.11e will be compatible with 802.11b and 802.11a devices, but will do a much better job of dealing with interference that would otherwise slow down the connection. Equipment that complies with this standard will be able to prioritize packets, sending the higher-priority packets first whenever congestion is apparent. Prioritization of packets is particularly important to a user watching a movie over a WLAN connection or participating in a video conference.

A protocol called *Whitecap2*, from the company ShareWave (owned by CirrusLogic at the time of writing), includes proprietary QoS mechanisms for 802.11 networks. Products from Panasonic using Whitecap2 are already on the market, so if you have a need for a wireless network that can handle voice, take a look at the Panasonic products with Whitecap2 technology.

Enhanced MAC Layer Security—IEEE 802.11i

According to October 2001 market research sponsored by Microsoft, WLAN security is a top concern for many corporation CIOs, negatively influencing their decisions to implement wireless networks. The publicity surrounding WEP's vulnerability to attack, as well as the overall economic and political environment in the aftermath of September 11th, probably has much to do with raising these concerns. Task Group I of the 802.11 Working Group is addressing the overall issue of WLAN security and authentication in the *medium access control (MAC) layer*.

Task Group E's focus originally included enhancement to the MAC layer, both for Quality of Service (QoS) and improved security. However, in May 2001, the 802.11 Working Group decided to split Task Group E into two groups. It assigned QoS to Task Group E and security to the new Task Group I.

The latest draft from Task Group I mandates the use of 802.1x for authenticating the wireless device to the network. The group has not mandated any specific authentication mechanism, leaving the decision to vendors and other industry bodies like WECA.

A major issue for Task Force I to resolve was whether to move to a variant of WEP for packet encryption or to scrap WEP and use a different encryption algorithm altogether. The group decided to propose two protocols—one protocol that uses the same building blocks as WEP but overcomes all the weaknesses and another based on the Advanced Encryption Standard (AES). The former could be implemented on current products via a firmware or driver update. The AES-based protocol is meant to provide long-term security for future products.

Because this task group has not yet submitted a draft amendment to 802.11, it is impossible to predict what its final recommendations will be. Keep an eye on these developments, however, so you can take advantage of security enhancements as soon as they become available.

Port-Based Network Access Control—IEEE 802.1x

One set of security enhancements is already available. IEEE 802.1x is a recently adopted standard, ratified in June 2001. It enables the network to authenticate and determine the identity of an entity, as well as the entity's access rights at the time the entity attempts to connect to a LAN port, without depending on the MAC address (see Chapter 13 for a full discussion of 802.1x).

Although 802.1x is not a wireless networking standard per se, several currently available WLAN products support it. For example, at the launch of Windows XP, Microsoft announced that the WLAN drivers now native in the operating system include support for 802.1x (see Figure 15-2).

Figure 15-2: The Authentication tab of the Wireless Network Connection dialog in Windows XP

At the same launch, ORiNOCO announced support for 802.1x in its high-end AP 2000 products. Since that time, ORiNOCO has released updates to its AP Manager software that also implement 802.1x support in its AP-1000 and AP-500 lines, as shown in Figure 15-3. In addition to ORiNOCO's products, APs from the other market leader, Cisco, now provide support for 802.1x over the following operating systems:

♦ Windows 9x

♦ Windows NT4

♦ Windows 2000

♦ Mac OS

♦ Linux

Notice that the ORiNOCO configuration dialog supports automatic key distribution. Using 802.1x, the WEP key is a single session key that is passed to the station from the authentication server rather than a multisession key that must be shared by all wireless stations using a common AP. Even if a hacker discovers the WEP key, it will be good for the current session only.

Figure 15-3: The 802.1x Authentication Setup dialog in ORiNOCO's AP Manager

The 802.1x authentication process uses *Extensible Authentication Protocol (EAP)*-compliant dynamic key derivation methods such as EAP-TLS, EAP-SRP, Kerberos, and Tunneled TLS. Keys are automatically derived on both the wireless station and the authentication server. All transmissions are encrypted using single session keys.

RADIUS servers that support EAP and, thus, 802.1x include the following:

♦ Microsoft Windows 2000 Server

♦ Windows .Net Server

♦ Cisco ACS

♦ Funk RADIUS

♦ Interlink Networks RADIUS servers

Power over Ethernet—IEEE 802.3af

Many companies and institutions select their WLAN equipment based on its capability to power the access points over the Ethernet cable—*Power over Ethernet (PoE)*. To date, each AP manufacturer has had to devise its own solution. Soon, there will be a standard for supplying DC power over Ethernet cabling. The IEEE 802.3af Task Force has been working on this project since January 2000. A major factor driving this initiative is the emergence of the WLAN market.

At the IEEE 802.3 Closing Plenary in November 2001, a motion was passed that approved the technical draft for IEEE 802.af Data Terminal Equipment (DTE) Power via the Media Dependent Interface (MDI). If the Task Force can stay on schedule, the official standard is expected as early as mid-2002. The existence of such a standard will enable WLAN manufacturers to focus on the communication aspects of their products. It should also give you a wider variety of PoE-compliant WLAN equipment from which to choose.

Plan for Change

When initial installations are planned with upgrades in mind, future upgrades are more likely to be successful. This is particularly true with wireless LANs. If you plan a large number of APs and client stations for your WLAN, your company will be making a significant investment. You certainly don't want to have to scrap the system and start over as soon as new technology is available.

The site survey that you performed at the beginning of your planning should give you enough information to predict which users or groups of users will use the WLAN most. These users will probably be the first to ask for more functionality from the WLAN. Ask yourself how difficult and costly it will be to upgrade the network a year from now and make your initial implementation decisions accordingly.

For example, if you expect that you will need to increase the network capacity in one of the WLAN cells, plan for adding an AP whenever needed. If you are connecting all APs with Ethernet cable, when you pull the cable for the first AP, pull a second cable so you won't have to do so later. Alternatively, you can purchase your first group of APs with two PC card slots, such as the ORiNOCO AP 1000 (shown in Figure 15-1) and AP 2000. If you use only one of the two slots initially, you can simply add a second PC card when you need to expand your network.

Implementing Firmware Updates

Many features of wireless LAN systems are implemented either in firmware in the PC card or AP, or in the client or AP management software that runs on your PC. Virtually all the manufacturers of WLAN equipment use flashable APs and wireless NICs. Each of these manufacturers periodically posts software and firmware updates on its company Web site. Sometimes the updates are mandatory in nature—for example, they might fix serious bugs—so you need to download them and update your products. Other times, the updates inform you how to add enhancements that you may or may not need.

When deciding whether to update the firmware in an AP or wireless NIC, consider that many bug fixes apply to features that you will never use. Many of the devices used in wireless networks contain chipsets that can be updated by running software that loads a new set of instructions into the chipset. This procedure is called *flashing the firmware* (a combination of hardware and software) that controls a device's features. By running a program to flash a device's firmware, you can upgrade the device without returning the device to the manufacturer. There is always a risk when you attempt to flash the product, that the power will go out and you will only partially load the update. This would be a major disaster for some products, because the factory settings may also be erased. Other products enable you to force a reset back to factory settings, even if the power fails while flashing the product.

In some cases, the update is significant—adding support for a new version of WEP, for example, or adding 802.1x support. Consequently, you need to periodically check for announcements in the technical support sections of the Web sites of access point and wireless NIC manufacturers.

Whenever you perform a firmware update, follow these general guidelines:

♦ Make a copy of the current configuration. If the product software enables you to save the configuration to a file that you upload later, do that first. Otherwise, print all the screens of configuration options. When you flash the product, you will probably reset everything back to factory defaults.

♦ Follow the manufacturer's instructions very carefully. Always perform the flash over a wired Ethernet connection or over a USB connection because you will probably lose any wireless connectivity after the new firmware is loaded.

♦ If you are doing more than one instance of a product, perform the upgrade on one and make sure you can get it running before you perform the remaining upgrades.

♦ Be very careful not to turn off the computer or unplug anything until the flash process is finished.

♦ After performing any upgrade, try to build in time for thorough testing, while you still have a chance to roll back the changes if something goes wrong.

New Site Survey

Your first WLAN will probably not be your last. The demand for this technology is on the rise, despite the downturn in the rest of the economy. When the inevitable call comes from a department head that needs wireless access *immediately*, you should be ready with your original site survey and questionnaires. Essentially, you need to perform a new site survey, at least for the group requesting more wireless network. Each time you make adjustments to the wireless network by adding, subtracting, or moving APs, record the changes on your site survey documentation. Armed with this information, you should find that planning the implementation of new wireless segments is relatively easy.

Summary

This chapter tells you how to keep up with the rapid changes in wireless LAN technology, and briefly discusses the criteria to use when choosing between several competing 802.11 protocols—802.11b, 802.11a, and 802.11g. This chapter also covers how to implement updates, and plan your upgrades.

This is the last chapter in Part III of the book. Part IV describes how people use wireless networks at work, at home, around campus, and on the go.

Part IV

Using Wi-Fi

Chapter 16

<u>Using Wi-Fi at Work</u>

In This Chapter

This chapter discusses the following topics:

♦ Wi-Fi basics from a user's perspective

♦ Connecting to a WLAN in Windows 9*x* and Windows 2000

♦ Connecting to a WLAN in Windows XP

♦ Connecting to a WLAN on a Macintosh

The chapters in this part of the book target individuals who use Wi-Fi wireless networks at work, at home, at college, and on the road. This chapter provides basic background information on wireless LANs, as well as a few pointers on connecting to a wireless LAN at work. If you are a network administrator, you might consider using this chapter as the basis for a wireless LAN user's orientation course.

The Big Picture

Networks, including wireless networks, are just tools to help you get your work done. Although most technophiles think wireless technology is unconditionally cool, "normal" people may not be enthusiastic about a particular technology unless it's useful. Fortunately, wireless technology has proven to be useful, at least in the context of wireless networks. The wireless network adapter in your laptop (or desktop) computer transmits a digital signal through the AP, back and forth to the other computers on your LAN, and, in most cases, to the computers on the Internet (assuming your LAN is connected to the Internet). The WLAN also enables you to print to network printers and to share files with other people on your company LAN.

Companies buy wireless networks to enable their employees to do the following:

- ◆ Share files
- ◆ Share printers
- ◆ Share schedules
- ◆ Share an Internet connection
- ◆ Make interoffice e-mail possible

Although wired LANs allow you to connect to the Internet, send e-mail, and share files and printers, a wireless LAN can facilitate all these activities from locations where wired network jacks are nonexistent. In some cases, a wireless LAN can even save your company a good deal of money by obviating the need to install network cable to every location that requires network access. If you have a laptop, a WLAN enables you to carry it, as well as its network, Internet, and printer connections, around your enterprise without ever losing a signal and without ever connecting a cable to the wall. Figure 16-1 depicts a typical wireless LAN with wireless laptops, an AP, a wired LAN, and devices connected to the LAN, such as printers and file servers.

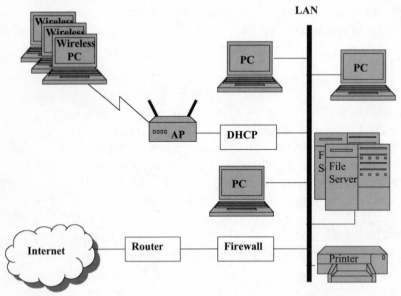

Figure 16-1: A typical wireless LAN, with wireless laptops, an AP, a wired LAN, and devices connected to the LAN, such as printers and file servers

Wi-Fi Basics

Wi-Fi is a trademarked logo owned by a nonprofit organization known as the Wireless Ethernet Compatibility Alliance (WECA). WECA's primary purpose is to certify the interoperability of wireless LAN equipment, specifically equipment that complies with IEEE 802.11b and IEEE 802.11a industry standards. You will see wireless LAN products that advertise compatibility with either of these standards, but the Wi-Fi logo means that the 802.11b-compliant product has passed a number of tests that determine whether the product can work with similar products from other vendors. Similarly, the Wi-Fi5 logo indicates that the 802.11a-compliant product has passed tests that demonstrate interoperability. Wi-Fi products and Wi-Fi5 products, however, are not interoperable. Odd as it may seem, 802.11a is a faster standard, but there are only a few Wi-Fi5 products on the market. Wi-Fi products, on the other hand, are widely available.

Whenever you use your computer at work, you seldom have a reason to think about the wired network that connects your computer to printers, file servers, e-mail, and the Internet—except, of course, if the network goes down. When you use a wireless LAN, however, you should know whether you have a good connection before you use the network. You should understand a few basics about the equipment so you can tell if it is working. Otherwise, wired local area networks and wireless local area networks (both Wi-Fi and Wi-Fi5) are essentially the same, except that WLANs use radios to make their connections.

For the remainder of this chapter, unless stated otherwise, everything covered applies to Wi-Fi and Wi-Fi5 products, as well as to other related products that will soon follow.

The Wireless Station

Wireless networking involves at least two radios. The computer or device that you use to connect to the wireless LAN is called a *station* or *client*. Most often, a WLAN station is a personal computer that contains a wireless network adapter, enabling the computer to communicate wirelessly with the LAN. The computer that your station talks to can be another station, but is more likely a *base station,* or *access point,* that connects your station to the larger LAN.

Most wireless stations are laptop computers or high-end *personal digital assistants (PDAs)* because the most compelling selling feature of wireless technology is its portability. Apple iBook laptop computers were the first to boast a wireless connection called an AirPort. Now, most laptop manufacturers provide built-in wireless LAN capability or PC card wireless LAN adapters (also called PCMCIA cards—short for Personal Computer Memory Card International Association cards) as options. (See Figure 16-2.)

Figure 16-2: A PC card wireless network adapter

If you use a desktop computer that is connected to a WLAN, the adapter inside the computer may, in fact, be a hardware adapter that enables the use of the PC card adapter in the desktop (see Figure 16-3). With this type of adapter, you can also remove the PC card (in many products, you must first turn your computer off) and use it in a laptop computer. However, wireless network adapters for desktop computers in which the radio is permanently mounted on the circuit board are becoming increasingly available. You will recognize these wireless products by their four-inch antenna attached to the back.

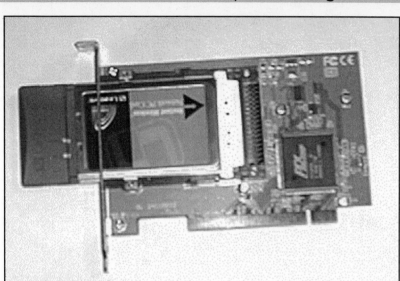

Figure 16-3: A PCI wireless network adapter

Access Points

In a workplace WLAN, the other side of the conversation is a device called an *access point (AP)*. (Apple calls its version of the device a *base station*, but most manufacturers use the term *access point*.) Regardless of terminology, both words refer to a device that communicates with wireless stations and connects these stations to the LAN. In many companies, access points are mounted on the wall, as shown in Figure 16-4, or even on the ceiling. Because each AP contains a radio, the AP should typically be mounted in a location that allows it to send and receive signals with the least amount of obstruction.

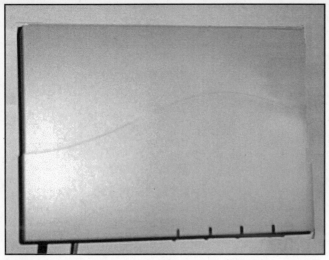

Figure 16-4: An access point, mounted on the wall, communicates with wireless stations and connects them to the LAN.

Each access point allows the network administrator to manage several parameters that enable each station to communicate with the AP and the LAN. These parameters include the following:

 ◆ The name of the wireless network

 ◆ The channel on which the AP is broadcasting (There are multiple radio channels available for use by wireless networks.)

 ◆ The Wired Equivalent Privacy (WEP) encryption key, which protects the data sent over the WLAN from eavesdropping

To ensure successful communication between the AP and the station, the network name (sometimes called the SSID) in your station must be set to the same value as the network name setting in the AP. Similarly, the WEP key in your station must be set to the same value as the WEP key setting in the AP. The radio in your wireless network adapter will automatically find the right channel.

Connecting to the WLAN

When connecting to the WLAN, you shouldn't have to do much more than insert a wireless network PC card into the computer's PC card slot or attach an adapter to the USB port. The person who set up your system should have configured the equipment to automatically connect to the WLAN as long as your computer is within range of the nearest wireless access point. In fact, if your computer uses Windows XP, your system can be configured to automatically connect to one of several different wireless LANs, depending on the strength of the signal that your wireless station is receiving.

To connect and remain connected to the WLAN, you must check the strength of the radio signal that your computer receives from the AP. If the signal is too weak, the radios will first try transmitting at slower speeds. Eventually, your wireless network adapter will disconnect itself from the LAN if it can't reestablish an adequate signal. Often, shifting the position of your computer can change the strength of the signal it receives. Ultimately, you may have to move closer to the AP, or move to a different location with a stronger signal.

Every Wi-Fi hardware manufacturer provides a software configuration utility that enables you to easily check signal strength. Most of these utilities are designed to run only on Windows. If you are using Windows XP, you can use built-in Windows XP software to check the signal. Similarly, Mac OS 9.*x* and Mac OS X have their own control panel utilities. If you are a Linux user, you are on your own to determine signal strength. I have not been able to find a utility for this purpose that runs on Linux.

The following sections discuss the steps involved in displaying signal strength information on Windows and Mac computers.

A Tale of Two Chipsets

A significant factor driving the rapid expansion of Wi-Fi-certified products is the existence of two high-quality radio chipsets (from Intersil and Lucent) that implement the 802.11b/Wi-Fi standard. One of these two chipsets is found in the majority of 802.11b access point and wireless network adapters available for sale.

Intersil's Wi-Fi-certified PRISM II chipset is clearly the most popular among wireless networking hardware manufacturers. Intersil also has a newer, more highly integrated PRISM 2.5 chipset. Manufacturers who use one of the PRISM chip sets include the following:

♦ 3Com	♦ Compaq (WL100)	♦ GemTek
♦ Addtron	♦ D-Link	♦ Intel
♦ Bromax	♦ Farallon	♦ LeArtery Solutions
♦ Cisco Aironet		♦ Linksys

- ♦ Nokia
- ♦ Nortel
- ♦ Samsung

- ♦ Siemens
- ♦ SMC
- ♦ Symbol
- ♦ Z-Com
- ♦ Zoom Telephonics

The Lucent technology chipset is used by another large group of manufacturers, including the following:

- ♦ 1stWave
- ♦ Agere ORiNOCO
- ♦ ARtem
- ♦ Avaya
- ♦ Buffalo

- ♦ Compaq (WL110)
- ♦ Dell (1150)
- ♦ ELSA
- ♦ Enterasys
- ♦ HP

- ♦ IBM
- ♦ Toshiba
- ♦ Sony

Windows 95, 98, Me, NT, and 2000 Users

Not all Wi-Fi equipment manufacturers use the same software to configure and test wireless network adapters, but most use one of two varieties: Lucent or Intersil. In Figure 16-5, you can see the icon that appears in the Windows Quick Launch toolbar if you are using a wireless LAN PC card designed by Lucent, and either Windows 95, 98, Me, NT, or 2000 as the operating system. Note that the icon is a miniature bar graph. When all five bars in the graph are filled with green, your WLAN radio is getting an excellent signal. As the signal gets weaker, the number of green bars shrinks until the entire graph turns yellow or goes blank, indicating a poor or nonexistent signal. You can also move the mouse pointer over the icon to see a message balloon that indicates an Excellent, Good, Fair, or Poor signal.

Figure 16-5: The icon that appears in the Windows Quick Launch toolbar if you are using a wireless LAN PC card manufactured by Lucent

To see a larger version of the signal strength graph, follow these steps:

1. Double-click the icon in the Windows Quick Launch toolbar to display the Client Manager window.

2. In the Client Manger window, click Link Test on the Advanced menu to display the Link Test window.

3. Click the Test Results tab in the Link Test window to display a screen similar to that shown in Figure 16-6.

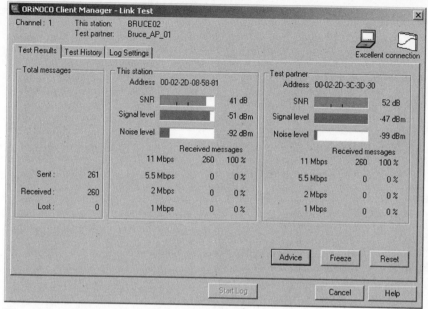

Figure 16-6: The Test Results tab of the Client Manager's Link Test window

4. In the Test Results and Test History tabs of the Link Test window, you can easily see signal strength, depicted in *signal-to-noise ratio (SNR)* format. The longer the green bar, the stronger the signal. You can also click the Advice button to obtain advice from the Help files, indicating whether the signal is strong enough.

5. When you are finished with this utility, click Cancel in the Link Test window, and then OK in the Client Manager window.

If you are using wireless network hardware that is based on the Intersil chipset, the icon shown in Figure 16-7 should appear in the Windows taskbar. This icon, which looks like a miniature computer, presents a green screen when the signal is adequate. When the signal is weak, the screen in the icon turns yellow. If it is too weak to receive information, the screen turns red.

Figure 16-7: The icon that appears in the Windows taskbar if you are using a wireless LAN PC card manufactured by Intersil

To see a larger signal strength graph, double-click this icon in the Windows taskbar to launch the Configuration software, as shown in Figure 16-8.

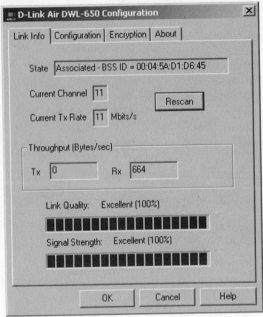

Figure 16-8: The Configuration screen for an Intersil chipset–based wireless network adapter card

Windows XP Users

Windows XP is the first version of Windows that comes with built-in support for wireless LANs in general and built-in drivers for some Wi-Fi equipment. A bit of configuration is still required when the wireless network adapter card is first installed in your computer, but it isn't necessary to install any software from the manufacturer of the wireless network adapter.

After you have inserted the wireless network adapter and started the computer, Windows XP displays a Network Connection icon, shown in Figure 16-9, in the Notification area of the Windows XP Taskbar. You can hover your mouse pointer over this icon to display a message like that shown in Figure 16-10, which indicates signal strength.

Figure 16-9: The Network Connection icon

Wireless Network Connection 7 (ORiNOCO_bruce)
Speed: 11.0 Mbps
Signal Strength: Very Good

Figure 16-10: Hover the mouse pointer over the Network Connection icon to display a message regarding signal strength.

To display a signal strength bar graph, follow these steps:

1. Right-click a Network Connection icon (there can be more than one if you have more than one network adapter in your computer) in the notification area of the taskbar at the bottom of the screen to display a pop-up menu.

2. Click the Status option. Windows XP displays the Wireless Network Connection Status dialog box, shown in Figure 16-11. This dialog contains a signal strength bar graph on the right side.

3. To close the window, click Close.

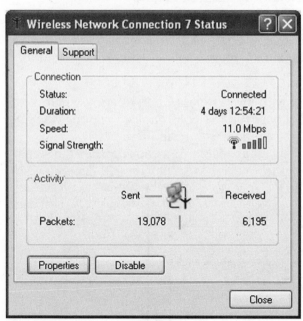

Figure 16-11: The Wireless Network Connection Status dialog shows signal strength.

Macintosh Users

Apple's iBook was the first personal computer to support 802.11b wireless networking with its AirPort Card wireless network adapter and AirPort Base

Station access point. Apple has recently announced the new AirPort 2, and will probably announce support for 802.11a in the near future.

If you are using a Mac with an AirPort Card, or another wireless network adapter, you can check signal strength from the Wireless control panel.

1. Open the Apple menu and choose Control Panels.

2. Select the Wireless control panel. The Wireless Configuration window, shown in Figure 16-12, should display. If it doesn't, click Windows in the Menu bar and choose the Configuration option.

☐	Wireless Configuration	目
Signal Strength:		
Status:	SSID 'ORiNOCO_bruce', channel 1, Encryption off	
Network (SSID):	Select the best ⬦	

Figure 16-12: The Macintosh Wireless Configuration window

The Wireless Configuration window contains a blue horizontal bar that depicts the strength of the signal that your computer is receiving from the AP.

To obtain a numeric read out, with the Wireless Configuration window open, click the drop-down list and choose the "Select from list" option. Mac OS displays the Wireless Networks window, shown in Figure 16-13. The Wireless Networks window lists all available APs and specifies the signal that your computer is receiving from each AP. Click the AP that you want to use, and then click Select. Click Cancel to close the window.

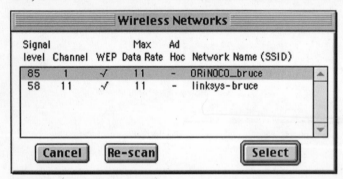

Figure 16-13: The Wireless Networks dialog lists all available access points, including the signal strenght, channel, and data rate.

If you don't want to choose the AP yourself, but would rather have Mac OS select the AP with the strongest signal, display the Wireless Configuration window and choose "Select the best " from the drop-down list.

Summary

This chapter provides basic background information on wireless LANs. It also gives a few pointers about how to connect to a wireless LAN at work using Windows, Windows XP, and Macintosh computers. The topic of the next chapter is using Wi-Fi at home.

Chapter 17

Using Wi-Fi at Home

In This Chapter
This chapter discusses the following topics:

- Wi-Fi basics, from a user's perspective
- Connecting to a WLA in Windows 9*x,* Windows 2000, Windows XP, and on a Macintosh
- Connecting to the Internet and to AOL over the WLAN

This chapter targets individuals who use Wi-Fi wireless networks. It gives the new home user of a wireless network some basic background information on wireless LANs, as well as a few pointers on connecting to a wireless LAN at home. If you are the person who installed your home network, this chapter is probably not for you; however, you may want to ask other members of your family to browse through it.

So What's the Big Deal?

If you're mostly interested in obtaining Internet access, a wireless network (several computers connected together) is an excellent tool for connecting all the computers in the house for shared Internet access. Connecting the computers also makes it easier to share document files and printers.

The wireless network PC card in your laptop (or desktop) computer, or the USB adapter connected to the back of the computer, transmits a digital signal to the other computers in your house. When computers in a home or business are connected, the network is called a *local area network (LAN).* A wireless LAN (WLAN) has the added benefit of allowing you to connect to the Internet from anywhere in your house without the limitations that electrical outlet placement can cause wired networks.

In most cases, people set up a home WLAN so they can share a single Internet connection, especially if it's a very fast connection using either DSL or a cable modem. When your computer is connected to the Internet through a WLAN, the computers on the Internet can't "see" the computers in your house. This gives everyone in the house access to the Internet at once, and protects everyone's computer from hackers. The hacker sees only the network's *gateway device*—the device that connects to the Internet and forwards information between the computers on the Internet and the computers in your house.

In addition to providing shared Internet access, your home WLAN also enables you to do the following from just about anywhere in your house:

♦ Share computer files, such as word processing documents, with the other computers in your house

♦ Share printers so you can print to any printer attached to any of the computers in the house

♦ Share schedules using programs such as Microsoft Outlook (which is part of Microsoft Office)

Figure 17-1 depicts a typical home WLAN. This WLAN comprises several wireless laptops and a printer connected to one of the laptops. The WLAN also includes a wireless device called an *access point (AP)*, which is also a *gateway*. APs and gateways are covered in more detail later in this chapter. Note also the DSL or cable modem that is connected to the Internet.

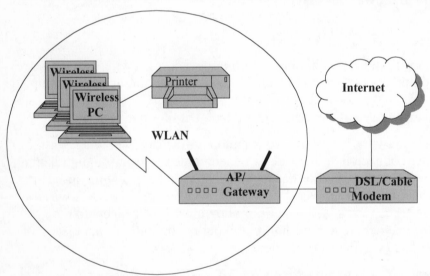

Figure 17-1: A typical home wireless LAN, with wireless laptops, a printer, an AP/gateway, and a wired LAN and devices connected to the LAN, such as a printer and file servers

All You Really Need to Know about Wi-Fi

You may see a Wi-Fi logo printed on the wireless network equipment that you use with your computer. Wi-Fi is a trademarked logo owned by a nonprofit organization called the Wireless Ethernet Compatibility Alliance (WECA). WECA's primary purpose is to certify that wireless LAN products from different companies work together. All the equipment that enables your computer to talk wirelessly to the network follows an industry standard called IEEE 802.11. The Wi-Fi logo means that each product has passed a number of tests that determine whether the product is interoperable with similar products from other vendors.

You may also see a Wi-Fi5 logo on your equipment. This logo indicates that the equipment can send information at a rate roughly five times faster than Wi-Fi equipment. Wi-Fi equipment works with other Wi-Fi equipment, but not with Wi-Fi5 equipment. Similarly, Wi-Fi5 equipment works only with other Wi-Fi5 equipment.

Because Wi-Fi network equipment is about eight times faster than the fastest home Internet connection currently available, it should be fast enough for your home WLAN.

Making Your PC a Wireless Radio Station

Wireless LANs communicate with radio signals. When it is connected to a wireless network, your computer becomes a wireless *station*. Most often, WLAN stations are laptop computers. Each computer contains a radio that enables it to communicate wirelessly with other computers over the WLAN. Apple iBook laptop computers were the first to boast a wireless connection called an AirPort. Now, you can add a PC card wireless LAN adapter to nearly any laptop. Two wireless LAN PC cards are shown in Figure 17-2.

If you don't own a laptop, you can install a wireless network adapter card inside a desktop computer, or attach a wireless network device to a USB port.

CROSS-REFERENCE

Refer to Chapter 8 for more information on installing wireless network adapters. Refer to Chapter 10 for details on implementing a home WLAN plan, network wiring issues, installing and configuring APs in your home, and Internet connection sharing.

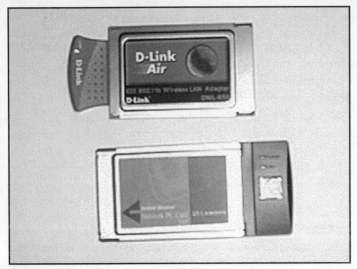

Figure 17-2: Two wireless network PC cards

Wireless networking involves at least two radios. The radio in each computer talks to a second radio. The second radio can be installed in another computer, but is most often a device called an *access point* (sometimes referred to as a *base station*). The access point receives signals from all the computers in the wireless network and passes them on to the other computers in the WLAN. Figure 17-3 depicts one of the more popular types of access points used in home WLANs.

The type of radio used by Wi-Fi equipment sends a digital signal over a radio channel in the 2.4 GHz radio frequency band. Some portable phones—the 2.4-GHz variety—use the same set of frequencies and can cause interference problems for WLAN equipment. You should also keep your WLAN equipment at least ten feet away from microwave ovens because they put out radio frequency (RF) "noise" in the 2.4 GHz frequency band as well.

Wi-Fi equipment, portable phones, and microwave ovens all operate in the same band because this band does not require a Federal Communication Commission (FCC) license. In 1985, the FCC made changes to the radio spectrum regulation and assigned three bands that it designated as the *industrial, scientific, and medical (ISM) bands*. These frequency bands are as follows:

♦ **902 MHz–928 MHz.** Some portable phones operate in this band.

♦ **2.4 GHz–2.4835 GHz.** Wi-Fi operates in this band, along with 2.4 GHz portable phones, microwave ovens, and other wireless devices.

♦ **5.725 GHz–5.850 GHz.** Wi-Fi5 equipment operates in this band, along with very few other types of devices, so potential interference is less likely.

Figure 17-3: A popular type of wireless network access point device used in homes

To encourage the development and use of wireless networking technology, the FCC regulation permits a user to operate radio equipment that transmits a signal within one of the three ISM bands (within certain guidelines) without obtaining an FCC license. HAM radio operators, commercial radio stations, and most other users of equipment that transmits radio frequency signals must obtain a license from the FCC before they can operate their equipment.

Getting Connected over the WLAN

Ideally, you shouldn't have to do anything special to connect to the WLAN other than turn on your computer. Now that your computer is connected to a network, you may need to sign on to the network each time you turn on the computer. Otherwise, using your computer for all its normal duties is exactly the same as before. The person who set up your computer system and/or who added the wireless station hardware and software in your computer should have configured the equipment to automatically connect to the WLAN when you turn it on, as long as your computer is within range of the nearest wireless access point.

NOTE
If you are setting up your computer for WLAN access for the first time, turn to Chapter 10 for more information about installing a home WLAN and wireless stations.

Before you attempt to use the network, you should determine if your computer has established a good connection with the AP. If the signal is not strong enough, the radios will first try to transmit at slower speeds. If slower speeds don't strengthen your signal, you may lose the connection completely. Shifting the position of your computer can often change the signal it receives. Ultimately, you may have to move closer to the AP, or move to a different location in your house that has a stronger signal.

Every manufacturer of Wi-Fi hardware provides software that enables you to easily see signal strength. Determining the strength of the WLAN radio signal is usually very easy. The following sections explain how to do this, depending on which operating system you are using.

Windows 95, 98, Me, NT, and 2000 Users

If you are using Windows 95, 98, Me, NT or 2000, either of the two icons shown in Figure 17-4 may appear in your computer's toolbar. These icons help you determine whether your computer is connected to the network.

Figure 17-4: One of these icons may appear in the Windows Quick Launch toolbar if you are using a wireless LAN PC card.

Not all Wi-Fi equipment manufacturers use the same software to configure and test wireless network adapters, but most use one of two varieties. The first icon shown in Figure 17-4 is used by most wireless LAN PC cards manufactured by Lucent. This icon is a miniature bar graph. A bar graph with all five bars filled with green indicates that your WLAN radio is getting an excellent signal. As the signal gets weaker, the number of green bars shrinks until the entire graph turns yellow, or goes blank, indicating a poor or non-existent signal. You can also move your mouse pointer over the icon to see a message balloon that indicates one of the following signal states:

◆ Excellent

◆ Good

◆ Fair

◆ Poor

The icon is probably all the information you need, but if you like to be well-informed, you can display a larger version of the signal strength graph:

1. Double-click the miniature bar graph on in the Windows Quick Launch toolbar to display the Client Manager window.

2. In the Client Manger window, click Link Test on the Advanced menu to display the Link Test window.

3. Click the Test Results tab in the Link Test window to display a screen similar to that shown in Figure 17-5.

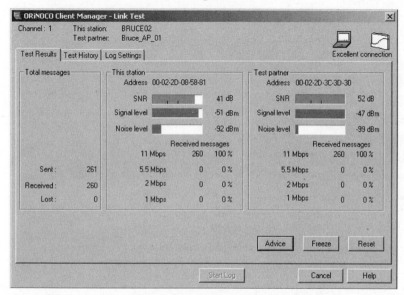

Figure 17-5: The Test Results tab of the Client Manager's Link Test window

From the Test Results and Test History tabs of the Link Test window, you can easily see the signal strength, depicted in *signal-to-noise ratio (SNR)* format—the signal level minus the noise level. The longer the green bar, the stronger the signal. You can also click the Advice button to obtain advice from the Help files, indicating whether the signal is strong enough. When you are finished with this utility, click Cancel in the Link Test window, and then click OK in the Client Manager window.

If you see the second icon shown in Figure 17-4 in the Windows taskbar, your wireless network hardware is based on a chipset designed by Intersil.

(Nearly all the wireless LAN cards sold today use either the Lucent chipset or the Intersil chipset.) This icon, which looks like a miniature computer, shows a green screen when the signal is adequate. When the signal is weak, the screen in the icon turns yellow. If the signal is too weak for the radio in your computer to receive information, the screen turns red.

To see a larger signal strength graph, double-click this icon in the Windows taskbar to launch the Configuration software, as shown in Figure 17-6.

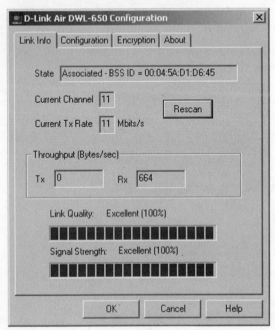

Figure 17-6: The Configuration screen for an Intersil chipset-based wireless network adapter card

Windows XP Users

If you are using Windows XP, you won't see the icons shown in Figure 17-4 in the taskbar. Instead, you will see the Network Connection icon shown in Figure 17-7. You can hover your mouse pointer over this icon to display a message similar to the one in Figure 17-8, which indicates signal strength.

Figure 17-7: The Network Connection icon

```
Wireless Network Connection 7 (ORiNOCO_bruce)
Speed: 11.0 Mbps
Signal Strength: Very Good
```

Figure 17-8: Hover the mouse pointer over the Network Connection icon to display a message similar to this one.

Notice that the message in Figure 17-8 states that signal strength is Very Good, indicating that you have a good signal between your computer's radio and the radio in the AP.

To display a signal strength bar graph:

1. Right-click a Network Connection icon in the notification area of the taskbar at the bottom of the screen to display a pop-up menu.

2. Click the Status option.

3. Windows XP displays the Wireless Network Connection Status dialog, as shown in Figure 17-9. This dialog contains a signal strength bar graph on the right side.

4. Click the Close button to close the window.

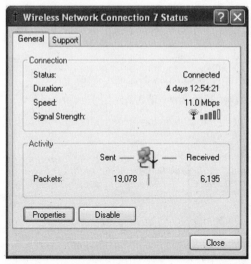

Figure 17-9: The Wireless Network Connection Status dialog shows signal strength.

Macintosh Users

The Apple computer company is known for creating innovative products, so it isn't surprising that the Apple iBook contained the first wireless Wi-Fi access point products. Apple sells the AirPort Card wireless network adapter, which works in newer Macintosh laptop and desktop computers. The Apple

AirPort Base Station is Apple's access point offering. Apple has recently announced the new AirPort 2 Base Station. Other Wi-Fi wireless network equipment is available that will work in Macintosh computers.

To check the signal strength of your Macintosh wireless connection, perform the following steps from the Wireless control panel:

1. Open the Apple menu and choose Control Panels.

2. Select the Wireless control panel. The Wireless Configuration window (see Figure 17-10) should display. If it doesn't, click Windows in the Menu bar and choose the Configuration option.

Figure 17-10: The Macintosh Wireless Configuration window

The blue horizontal bar in the Wireless Configuration window depicts the strength of the signal that your Macintosh is receiving from the base station. If you prefer a numeric read out:

1. Click the drop-down list in the Wireless Configuration window.

2. Choose the Select from list option to display the Wireless Networks window shown in Figure 17-11.

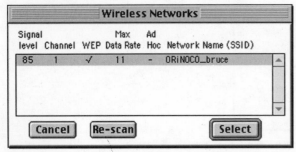

Figure 17-11: Use the Wireless Networks dialog to see a numeric readout of the signal level that your computer's wireless network adapter is receiving from the base station.

3. The Wireless Networks window lists all available wireless networks and specifies the signal that your computer is receiving from each base station. Click the network that you want to use.

4. Click Select to complete the selection or click Cancel to close the window.

Connecting to the Internet

Most home WLAN users set up a network in order to connect to the Internet over a fast DSL or cable modem connection. If your WLAN is connected to one of these Internet services, it is connected 24 hours a day. Now that you have determined that the radio signal is sufficient between your computer and the wireless LAN, connecting to the Internet should be a piece of cake. Just open a Web browser, such as Microsoft Internet Explorer. It should open to the Web site that is stored in the program as the home page. You can also type a valid Web address in the Address line and press Enter. If you know that you have a strong WLAN signal, but your Web browser doesn't display a Web page, the culprit is most likely the Internet settings on your computer, rather than the wireless network.

If you are an AOL user connecting to the Internet, you must first change your AOL connection type from Modem to TCP/IP:

1. From the AOL opening screen (before you attempt to sign on), click Setup and then Add Modem.

2. AOL will detect that you have both a modem and a high-speed Internet connection and will prompt you to select either the modem or the TCP/IP connection.

3. Select TCP/IP, and click Next at each of the screens until AOL returns to the login screen.

4. AOL will then attempt to log you in over the WLAN and out through the fast Internet connection. If AOL starts dialing numbers instead, select Setup and then Edit Numbers, and delete any phone numbers you see there. The ISP/LAN Connection selection is the only one you need.

5. Click OK.

6. When AOL returns to the Sign On screen, click the SIGN ON button. AOL should sign you on to AOL over the WLAN/DSL/cable modem connection.

Summary

This chapter provides basic background information on wireless LANs, as well as a few pointers on connecting to a home WLAN using Windows,

Windows XP, and a Macintosh computer. Chapter 18 tells you how to use Wi-Fi around town and on the road.

Chapter 18

<u>Using Wi-Fi on the Go</u>

In This Chapter

This chapter discusses the following topics:

- ◆ Wi-Fi security when using wireless LAN equipment away from home or the office
- ◆ Connecting to other computers using an ad hoc wireless network
- ◆ Accessing the Internet over a public wireless network

This chapter targets individuals who will be using Wi-Fi wireless networks and helps users get connected to *public wireless networks* that are available in places such as coffee shops, hotels, and airports.

Public Wireless LANs

As of this writing, the emerging wireless LAN technology has produced two types of public wireless networks:

- ◆ **Commercial WLAN Internet service providers.** Public wireless LANs of this type provide Internet connectivity for a fee in public places such as coffee shops and airports, as well as hotels—locations sometimes called wireless *hot spots*.
- ◆ **Community wireless networks.** Several communities in the United States have collaborated to set up a wireless network that connects interested members of the neighborhood free-of-charge.

The following sections describe each of these wireless services in more detail.

Commercial Wireless LANs

Anyone who habitually accesses the Internet over a T1 line at work or a DSL or cable modem line at home will find being connected by a 56K bps modem to be painfully slow. Yet most business travelers connect their laptops to the hotel telephone and dial up their companies' e-mail servers. In my experience, downloading a day's worth of e-mail over a 56K line may sometimes take hours. The same exchange of outgoing and incoming e-mail messages would take only seconds over a T1 line at work, or slightly longer over a cable modem at home.

Fortunately, high-speed Internet connections are becoming more common in the major hotel chains frequented by business travelers, and even in a few of the smaller nationwide hotel chains, such as Summerfield Suites, Fairfield Inn, Hampton Inn, Comfort Inn, and Courtyard by Marriott. The typical hotel-based high-speed connection requires that your laptop have an Ethernet port and that you pay about $9.95 for 24 hours of service.

The availability of a high-speed connection in your hotel room is convenient; however, it only gives you connectivity in a single location. If you're attending a conference in the hotel, it would be much more convenient if you could access the Internet and download company e-mail from anywhere in the building.

Wayport

Wayport, Inc. (www.wayport.com), based in Austin, Texas, is one of the leading providers of high-speed Internet connections in hotels. Wayport provides high-speed Internet access in more than 400 hotels across the United States, airports, and conference centers at speeds up to 50 to 200 times faster than traditional dial-up modem services. WayPort also has a European operation with an office northwest of London's Heathrow Airport. They have been providing wired Ethernet Internet connections to customers worldwide in a growing number of hotels and other public venues since 1997.

In the last year, Wayport has extended its service to Wi-Fi wireless equipment users. Wayport has started to set up major U.S. airports and hotels for all-wireless LAN connectivity.

Wayport charges for connectivity on a pay-as-you-go, daily basis—providing user connectivity from one of their properties for up to 24 hours a day (usually until midnight)—or on a monthly basis. Travelers can use Wayport's wireless Internet services by signing up on the spot and paying by credit card for service until midnight. Frequent business travelers who expect to use Wayport's services more than a couple times a month may prefer to sign up for a monthly account.

In addition to the à la carte daily charges, Wayport offers three plans:

- ◆ **Yearly Corporate Membership.** Organizations who recruit fifty or more members and commit to a year-long contract can sign up for a Wayport Corporate Membership, which entitles members to unlimited connectivity at any of Wayport's hotels or all-wireless airport locations for a set monthly rate that is based on volume of users.

- ◆ **Yearly individual membership.** Individuals can sign up for unlimited connectivity by committing to a yearly contract, but at a higher monthly rate than the Corporate Membership.

- ◆ **Prepaid plan.** This plan, designed for less-frequent users, is similar to a phone card. Members establish an account by prepaying a set amount. They can then connect at any Wayport hotel or all-wireless airport location at up to a 30 percent discount. The members' account is debited each time they use the service.

Several WLAN hardware manufacturers have partnered with WayPort to introduce potential customers to the service by providing coupons to users for a free day of access.

As part of a test project co-sponsored by Wayport and Microsoft, users of Windows XP and Wi-Fi WLAN equipment benefited from free wireless Internet service in participating hotel lobbies and throughout all gates and terminals at Wayport's all-wireless airports for three months at the end of 2001 and beginning of 2002. Free wireless connectivity was available in major travel hot spots such as Dallas/Fort Worth, San Jose, Seattle-Tacoma, and Austin-Bergstrom International airports. Participating hotels included select Sheratons, Marriotts, Westins, Radissons, Doubletrees, and Embassy Suites managed by MeriStar Hotels & Resorts, as well as Four Seasons, Wyndham, and many others.

This Wayport/Microsoft test program not only enabled users to try out Wayport at no cost, but also enabled Microsoft to test the new *Wireless Zero Configuration* feature of Windows XP. In addition, Microsoft was able to test Windows XP's support for IEEE 802.1*x* port-based authentication. According to press reports, Microsoft had run a successful smaller test of this enhanced security feature in the Seattle-Tacoma (SeaTac) airport in May 2001.

MobileStar

MobileStar Network Corporation (www.mobilestar.com), headquartered in Richardson, Texas, now owned by VoiceStream Wireless of Bellevue, WA (a subsidiary of German phone company Deutsche Telekom AG), is another leading provider of high-speed Internet access for business travelers, with an exclusive focus on wireless connectivity. MobileStar has hot spots in airports, hotels, conference centers, restaurants, coffee houses, and other public places in the United States. In its press releases, MobileStar states that since its inception in 1996, it has created the largest wireless broadband Internet access network designed to give mobile professionals access to their corporate intranets remotely. MobileStar is the first to provide a wireless-only subscription service. The MobileStar service also includes authorization and authentication specifically designed for wireless Internet access.

MobileStar has partnered with Starbucks to provide broadband wireless Internet access in many of the Starbucks coffee houses across the country, with over 500 coffee houses already active. The service provider originally planned to operate a wireless Internet service at each of Starbucks' 3,900 or so locations in North America, but the slowdown of the personal computer industry and the overall weak economy has convinced MobileStar to put those plans on hold. In October 2001, it was widely reported that MobileStar had closed up shop; but in February 2002, MobileStar was purchased by VoiceStream, a subsidiary of German phone company, Deutsche Telekom AG, and continues to operate hundreds of hotspots around the United States.

Like WayPort, MobileStar offers several subscription options. These plans will probably change over time and are provided here simply as examples of what is currently available:

♦ **Pulsar.** This pay-as-you-go metered plan allows users to pay a flat fee for the first 15 minutes and a set rate per minute thereafter.

♦ **Prepay 120/300.** MobileStar sells prepaid cards in either 120-or 300-minute denominations. When the initial quantity of minutes is used, the user buys another card.

♦ **Local Galaxy Plan.** In six U.S. metropolitan areas, MobileStar offers unlimited usage in the local area for a year-long commitment and a flat monthly fee, with a cap on the amount of data that can be transferred per month. This service is available in the following areas:

- Dallas/FortWorth, Texas Metroplex
- Seattle/Tacoma, Washington
- San Francisco Bay Area (East Bay), California
- New York City metro area (New York, New Jersey, Connecticut)
- Houston, Texas
- Austin, Texas

Cities planned for extensive coverage through Starbucks stores include Atlanta, Chicago, Boston, and the Washington, D.C. metro area.

♦ **National Galaxy Plan.** This plan offers unlimited nationwide coverage at all MobileStar locations, including Starbucks, airports, hotels, and conference centers.

♦ **StarPlan 500.** 500 minutes are allotted per month for a flat rate, plus additional minutes can be purchased at a 50 percent discount over the prepaid card rates.

♦ **StarPlan 200.** 200 minutes are allotted per month for a flat rate, plus additional minutes can be purchased at a 40 percent discount over the prepaid card rates.

Aggregators

Wireless connectivity from MobileStar, Wayport, and other public wireless LAN service providers is also marketed through wireless LAN service *aggregators*. A wireless LAN aggregator offers regional or nationwide subscriptions that provide access to wireless networks that may be maintained by many different vendors.

WiFi Metro (`www.wifimetro.com`) is an example of a regional aggregator. WiFi Metro sells subscriptions to wireless hot spots in the San Francisco Bay area of California, including all MobileStar hot spots, the Le Boulanger Café chain, and local restaurants such as Kokkari.

hereUare Communications (`www.hereuare.com`) and Boingo Wireless (`www.boingo.com`) are examples of national aggregators. hereUare subscriptions include access to all MobileStar hot spots, as well as many other regional and independently run public wireless LANs. Boingo Wireless subscriptions include access to all Wayport hot spots, as well as many independently run hot spots.

If you are a frequent business traveler, you may find that subscribing to public wireless LAN access through an aggregator is the most economical way to stay wirelessly connected to e-mail and the Internet.

Wi-Fi Security on the Go

As discussed in several earlier chapters, WEP encryption is the standard Wi-Fi method of ensuring private data transmission. Although you should make a habit of using WEP, you will have to turn it off when using a public wireless network.

Hopefully, Microsoft's tests of 802.1*x* security in SeaTac Airport will lead to the widespread availability of this authentication and WEP key delivery system. Until that happens, however, you should consider all public networks as just that—public, not secure.

Many corporations have implemented *virtual private networks (VPNs)* for connecting remotely to the company LAN. If you need to have users remotely connect to your company network from a public wireless network, set up a VPN. The VPN will not only protect the LAN, it will also protect all the data transmitted by the wireless station on the public WLAN.

Accessing a Public WLAN

Because wireless network technology is still evolving and public wireless networks are still a bit of a novelty, the services available a year from now will certainly be different than they are now. Nonetheless, you will still want to know how to use the services that are currently available.

The following sections walk you through logging on and logging off—using WayPort and MobileStar as examples—to give you an idea how to operate public wireless LAN services.

Nonfat Latté and a Wireless Internet Connection, Please!—Using Wi-Fi at Starbucks

Connecting to the Internet from a *wireless Starbucks store* is almost as easy—maybe easier—than saying "Double nonfat latté and a single mocha with whipped cream, please." Follow these steps:

1. Using the configuration program for your wireless network adapter, create a new configuration and set the SSID (network name) to

MobileStar. (Both the letters "M" and "S" must be uppercase and the other letters lowercase.)

TIP

If you want to connect to some other public wireless network and you don't know the SSID, you should be able to use the *scan* feature of your wireless network adapter's configuration program to identify the SSID. Public wireless LAN service aggregator, Boingo, supplies a utility program to its subscribers that facilitates locating, identifying, and connecting to public hot spots. Another aggregator, hereUare, provides software that includes a searchable database of all the currently available hot spots along with street address, phone number, and wireless network name.

---

2. Turn off encryption.

3. Set this configuration to renew the IP address when selected. When you sign on to MobileStar, the service will assign a new IP address to your computer for use while connected to the service.

4. When you save this configuration, your wireless client/station software should be able to detect the signal from the MobileStar network. If your client software does not "see" the MobileStar network, check Steps 1 through 3 above to make sure you entered the correct information.

5. Open your Web browser. When it attempts to open your default home page, MobileStar will display a screen similar to that shown in Figure 18-1.

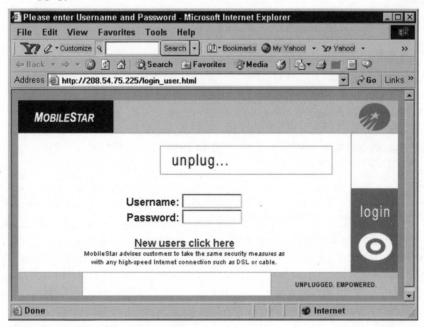

Figure 18-1: The MobileStar sign-on screen

6. If you have already established an account, enter your username and password, click the login button on the right side of the screen, and go to Step 8. Otherwise, click New users click here to display a screen similar to that shown in Figure 18-2.

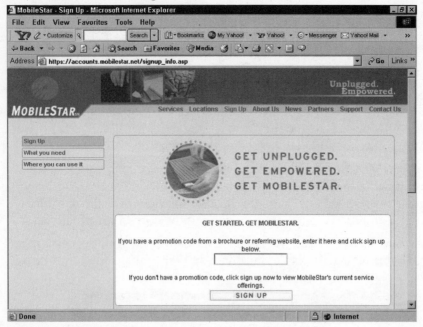

Figure 18-2: Use this screen to enter a promotion code or to select SIGN UP.

7. Either enter a promotion code for any special offer that you may have obtained from a WLAN equipment manufacturer, or click the SIGN UP button to go to the screen where you can choose one of the MobileStar payment options. When you have signed up for a plan, MobileStar displays a screen similar to that shown in Figure 18-3.

> **NOTE**
>
> Notice that the screen in Figure 18-3 consists of two windows: a small window hovering over a larger window. When you use the large window to browse the Internet, the small window will seem to disappear. But don't forget that it is still open in the background. You will use the small window to log off.

8. If you want to see the status of your MobileStar account or make changes in your account, click the Account Management link shown in Figure 18-3. Otherwise, from this point, you can use your Web browser to navigate the Internet as you always do, keeping in mind that you are using up your MobileStart minutes (if you have chosen an à la carte style plan).

You may also be able to access e-mail, depending on the type of account you use. If you have a HotMail account, for example, you should be able to access your e-mail through the MobileStar connection the same way you always do. You should also be able to access your company VPN.

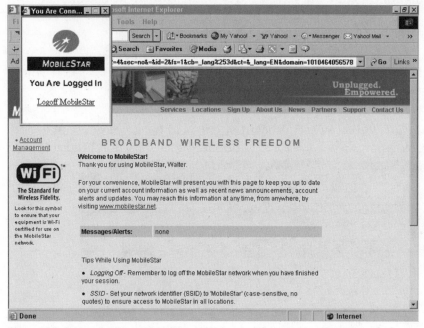

Figure 18-3: Browse the Internet from this screen, but don't forget the Logoff window.

9. When you have finished using the Internet connection, find the small window (which should still be open) and click the LogOff MobileStar link. MobileStar closes the window and stops charging your account for access.

Using Wi-Fi at the Airport and Hotel

Some airports are served by MobileStar. In these cases, the instructions found in the preceding section still apply.

Wayport is the service provider in many airports and in over 400 hotels. If you find that you need to connect via Wayport, follow these steps:

1. Using the configuration program for your wireless network adapter, create a new configuration and set the SSID (network name) to *Wayport Access*. (Both the letters "W" and "A" must be uppercase and

the other letters lowercase, and you must type the underscore(_) that connects the two words.)

2. Turn off encryption.

3. Set this configuration to renew the IP address when selected. When you sign on toWayport, the service will assign a new IP address to your computer for use while connected to the service.

4. When you save this configuration, your wireless client/station software should be able to detect the signal from the Wayport network. If your client software does not "see" the Wayport network, check Steps 1 through 3 for possible errors.

5. Open your Web browser. When it attempts to open your default home page, Wayport displays a screen similar to that shown in Figure 18-4.

Figure 18-4: The Wayport Welcome screen

6. If you have already established an account, click "Use Wayport Membership" to display the sign-on screen shown in Figure 18-5. Otherwise, either click Purchase a Connection or Use a Coupon, depending on whether you have a promotional coupon. (Some WLAN equipment manufacturers issue a coupon to new customers good for a free Wayport connection.) If you click Purchase a Connection, you see a screen like that shown in Figure 18-6.

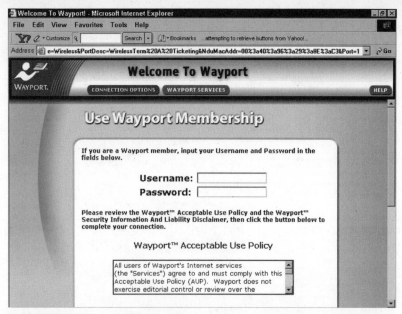

Figure 18-5: The Wayport sign-on screen

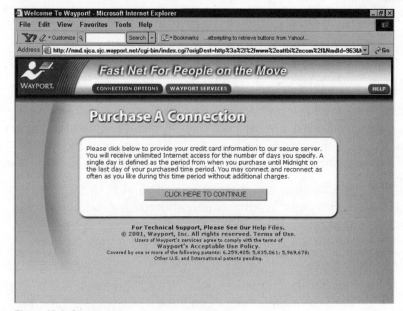

Figure 18-6: Start here to purchase a connection.

7. After you log in, Wayport displays a screen like that shown in Figure 18-7.

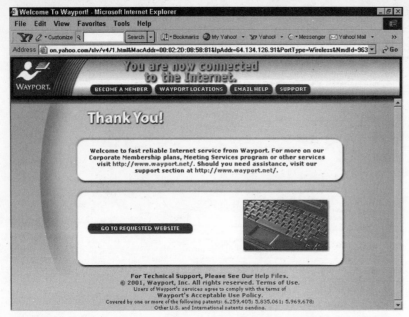

Figure 18-7: Click Go to Requested Website to begin browsing the Internet.

8. Click Go to Requested Website to begin browsing the Internet.

9. When you are finished, simply close the Web browser.

Community Wireless LANs

Someone has to pay for the Internet service for community wireless LANs. Ideally, the community finds a sponsor, but more typically, several members of the community share the cost of the high-speed Internet connection, as well as the cost of transmitting the signal to the neighborhood.

In some cases, the signal is transmitted by an access point in one neighborhood to an access point in another neighborhood. A wireless network is established in the second neighborhood. The result is that residents in both neighborhoods can access the Internet through wireless LAN connections.

The steps for connecting to a community public WLAN are beyond the scope of this book, mainly because each network can have a very unique sign-on process.

Summary

This chapter describes how to connect to public wireless networks that are available in places like coffee shops, hotels, and airports. The last part of the book, Part V explains how to plan and implement a multisite wireless network.

Part V

Connecting Sites with Wireless Technology

Chapter 19

Planning a Multisite Wireless Network

In This Chapter

This chapter discusses the following topics:

- ♦ Using 802.11 wireless equipment to connect multiple network sites
- ♦ Different types of wireless bridges
- ♦ Fresnel zones
- ♦ Link budgets

This chapter explains how to use license-free 802.11 wireless network equipment to *bridge* (connect) two or more sites.

Wireless Bridges

Many companies and institutions have operations at more than one physical site. Connecting networks at multiple sites has traditionally required leasing a line from the phone company at significant expense. In some cases, companies have connected networks wirelessly, but at radio frequencies that have to be licensed. Again, the cost can be high.

The standard operation of an 802.11 (b, a, or g) wireless access point includes passing network packets between the wireless stations and the rest of the LAN—a typical network bridging function. This raises the question of whether or not 802.11 equipment can be used to create a wireless bridge between two sites. Unfortunately, only some AP equipment is capable of establishing a wireless-to-wireless bridge.

As shown in Figure 19-1, most APs are used to support a group of wireless devices that need to be connected to a LAN.

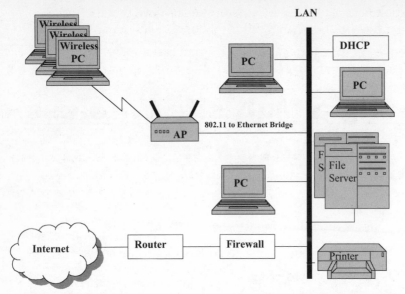

Figure 19-1: In a typical 802.11 wireless LAN, an AP is a bridge between wireless and wired portions of the LAN.

Nonetheless, some 802.11 devices can also be used to connect two wired or wireless LANs through a wireless-to-wireless bridge, as shown in Figure 19-2. This type of bridge is often called a *point-to-point* or *LAN-to-LAN* bridge.

Figure 19-2: A point-to-point, wireless-to-wireless bridge between two sites

Using 802.11 wireless equipment to bridge two geographically remote LANs has several advantages over alternative bridging methods:

♦ **Lower cost.** The cost of installing an 802.11 bridge is a one-time expense that is normally less than the cost of leasing a line for a single year. Depending on the type and brand of equipment you buy, the distance between points, and the speed of the connection, the cost of installing a single bridge between two points ranges in price from about $1,000 to about $30,000. In the last year, the average cost of wireless access points capable of wireless-to-wireless bridging has dropped significantly—to less than $200 for the most economical units.

♦ **No license required.** Because 802.11 radios do not require a license (within set power and gain restrictions), setting up a bridge is much faster and easier than setting up traditional wireless bridges.

In many cases, however, setting up a wireless, point-to-point bridge between two sites is impractical because of one or more of the following reasons:

♦ **Line-of-sight.** The antennas at each end of the proposed connection must be able to "see" each other, which may require mounting an antenna on a mast or tower at heights that may not be practical or even legal in certain situations.

♦ **Distance.** In ideal conditions, the maximum distance that an 802.11 signal can reliably be sent is about 25 miles. The signal that can be detected at the receiving end decreases as the distance between endpoints increases. Eventually, the signal will be too weak for the receiving AP to detect.

♦ **Obstructions.** Buildings, hills, trees, electrical transmission towers, and so on can block enough of the signal to prevent a good connection between point-to-point bridging APs.

The following sections describe the operation of wireless bridges, as well as how to plan point-to-point bridging.

How Wireless Bridges Work

Every standard wireless access point is a wireless-to-Ethernet bridge. This bridging function, between the AP's wireless and wired interfaces, takes place in the MAC layer of the OSI network model and is based on frame addresses.

A typical AP builds an internal database that lists all the MAC addresses of devices that have sent or received messages through the AP. The database also tracks the interface through which each MAC address communicates. When a wireless device sends an *Address Resolution Protocol (ARP)* request frame, the AP forwards it over all active interfaces except the interface through which the ARP request packet was received. After receiving the ARP response frame, the AP places a record of the destination address in its database, along with the receiving interface. After an AP has "learned" a particular MAC address in this way, the AP forwards frames addressed to that MAC address only to the interface where the MAC address is located, based on the information it has stored in a bridging database.

Of course, the AP will still receive frames from MAC addresses that are not found in its database. For this reason, until it learns the location of a particular MAC address, the AP forwards frames for unknown destinations to the *default interface,* which is typically the Ethernet interface.

The AP continually updates its database by removing destinations or interfaces not used for a specified time and by refreshing the database when it transmits or receives data from destinations and interfaces that have already been stored there. This intelligent bridging function helps minimize network traffic and enables roaming of wireless stations.

Many APs offer tools that allow network administrator to limit which network devices are permitted to associate with a particular AP. Using filters, an administrator can provide network security or improve performance by eliminating packets that are sent to and from unauthorized MAC addresses.

Wireless-to-Wireless Bridges

When used as a typical wireless access point, an AP is more than an intelligent bridge. In addition to bridging, each AP also broadcasts messages on the WLAN and responds to wireless station association requests. To connect two geographically remote sites, however, you may want the AP to perform bridging only. APs used as point-to-point wireless bridges typically communicate only with other APs and do not provide an interface for connection to wireless stations (see Figure 19-3).

Several WLAN equipment manufacturers sell APs that can be used either as a wireless-to-Ethernet bridge or as a wireless-to-wireless bridge. In addition, ORiNOCO, Cisco, Intel and other manufacturers produce packaged 802.11b bridging solutions that include two APs, high-gain antennas, and the necessary cable to connect the antennas to the APs. Other high-end vendors, such as Alvarion (formerly Breezecom), sell wireless bridges that use proprietary standards that are faster than 802.11b wireless networks, but that won't interoperate with 802.11b equipment.

Wireless-to-wireless bridges come in a number of varieties, including the following:

♦ **Point-to-point.** In this simplest form of a wireless bridge, two APs communicate wirelesssly only with each other. As shown in Figure 19-3, each AP also acts as a bridge to a wired LAN. The antennas used in a point-to-point bridge are typically highly directional, reducing the interference to other equipment and increasing the effective transmission range.

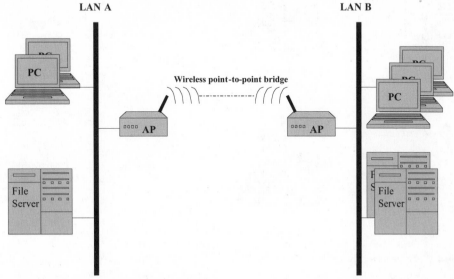

Figure 19-3: A point-to-point wireless bridge

♦ **Point-to-multipoint.** This type of bridge has a *master* or *central* AP that broadcasts to several *slave* or *client* APs (see Figure 19-4). The slave APs communicate wirelessly only with the master AP, not with the other slave APs. Devices on any of the LANs connected by this point-to-multipoint bridge can communicate with any of the other devices on any of the LANs bridged by the point-to-multipoint bridge.

♦ **Master/AP-to-slave.** In this type of bridge, the master AP in a point-to-multipoint bridge can also fill the role of an AP. The master AP communicates wirelessly with the slave APs as well as with local wireless stations that are within range of the master AP. Sometimes this type of bridge is accomplished with two radios in the AP, one acting as the bridge and one acting as the AP.

♦ **Repeater.** The repeater is a special point-to-multipoint bridge in which all APs can act as wireless-to-wireless bridges and as APs at the same time.

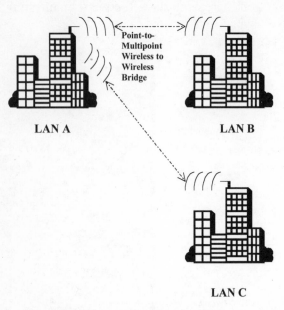

Point-to-
Multipoint
Wireless to
Wireless
Bridge

LAN A

LAN B

LAN C

Figure 19-4: A point-to-multipoint, wireless bridge

Although 802.11 products have been available for several years, 802.11b products have been available in quantity and from numerous vendors for only the last year or so. The increasing competition seems to have sparked the rapid introduction of new products—and new features to old products. Wireless bridges are no exception. The leading manufacturer of APs for home/office use, Linksys, recently upgraded its basic wireless AP (model WAP11) to include bridging, with point-to-point, point-to-multipoint, and a mode Linksys calls Access Point Client. Yet this product sells for less than half the price of wireless bridges from the leading manufacturers of enterprise-level APs.

Planning the Path

Determining whether a wireless station can connect to an AP in your office is relatively simple. In most cases, the antennas attached to both the AP's radio and the station's radio are omnidirectional—transmitting in all directions at once. After turning on the station's wireless configuration software, you can view the signal-strength meter and determine whether you are close enough to the AP to make a connection.

Connecting an 802.11b wireless bridge is not quite as simple. You must consider certain factors that operate on a microwave signal as it moves through space For example, radio signals dissipate as they travel, and obstructions in the path will attenuate the signal.

Line-of-Sight

A major factor that determines whether you can successfully link two sites with a wireless bridge is called *line-of-sight*. If the two radios can't "see" each other—in other words, if one or more structures or objects block the physical view between the two radios—you probably won't be able to create the bridge.

Earth Bulge

Typically, you need to mount the antennas used in site-to-site bridges on the top of a tall building or a tall tower in order to achieve a clear line-of-sight. This is especially true in areas where the terrain is hilly. Even on completely flat terrain, at a distance of about six miles, you must increase the elevation of the antenna to accommodate for the curvature of the earth (commonly called *earth bulge*). The further apart the sites, the higher you need to mount the antennas.

For the sake of simplicity, assume that both antennas are positioned at the same height. You can use the following formula to determine how high an antenna needs to be to clear the earth bulge:

```
Antenna Height=(D/2.448)² feet
```

D is the distance in miles between the two antennas. If the antennas are ten miles apart on flat land, both antennas should be mounted at least 16.7 feet high $((10/2.448)^2 = 16.7)$ to clear the earth bulge. If you have other obstructions to clear, the antennas may need to be higher than this minimum. Keep the earth bulge in mind as you determine how high to mount the antennas.

Topographical Tools

If the sites in question are not on flat land, you may need access to topographical maps to determine line-of-sight. Several excellent online and software products are available—some designed with radio frequency (RF) propagation in mind.

◆ **TopoZone** (`www.TopoZone.com`). This Web-based center for recreational and professional topographic map users has worked with the *U.S. Geological Survey (USGS)* to create the Web's first interactive topographical map of the entire United States.

◆ **TOPO! and Terrain Navigator.** These two relatively low-cost topographical software products are also based on USGS maps. These products enable you to generate detailed 2D and 3D topographical maps that show you elevation profiles. Both products can integrate with a GPS unit for precise locations. These "budget" products may not, however, properly adjust for the curvature of the earth.

◆ **Professional products such as GeoCAD and Terrain Professional.** These include many additional features, with appropriate allowance for the curvature of the earth.

◆ **Products from companies such as Comarco Wireless Technologies** (`www.edx.com`) **and V-Soft** (`www.v-soft.com`). These companies offer high-end (and high-priced) tools, complete with features designed specifically for determining RF paths between two or more points.

Fresnel Zones

Radio signals are made up of waves of electromagnetic energy. Like ripples on a pond, RF waves travel out in a straight line until they encounter an object through which they cannot pass. The RF waves spread out as they travel and are reflected by the earth and other large objects. The net effect of RF waves traveling outward and being reflected is to create an RF signal pattern of concentric cones, which start at the transmission point and grow in size. This RF signal pattern surrounds the direct line-of-sight between the two radio antennas in an elliptical cone shape. The diameter of each cone can be calculated depending on the wavelength of the signal. Each cone-shaped signal path is called a *Fresnel zone* (pronounced *free*-nel, with a silent s—named after the Frenchman Jean Augustin Fresnel). The center cone contains the strongest signal and is called the *first Fresnel zone*. Figure 19-5 shows a point-to-point bridge with its first Fresnel zone.

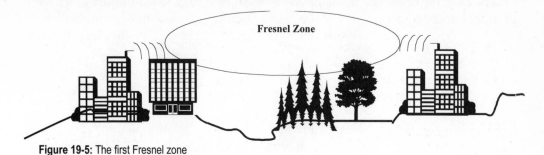

Figure 19-5: The first Fresnel zone

Clearing the First Fresnel Zone

At least 60 percent of the first Fresnel zone's radius must be unobstructed to allow a sufficient signal to reach the destination antenna for effective wireless communication. In other words, if more than 40 percent of any portion of the bottom half of the first Fresnel zone is blocked by trees or buildings, you probably won't get a sufficient signal to create the link.

Although 2.4-GHz signals pass well through walls, they have difficulty with entire buildings. Because of their water content, trees also pose an almost impenetrable barrier to RF waves. Water absorbs the waves, causing a substantial signal drop. And, of course, RF signals can't pass through hillsides.

If you are concerned that an object may encroach upon the first Fresnel zone, you can use the following formula that calculates the radius of the first Fresnel zone at any point on the path between the endpoints:

$$R = 72.1 * \sqrt{\frac{D_1 * D_2}{F * D_T}}$$

This formula uses the following variables:

- ♦ R = Radius of the first Fresnel zone in feet
- ♦ D_1 = Distance along the line-of-sight from the first antenna to the point directly above the obstruction (tree, building, and so on)
- ♦ D_2 = Distance along the line-of-sight from the point directly above the potential obstruction to the second antenna
- ♦ D_T = Total distance along the line-of-sight between the two antennas
- ♦ F = Frequency in GHz

If the two antennas in a point-to-point 802.11b bridge are 20 miles apart, and a tree that is 35 feet tall sits at the 5-mile point, you need to determine how high to mount the antennas in order for the first Fresnel zone to clear the tree. Use the formula:

$$R = 72.1 * \sqrt{\frac{5 * 15}{2.4 * 20}} = 90.125 \text{ feet}$$

Because 60 percent of the first Fresnel zone radius should be unobstructed, you need to mount the antennas at least 54.075 feet (60% of 90.125 feet) above the top of the tree, or 89.075 feet up.

The widest part of the first Fresnel zone is the point equidistant from both ends. Using the same formula, you can determine that you need at least 62.44 feet to clear the first Fresnel zone, plus an additional 66.75 feet for the earth bulge ($[20/2.448]^2$) for a total of 129.19 feet. Therefore, in this example, if you mount each antenna at least 130 feet up, the signal clears the first Fresnel zone both at the center of the path and at the potentially troublesome tree.

> **TIP**
>
> Quite a few Fresnel zone calculators are available online. To find one, just search for "Fresnel zone" in your favorite Internet search engine. You can also find a multifunction Microsoft Excel spreadsheet written by Tim Posar at `www.lns.com/papers/pathcalc/`. This spreadsheet calculates the first Fresnel zone radius, as well as several other useful statistics.

Looking for Reflection Points

Fresnel zone information can also be used to determine whether the signal may be disrupted by signals bouncing off a good reflecting surface such as a lake, desert, or roadway. The first Fresnel zone formula described in the preceding section defines the set of points where the distance from the transmitter to the Fresnel zone, then to the receiver, is longer than the direct path from the transmitter to the receiver by exactly one wavelength, which tends to strengthen the signal. By contrast, for even-numbered Fresnel zones (N = 2, 4, and so on), the difference between the direct path and the indirect path defined by the Fresnel zone distance is a multiple of one-half wavelength. If an even-numbered Fresnel zone happens to be tangential to a lake, desert, roadway, or other reflective surface, signal cancellation will occur.

Using a Fresnel zone calculator, such as Tim Pozar's PathCalc (`www.lns.com/papers/pathcalc/`), you can determine whether your RF path may run into a destructive signal reflection.

Computing Link Budgets

When you plan the link between two bridge antennas, you need to determine whether you have sufficient signal at each end to make the connection. Many factors affect the signal strength. When all these factors are taken into account, you are computing the total expected signal. You need to compare this computed signal against the required signal minimums to determine whether the signal will be adequate—in other words, to determine whether the actual signal will meet the required *link budget*.

To compute a *link budget*, you need the following information:

♦ Frequency of the link

♦ Free-space path loss

♦ Power of the transmitter

♦ Antenna gain

♦ Total length of transmission cable and loss per unit length at the specified frequency

♦ Number of connectors used

♦ Loss of each connector at the specified frequency

♦ Path length

Free-Space Path Loss

As a signal moves through space, it loses some of its power. This *free-space path loss* is easy to calculate using the following formula:

```
Free-space path loss (in dB) = (96.6 + 20 log10 F) + (20
log10 D)
```

where F equals the frequency in GHz, and D equals the path length in miles. Or you can use this formula:

```
Free-space path loss (in dB) = (92.4 + 20 log10 F) + (20
log10 D)
```

where F equals the frequency in GHz and D equals the path length in kilometers.

Antenna Gain

Antenna gain, expressed in dBi (the ratio of the power radiated by the antenna in a specific direction to the power radiated in that direction by an isotropic antenna fed by the same transmitter), is a measurement of how well an antenna focuses RF energy in a given direction. Antenna manufacturers typically specify the antenna gain for each of their antennas.

FCC regulations limit the maximum effective isotropic radiated power (EIRP) of point-to-multipoint systems to 36 dBm. EIRP consists of transmission power plus antenna gain. When an a AP/antenna system is already producing 36 dBm and you decide to use an antenna with more gain, for every 1 dB added gain, you must decrease the AP's radiated power by 1 dB.

In point-to-point systems for 2.4-GHz systems using high-gain directional antennas, FCC regulations are more lenient. High-gain directional antennas focus the RF beam more narrowly than other types of antennas, reducing the likelihood of interfering with RF equipment in use by other individuals. FCC regulations provide that for every dB the transmitter is reduced below 30 dBm, the antenna may be increased by 3 dB from the 6 dBi starting point. For example, a 29-dB transmitter can use a 9-dBi antenna, and a 28-dB transmitter can use a 12-dBi antenna.

Cable and Connector Loss

Whenever you connect an antenna to an AP using a cable, some loss of signal strength always occurs through the cables and connectors. This loss is directly proportional to the length of the cable and inversely proportional to the diameter of the cable. The more connectors you use, the more loss of signal occurs. Check with your cable vendor for a chart indicating the loss for various types and lengths of cable.

Sample Link Budget Calculation

The example below is based on the following assumptions:

- **Frequency:** 2.4 GHz
- **Length of path:** 20 miles
- **Free-space path loss:** 125.7 dB
- **Transmitter power:** 22 dBm
- **Cable:** Two cables—25 feet-LMR 400 (~10.7 dB loss per 100 feet at 2.4 GHz)
- **Number of connectors used:** 4 (~ 0.5 dB loss per connector)
- **Antenna gain:** 24 dBi transmit/receive

♦ **Receiver threshold:** 80 dBm

♦ **Required fade margin:** 20 dB (minimum)

Using the following formula, you can determine if the fade margin meets the requirement:

```
Fade margin = received signal - receiver threshold
```

Using the following formula, you can calculate the received signal:

```
Received signal = transmitter power - transmitter cable and
connector loss + transmitter antenna gain - free-space path
loss + receiver antenna gain - receiver cable and connector
loss
```

Plugging in all the preceding assumptions, the formula becomes:

```
Received signal = 22 dBm - 2 dB (25 ft) + 24.0 dB - 125.7 dB
+ 24.0 dB - 2 dB (25 ft) = -59.7 dBm
```

To calculate the fade margin, use the following formula:

Fade margin = -59.7 dBm – (-80 dBm) = 20.3 dBm

This fade margin of 20.3 dBm is above the required fade margin (20 dB) for this example.

Multipath

Radio signals can take several paths to the same destination. When the same signal arrives at different times or out of phase with other instances of the same signal, interference and distortion may result. This problem, commonly called *multipath,* typically results when the signal reflects off several objects and arrives at the receiver at different times.

The most severe type of multipath causes received signals to spread out over time, sometimes resulting in frequency selective fading. Delay spread, at its worst, can cause bit errors in phase shift modulation. Spread spectrum modulation's correlation process, used in 802.11b, helps reduce this delay spread. If you intend to establish a long point-to-point link over a highly reflective surface, such as a lake, ocean, or desert, you should probably invest in the services of a wireless engineer to help you avoid severe multipath problems.

Towers

When designing antenna placement, be aware that the height and location of towers in the vicinity of airports, runways, and airplane approach paths are controlled by FAA rules and regulations. In some circumstances, tower installations must be pre-approved by the FAA, registered with the FCC, or both. Make sure you are familiar with the current FCC regulations regarding antenna structures (www.fcc.gov/wtb/antenna/) before you get too far into planning the installation of free-standing antenna towers.

Amplifiers

You may wonder whether you can add an amplifier to an AP to extend the range of a wireless-to-wireless bridge. The FCC rules Section 15.204-Part C states "External radio frequency power amplifiers shall not be marketed as separate products." Part D of the same rule also states "Only the antenna with which an intentional radiator (transmitter) is originally authorized may be used with the intentional radiator." Each amplifier manufacturer is required to submit the amplifier for testing with the radio and antenna as a complete system. Otherwise, it cannot be sold in the U.S. Certified systems are required to be marketed, sold, and installed as a complete system, including transmitter, antenna, and coax. Adding an aftermarket amplifier to an AP is illegal. Consequently, your best solution is probably to purchase a complete system that has received FCC certification as a unit.

Summary

This chapter describes how to use 802.11 wireless equipment to connect multiple network sites through wireless bridges. It also discusses Fresnel zones and link budgets. Turn now to Chapter 20 for details about how to select and install site-to-site bridges and antennas.

Installing Site-to-Site Bridges and Antennas

In This Chapter

This chapter discusses the following topics:

♦ Choosing the type and brand of equipment you will use to create one or more wireless site-to-site bridges

♦ Installing wireless bridges

♦ Installing antennas

This chapter, like the others in this part of the book, is about the site-to-site bridging of two or more LANs using 802.11b equipment. Using the information in Chapter 19 and your analysis of the physical environment, you should decide whether it is even possible to connect your sites using wireless technology, and if so, where and how high you need to mount the antennas. After you decide to install a wireless bridge, this chapter will provide additional information and guidance on selecting and installing the 802.11b equipment—specifically, access points and antennas.

Choosing Wireless Bridging Equipment

If you decide to build a wireless bridge around the IEEE 802.11b standard, you should look for the Wi-Fi logo on the products you buy. It is not, however, necessary to stick with 802.11b equipment for bridging, even if the remainder of your network uses equipment that complies with that standard. You could decide, for example, to use 802.11a, 802.11g, or even proprietary wireless equipment to accomplish each bridge. You should base your decision on the specific circumstances, needs, and budget of your company or client. Because this book is primarily about 802.11b equipment, this chapter uses 802.11b as an example. In most cases, however, the principles are the same should you decide to use a different type of wireless bridging equipment.

Selecting Wireless Bridges

The key elements of any 802.11b wireless bridging system are the APs that are used to make the wireless connection. Chapter 5 covered the most important points to consider when selecting APs for use as standard access points. Most of the same factors are still important when selecting APs for use as wireless bridges:

- **Ease of installation, setup, and maintenance.** Some wireless bridge systems are sold as a package, complete with APs, cable, and antennas. If one of these systems fits your needs, installation and setup should be relatively simple.

- **Availability of reliable technical support.** Some vendors advertise 24-hour technical support, but they really mean that they have a Web site with several FAQs. If you desire more personal attention, consider acquiring your bridging system(s) through a *value added reseller (VAR)*, who will help you before and after the sale.

- **Range.** When using an AP as a wireless bridge, the signal range is a function of several factors taken together:
  - transmission power
  - antenna gain
  - distance
  - interference
  - attenuation

  Refer to the section on *link budgets* in Chapter 19. Some APs, however, allow you to "tune" the range by adjusting the output power. Cisco APs, for example, can be adjusted to transmit at different power levels.

- **Security.** All brands of 802.11 wireless bridges have WEP as a security feature. Most bridges also enable you to control which MAC addresses are permitted to communicate with the bridging AP. The best systems also support advanced authentication features.

- **Total cost of ownership (TCO).** As always, TCO is a subjective concept, but as you decide which system to purchase, keep in mind that the cost of training, operation, maintenance, and upgrades should be included in your cost comparisons.

As is the case with standard APs, many bridge vendors target and market their product lines to enterprise customers. This is logical, because home users and small businesses probably won't need to bridge LANs in multiple sites.

Standard enterprise-level APs typically don't include the capability to act as a wireless-to-wireless bridge. Bridges and APs are usually sold as separate products, or sometimes as an additional license.

Several of the least expensive APs on the market (for example, Linksys WAP11, which is shown in Figure 20-1) can be used as a standard AP and can also be configured to operate in point-to-point, point-to-multipoint, or client/AP mode at no additional cost. The main difference between the bargain units and the more expensive variety lies in the utility software. If you need to set up a small number of bridges, you may find the software adequate and save your company or client a few dollars without sacrificing performance.

Figure 20-1: The Linksys WAP11 can be used as a standard AP and can also be configured to operate in point-to-point, point-to-multipoint, or client/AP mode at no additional cost.

Cisco, ORiNOCO, Proxim, Intel, Symbol, Enterasys, and other companies that produce wireless bridges for enterprise use provide AP management software with excellent support for the following:

♦ **Remote configuration.** The setup and configuration software enables you to make changes to the AP's configuration over the network, in addition to or instead of connecting a computer directly to the AP through a serial or Ethernet port. These utilities should enable you to set up AP groups that you can configure as a group, rather than having to configure them individually. For example, if an AP is mounted inside a metal enclosure on a platform two hundred feet in the air, you probably don't want to climb the tower every time you need to reconfigure the unit, update its firmware, or determine the signal strength.

♦ **SNMP configuration.** Many enterprises manage their IS equipment through *Simple Network Management Protocol (SNMP)* software such as IBM NetView. If an AP can be managed using SNMP, any SNMP management tool can be used over the network to set up, configure, and maintain the AP. A database file called a *management information base* (MIB) accompanies each SNMP-configurable device. The MIB contains information that informs the SNMP management software of the features and options available in the device.

♦ **802.1☐ authentication.** As discussed in Chapter 13, IEEE 802.1x defines a port-based authentication scheme that provides enhanced security to any wireless LAN.

♦ **MAC address filtering.** This feature enables the AP to recognize only a finite list of MAC addresses. All devices with MAC addresses not on the list are not permitted to associate with the AP. When you set up point-to-point bridging, the configuration software typically requires that you enter a single MAC address (the MAC address of the AP at the other end of the link). Consequently, the AP with the specified MAC address is the only wireless device that will be acknowledged by this AP. Be aware, however, that changing the MAC address that is broadcast by a wireless device is trivial. Many of the setup utilities that ship with APs and wireless NICs include a feature that enables you to enter a new MAC address, so don't consider MAC filtering a foolproof security feature.

♦ **Protocol filtering.** Protocol filtering enables the network administrator to manage the traffic over the bridge by limiting the type of packets that are forwarded to the bridged LAN.

♦ **SSID suppression.** The IEEE 802.11b standard requires that an AP broadcast its SSID in the beacon frames that it sends out periodically. This requirement makes it easier for a device to attach to a wireless

LAN for the first time. Shared-key authentication and 802.1*x* authentication are available to permit only authorized parties to associate with the AP, as well as WEP encryption to protect the privacy of the data transmitted over the WLAN. Some enterprise-level APs also provide an option for setting up a *closed* system. When this feature is used, the AP does not broadcast the SSID and only acknowledges stations that already know the SSID.

♦ **Extensive diagnostic utilities.** The best AP management software includes utilities that enable you to do the following:

- Poll all the APs on the system
- View the ARP table
- View the learned MAC addresses
- Monitor each AP
- Perform link analysis
- View the signal strength of each AP

Figure 20-2 shows the suite of utilities available in ORiNOCO AP and Outdoor Router (bridge) products.

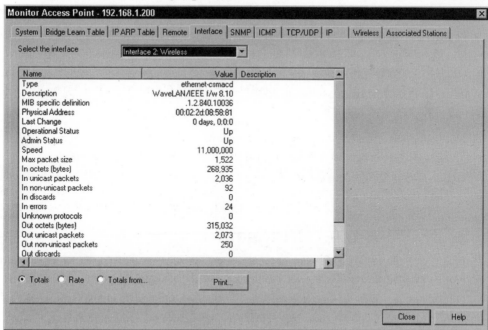

Figure 20-2: AP/bridge monitoring utilities available in ORiNOCO AP and Outdoor Router (bridge) products

◆ **Support for the IEEE 802.1d Spanning Tree.** If your network contains more than one bridge, several different paths may exist between two devices on the network. Multiple paths can result in the endless circular routing of packets. Typical networks are set up to turn off a connection if such a loop occurs; nonetheless, you should design the network to eliminate that possibility. The IEEE 802.1d Spanning Tree algorithm enables the network administrator to assign priority values to each bridge (see Figure 20-3). Bridges trade messages, called *configuration bridge protocol data units,* that contain enough information to enable the bridges to select a *root bridge* and to calculate the shortest route for packets to travel from each bridge to the root bridge.The result is a loop-free topography with exactly one path between every pair of network nodes.

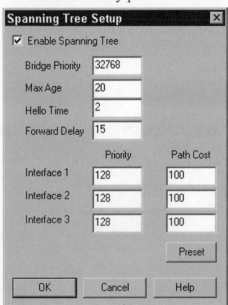

Figure 20-3: Assigning bridge priority for use by the Spanning Tree algorithm

Software-Based Bridges

In addition to using hardware-based access points, you can create a wireless bridge using one of your existing wireless NIC cards as the radio but using a PC to manage the bridge. In fact, Windows XP makes it quite easy to set up a bridge between a wireless NIC and an Ethernet card installed in the Windows XP PC.

The major drawback of using a PC to create a bridge is that you can't easily mount the PC close to an outdoor antenna. If you need to create a bridge inside a building, however—to link LANs from two different parts of the building perhaps—and have a standard AP and a Windows XP PC, you may want to consider this option. The PC that acts as a wireless bridge must be equipped with both a wireless NIC and a wired Ethernet card.

Follow these steps on the Windows XP PC to set up the bridge:

1. Right-click a Network Connection icon in the Notification Area of the Taskbar and select Open the Network Connections to display the Network Connections window.

2. Press the Ctrl button on the keyboard while clicking the icon for each of the two network connections that you want to bridge. The names of both connections should now be highlighted.

3. Right-click either of the highlighted network connection names, or click Advanced in the Network Connections window's menu bar. Select Bridge Connections from the menu. Windows displays this message: "Please wait while Windows bridges the connections…" After a few seconds, Windows creates a new connection called Network Bridge (Network Bridge) #, where # is a number assigned by Windows. Figure 20-4 shows a Network Connections window that lists a network bridge between a wired local area connection and a wireless network connection.

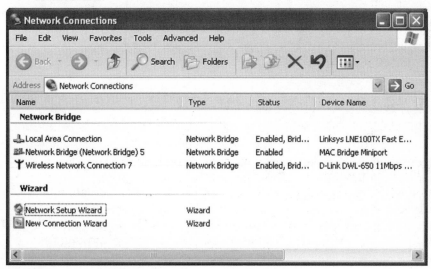

Figure 20-4: Creating a wireless network bridge in Windows XP

4. Right-click the Wireless Network Connection item in the Network Bridge section of the Network Connections window and select the Properties option to display the Network Bridge Properties dialog.

5. Click the Wireless Networks tab. Use the Preferred Networks portion of the dialog to configure a wireless network connection that matches the AP that will be the other end of the wireless-to-wireless bridge. Move this connection so that it is at the top of the list of preferred networks.

6. Click OK to save the changes.

When you use a PC as a bridge, keep in mind that the bridge can only work if the PC is running.

Security

Unlike standard APs, which are used to communicate with stations, most point-to-point and point-to-multipoint wireless bridge APs communicate only with other APs. Consequently, you should be able to implement and enforce stringent security policies to protect the privacy of the data transmitted over the bridge. In all 802.11b systems, you should definitely use the available WEP. Ideally, you should also frequently change the WEP key. As wireless networking equipment manufacturers and WECA approve and implement new WEP and other security features, you should keep up with the changes and upgrade each wireless bridge to the newest security scheme. Most enterprise-level APs should now support 802.1x authentication, which includes support for the automatic distribution of keys. By the time you read this chapter, new firmware should also be available for these APs that enables rapid rekeying of APs and stations to eliminate the security risk that currently exists when using WEP.

Choosing the Optimal Antenna

Besides the APs, the other key ingredient to successful wireless bridging is the antenna. The obvious difference between antennas used inside and those used outdoors is the distance the signal must travel. Radio signals always travel further outdoors than indoors simply because there are fewer objects outdoors to attenuate the signal.

Ironically, the same radio that doesn't penetrate one floor above may be able to transmit a signal to an AP 20 miles away. The determining factor is the antenna.

Omnidirectional Antennas

As implied by the name, omnidirectional antennas, such as dipole antennas, send their signals in all directions at once. In fact, the signal pattern of an omnidirectional antenna is shaped a bit like a bagel or doughnut—with a small hole in the center. The signal is weakest directly above and below the antenna. Omnidirectional antennas are appropriate for use when the other AP (in a point-to-point bridge) or APs (in point-to-multipoint bridges) are located within about one-half mile. As discussed in Chapter 19, you should calculate the link budget to determine whether the gain of a particular omnidirectional antenna is sufficient for your particular situation.

A typical example of an omnidirectional antenna for use with a 2.4 GHz wireless bridge is the HyperLink 2.4 GHz High Performance Omnidirectional Antenna system, which features fiberglass construction and an extruded aluminum mounting bracket. This antenna has a 15dbi gain and a height of 70 inches; it is designed for outdoor use and sells for a little over two hundred dollars.

Directional Antennas

For longer distances, you need to use directional high-gain antennas. Directional antennas provide a stronger signal at long distances than omnidirectional antennas and are much less likely to cause interference to other RF systems.

Several types of directional antennas are available:

♦ **Patch.** This type of antenna is flat and either square-shaped or round. It can be mounted to a wall or a mast. HyperLink, for example, produces patch antennas for outdoor use that have signal patterns that cover from 30-degree to 90-degree beams with gain from 8dbi to 14dbi. These antennas vary in price, up to about $100. Patch antennas can effectively transmit the signal from the master AP in a point-to-multipoint configuration, depending on the relative location of the various sites you are connecting.

♦ **Yagi.** The cylinder-shaped yagi antenna is typically mounted at one end and pointed toward the corresponding antenna on the other end. Typical 2.4 GHz yagi antennas have a solid aluminum boom enclosed by a UV-inhibited PVC (or similar substance) radome. HyperLink makes a yagi antenna that has a 30-degree beam and 14dBi gain. The radiation pattern of yagi antennas has large side lobes that extend up to 45 degrees from the center of the radome. When aiming a yagi, don't point directly at the antenna at the other end. Rather, aim at a slightly elevated angle just to the right or left.

THE PRINGLES YAGI DO-IT-YOURSELF

Although yagi antennas are of excellent quality and not that expensive, you may want to experiment with building your own high-gain antenna out of an empty Pringles potato chip can. Instructions—including text and photographs—can be found online at several locations: www.oreillynet.com/cs/weblog/view/wlg/448, www.arwain.net/evan/pringles.htm, and http://verma.sfsu.edu/users/wireless/pringles.php. You can view a video at http://airshare.org/sd/installfest.html.

- **Panel.** 2.4 GHz panel antennas are typically used by wireless Internet Service Providers (ISPs) to cover multiple customers in a point-to-multipoint configuration. These antennas are available in many different gain and radiation pattern combinations. Typical examples include radiation patterns from 90 degrees to 180 degrees and gains from 15dBi to 20dBi.

- **Parabolic grid.** If you want to span a great distance, choose a 2.4 GHz parabolic grid antenna. This type of antenna is similar in appearance to a small satellite dish, but is made of a grid of wire rather than a solid dish, which keeps its weight and cost down. Parabolic grid antennas are designed for long-range operation. You can set them up for either vertical or horizontal polarization. Typical parabolic grid antennas have very narrow radiation patterns, from 8 degrees to 15 degrees, but provide gain from 15dBi to 24dBi.

THE TIN CAN-PRIMESTAR DO-IT-YOURSELF

The PrimeStar satellite TV company has been sold to Direct TV, which seems to be systematically switching customers to new equipment, leaving countless parabolic dish antennas orphaned all over the U.S. If you own one of these antennas and need a long-range 2.4 GHz antenna, you can build one yourself. Instructions can be found online at: www.wwc.edu/~frohro/Airport/Primestar/Primestar.html. If you are careful, this project should produce an antenna with as much as 22dBi gain.

Installing a Wireless Bridge

Some brands of wireless bridges are designed for indoor installation, with a cable running to the antenna mounted outdoors. Some ORiNOCO products, for example, have slots for two radios. You can set up one radio as a standard AP, serving wireless stations, and use the second radio as a wireless bridge to another part of the same building or to a separate building. (If you use ORiNOCO APs in this manner, you must purchase a software license from an ORiNOCO vendor for special Outdoor Router software that will enable the bridging features.) This setup requires you to run a low signal-loss cable to the antenna. The installation instructions from ORiNOCO, however, suggest that you mount the AP as close as possible to the antenna.

If you need to mount the antenna high on a rooftop or on a tower, you may have to run a very long cable. The longer the cable, the more signal lost. The best configuration, therefore, is to mount the AP outdoors along with the antenna to reduce the signal loss due to the transmission cable. The ideal system will enable you to install the AP inside a weatherproof enclosure, on or near the same mast that holds the antenna.

Any outdoor AP installation must take weather conditions into account. Make sure the AP is not directly exposed to rain or snow, and follow the manufacturer's guidelines with respect to temperature. If you are installing the AP on the top of a building or on a tower, near the antenna, you should install the wireless bridge device in a weatherproof enclosure that can withstand high winds as well as rain and sun. In very cold environments, you may need to install a small electric heater in the enclosure.

Power over Ethernet

You need to provide electrical power to each wireless bridge device. As with indoor APs, models that enable you to provide power over the Ethernet cable are more convenient than models that need AC power running to the point where the AP will be mounted.

Mounting Antennas

Every antenna must be securely mounted. Most antennas come with the necessary mounting hardware. If you are using an omnidirectional dipole antenna, for example, you should mount the antenna either to 3/-inch or 1-inch electrical conduit for indoor use or to a heavy-duty galvanized wall mast for outdoor use (see Figure 20-5).

Whenever you install an antenna outdoors, you should install a lightning/surge arrestor indoors between the antenna cable and the wireless bridge device. The arrestor should be attached to the same grounding system as the mast to which the antenna is attached. A lightning/surge suppressor protects the wireless bridge equipment from being damaged by potential charges developing on the antenna and cable, or surges induced from nearby lightning strikes. Typical arrestors protect equipment from surges up to 5,000 Amperes, but will not prevent damage from a direct hit by lightning.

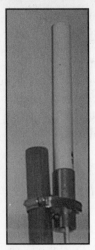

Figure 20-5: An omnidirectional antenna and mounting hardware

Aiming Antennas

When your wireless bridge is going to cover a long distance, aiming the antennas becomes tricky. The further apart the antennas, the more directional the antenna needs to be. It is much more difficult to aim antennas that are highly directional than to aim antennas with a broader radiation pattern, simply because the target at each end of the link is smaller. To aim the antenna, you need the following equipment:

♦ Good binoculars or a telescope (or surveying equipment, if you can get it and know how to use it)

♦ Two cell phones

♦ The APs that will be used in the wireless bridge

♦ Two laptop computers equipped with the AP-bridge management software and utilities, including a link test utility

If you can, you should also obtain a drawing or graph that shows the radiation pattern of your antennas from the antenna manufacturer. Make sure that both antennas use the same polarization (horizontal or vertical). If the polarization doesn't match, you won't be able to get the antennas to talk at a long distance. You obviously need someone at each end communicating over the cell phones.

The type of antennas you use determines the exact procedure you will need to follow. If you are setting up point-to-multipoint bridges, for example, you will probably have one broad-radiation-pattern antenna (such as a panel or omnidirectional antenna) as the master AP and a highly directional antenna (such as a yagi or parabolic grid antenna) at each of the other APs, pointing toward the master AP's antenna. In such a case (see Figure 20-6), you should set up the broad-pattern antenna first and then work at aiming the other antennas to connect each slave AP to the master AP.

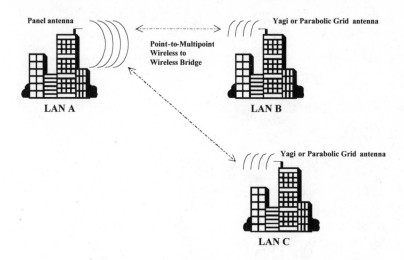

Figure 20-6: A point-to-multipoint wireless-to-wireless bridge with panel antenna and two directional (yagi or parabolic grid) antennas

Attach each antenna to its respective AP. For the purpose of aiming the antennas, attach a laptop computer to each AP (either by Ethernet connection, wireless connection, USB, or serial port, depending on the AP model that you have selected). In each laptop computer, activate the link test utility that shows the strength of the signal and noise received by each AP. The laptops will act as your signal strength meters. You can use standalone signal-strength analyzers if you have them, but the 802.11b packets include enough signal-strength information to indicate whether the signal will allow the wireless bridge to function. In addition, when using the AP utility software, you can precisely identify the source of the signal.

USING NETSTUMBLER TO AIM AN ANTENNA

Another very useful utility is the program NetworkStumbler (usually called just NetStumbler), which you can download for free at www.netstumbler.com. This program is best known for enabling so-called "war driving," but is a very useful utility when you are working with multiple APs or trying to link up to one particular AP. NetStumbler is designed to locate APs, not bridges, so you may not be able to "see" the signal of an AP operating in bridge mode. In addition, NetStumbler works only with wireless PC cards based on the Lucent chipset. If you own a Lucent-based card and an adapter cable that matches the antenna you are aiming, you can use NetStumbler to help aim the antennas.

If you have trouble linking two APs in bridge mode, switch the devices to standard AP mode. Detach the antenna you want to aim from the AP and attach the adapter cable from the antenna to the Lucent-based wireless PC card, which has been inserted into your laptop. Now, use NetStumbler to identify the signal of any AP in the range of the antenna. As you slowly move the antenna from side to side, NetStumbler displays a list of all the APs that the radio in your laptop can "see." When you spot the AP with which you want to connect, use the NetStumbler signal/noise meter (see Figure 20-7) to find the antenna position that produces the best signal. After you have found the best signal by moving the antenna horizontally (left and right), find the best vertical postion by pointing the antenna slightly upward and then slowly moving it downward. After the antenna is optimally positioned at one end of the link, repeat the process at the other end. When both antennas achieve the best signal, you are ready to switch the APs back to bridge mode.

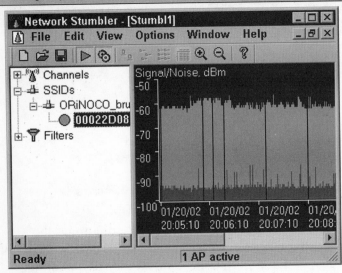

Figure 20-7: Using NetStumbler to help aim an antenna

Use your binoculars or telescope (or surveying equipment) to locate the antenna site on the other end. Hold the antenna from behind its swivel connector and point it just to the left or right of the target. Very slowly, sweep the antenna across the target area while watching the link test screen for an indication of a signal. If you possess a drawing of each antenna's radiation pattern, make note of the shape of the largest lobes and adjust the direction that the antenna is pointing—left or right, up or down—to take advantage of the strongest lobe.

Long-distance point-to-point connections are the most difficult connections to make. Both antennas radiate a narrow signal that may be just barely strong enough to produce a connection. Make sure you do the "math" first—that is, calculate the link budget—to make sure you'll have sufficient signal to produce a connection. If the link budget is sufficient, after accounting for cable loss, earth bulge, Fresnel zone, and so on, you may just need a steady hand and some patience to get the two antennas lined up.

WARNING!

Never install an antenna mast near power lines. Doing so can be extremely dangerous — even life-threatening. In addition, never use a metal ladder when installing an antenna on a tower or other high platform. You don't want to become a human lightning rod!

Summary

This chapter covers the factors you should consider when selecting 802.11b wireless-to-wireless bridge equipment for your company or client's network. It also provides a few guidelines on installing wireless bridges, as well as antennas. Because there are many different brands and equipment configurations, the precise details of your situation will vary.

Glossary

100BaseT

The specification for an Ethernet cable that will support transmitting data at 100 Mbps on a baseband signal over twisted pair cable. Short for *100* Mbps, *Base*band, *Twisted* pair.

10BaseT

The specification for cable that supports transmitting data at 10 Mbps on a baseband signal (that is, standard Ethernet) over twisted pair cable. Short for *10* Mbps, *Base*band, *Twisted* pair.

802.11a

See *IEEE 802.11a.*

802.11b

See *IEEE 802.11b.*

802.11e

See *IEEE 802.11e.*

802.11g

See *IEEE 802.11g.*

802.1x

See *IEEE 802.1x.*

802.3

See *IEEE 802.3—Ethernet.*

A

AAA

An acronym for authentication, authorization, and accounting; a network management and security framework that controls access to network resources by uniquely identifying users, authorizing the level of service, and tracking resource utilization.

access point

A special type of wireless *station* in a wireless network. An access point can be a computer that contains a wireless network adapter as well as access point management software. It is more common, however, for an access point to be a dedicated standalone device whose purpose is to receive and forward to the rest of the network radio transmissions from all the other stations on the wireless LAN (WLAN). An access point can also act as a *bridge* between wireless stations and a wired network. Some access points can work with a second access point to create a wireless bridge between two wired LANs.

ad hoc mode

If you are setting up a wireless NIC solely for the purpose of communicating with other wireless NICs, in a peer-to-peer fashion, you need to set up the device for *ad hoc mode*. If you are using wireless NICs from different manufacturers, different terminology may be used for the same mode. For example, one manufacturer's configuration software may refer to *ad hoc* mode while another may call it *peer-to-peer* mode. At least one manufacturer uses the term *ad hoc* to refer to a proprietary mode that communicates only with other cards from the same company and uses the term *802.11 ad hoc mode* to refer to the mode that interoperates with cards from other manufacturers.

ad hoc network

Whenever two wireless stations are close enough to communicate with each other, they are capable of establishing a form of peer-to-peer network called an *ad hoc network*. In small offices and homes, you may be able to use an ad hoc wireless network as the only network, without using an access point. However, in most cases, ad hoc networks are temporary in nature — hence the name "ad hoc." Ad hoc wireless networks occur spontaneously and dynamically. Whenever two stations are close enough together to communicate (and their network adapters set to *ad hoc mode*), the stations form a *basic service set (BSS)*.

algorithm

A process, procedure, or formula for solving a problem or determining an outcome.

antenna

The transmitting and receiving device for RF transmissions.

AP

See *access point.*

API

An acronym for Application Program Interface; a library of application-, or operating-system-specific routines or subprograms through which other software can interact with a hardware or software feature.

Application layer

The final layer in the OSI reference model, where applications gain access to network services. The Application layer is intended for use by application software that is written to operate across a network, such as e-mail software, FTP, DNS, SNMP, and TELNET software.

application server

A computer that runs centralized application software such as mission-critical database software or enterprise resource planning software that provides service to workstations on the network (also called an appserver).

application software

Special-purpose software, created to perform a specific task, that runs on top of a computer's operating system. Examples include MS Word, Corel's Word Perfect, or Intuit's Quicken.

ASCII

An acronym for American Standard Code for Information Interchange; the standard data code used by computer and data communication systems for translating characters, numbers, and punctuation into digital form.

ASP

An acronym for Application Service Provider; an Internet company that provides online access to one or more applications and related services.

asymmetric cryptography

A form of encryption in which both a private key and a public key is used. As the names imply, the key's owner keeps a private key secret, but makes a public key intentionally public in a directory maintained for that purpose. In effect, both keys are used together, but not at the same time. That is, if one key is used to encrypt data, the other key must be used to decrypt the data. Asymmetric cryptography only works if both keys are created at the same time using a complex mathematical algorithm.

ATM

An acronym for Asynchronous Transfer Mode; a dedicated-connection cell switching high-speed communication technology that transmits data in 53-byte cells over a physical medium using digital signal technology.

Authentication

The process of proving the identity of a computer user that generally involves the verification of a user name and password.

B

backbone

The primary medium or device of a network that ties the segments and nodes of the network together. Backbone devices include switches, hubs, routers, and gateways.

baseband

In a *baseband* transmission, electrical impulses are sent out without the need to change the frequency of the signal.

basic service set

See *BSS.*

bit

The smallest unit of data storage in a computer capable of storing one binary digit.

BIOS

An acronym for Basic Input/Output System; firmware used to start up a PC and provide an interface between the PC's operating system and its attached hardware devices.

Bluetooth

In 1994, the *Bluetooth* wireless technology, named for the tenth-century Danish King Harald Blaatand "Bluetooth" II, was invented by the L.M. Ericsson Company of Sweden. In February 1998, Ericsson, IBM, Intel, Nokia, and Toshiba founded the Bluetooth Special Interest Group (SIG) Inc. to develop an open specification for always-on, short-range wireless connectivity, based on Ericsson's Bluetooth technology. Their specification was released publicly on July 26, 1999. The SIG now includes 3COM, Microsoft, Lucent, Motorola, and nearly 2,000 other companies.

Bootstrap protocol

Also known as BOOTP; the protocol used to automatically configure a node by obtaining required parameters over a network from a host device.

Bps

An acronym for bits per second; the most commonly used transmission rate unit of measurement.

bridge

A network *bridge* provides a pathway for electronic packets of data to cross between networks or segments of networks. Network bridges are sometimes used to connect networks on different floors in the same building or in different buildings; sometimes, they connect networks of different types. A bridge is "simple-minded" in its approach to passing network traffic from one end of the bridge to the other. It simply gives the signal a boost and sends it on its way—no analysis and no discrimination. All packets are treated the same.

broadband

A *broadband* transmission requires that the signal be modulated to change its frequency so that it can be transmitted within a particular frequency range or *channel*. By using a frequency division multiplexing (FDM) technique, many different channels can be transmitted simultaneously over some types of media, including coaxial cable. Thus, you can use the same wide bandwidth cable to transmit both data and television without interference by using a broadband signal.

BSS

An acronym for Basic Service Set; the area in which wireless stations can remain in communication. The most basic type of BSS is an *independent basic service set,* also known as an *ad hoc network,* and consists of at least two wireless stations that have no mechanism for communication with stations outside the BSS.

C

Cascading

The method of linking two network connectivity devices, such as a hub or a switch, using an uplink port.

category 5 unshielded twisted pair cable

Also called cat 5 UTP cable; the most common type of cable used for network cabling. Category 5 cable has four pairs of wires inside the jacket. Each pair is twisted together and then all four pairs are twisted. The number of twists per foot is one aspect of the cable specification that gives it the category 5 rating, a rating scheme established by the Telecommunication Industry Association/Electronic Industry Association (TIA/EIA) standards group.

CDMA

An acronym for Code Division Multiple Access; a spread spectrum wireless technology used in digital cellular communications and wireless networks.

CF card

An acronym for Compact Flash card; a CF card wireless networking adapter enables you to connect PDAs and other devices with Compact Flash interfaces (such as a Visor PDA) to a WLAN. At least one vendor even offers an adapter for the CF card that converts the CF wireless NIC into a PC card.

channel

Multiple radio *channels* are available for use by wireless networks. The exact number of channels varies according to which type of wireless network you are using and the country in which you install the WLAN.

client

See *workstation*.

collision domain

A group of network devices connected so that they receive all messages sent by any member of the group.

cryptography

In the world of computers, the science of writing and deciphering computer data in secret code for the purpose of protecting the data from unauthorized access.

CSMA/CA

An acronym for Carrier Sense Multiple Access/Collision Avoidance; the principle medium access method used on IEEE 802.11 LANs.

CSMA/CD

An acronym for Carrier Sense Multiple Access/Collision Detection; the LAN access method used in Ethernet.

CSU/DSU

An acronym for Channel Service Unit/Data Service Unit; a hardware device that converts a digital signal from a LAN to the signal used on a WAN, and vice versa.

D

Data Link layer

The second layer of the OSI model, responsible for the physical connection between the two systems.

Data Over Cable Standard Interface Specifications

Also known as DOCSIS; a cable modem standard that establishes an industry standard for cable modems that connect consumers to the Internet over cable TV infrastructure.

demilitarized zone

Also called a DMZ; in the "real" world, a physical area—usually a strip of land—that provides a buffer between two countries that do not trust each other. For example, the cease-fire agreement at the end of the Korean War established a DMZ between North Korea and South Korea that exists to this day. In a LAN, a DMZ is usually a network added between an internal network, such as a company intranet, and an external network, such as the Internet. This type of DMZ may contain an HTTP/FTP proxy server, an HTTP/FTP Web server, and a News proxy server. Like the real-world DMZ, a DMZ in a LAN provides an added layer of security between the internal (trusted) network and the external (not trusted) network. DMZ networks are also sometimes called *perimeter networks*.

DHCP server

An acronym for Dynamic Host Configuration Protocol server; a server that automatically assigns IP addresses to the computers on a network, instead of requiring the system administrator to manually assign an IP address to each computer.

digital signature

A process that uses a portion of an electronic file to enable a recipient of the file to prove that the purported sender really sent the file. A recipient of a file that includes a digital signature can compare the electronic signature to the electronic equivalent of the signature on the back of a credit card to determine the file's authenticity.

Direct-sequence spread-spectrum

Another physical layer modulation technique included in the IEEE 802.11 specification. The IEEE 802.11 physical layer that uses direct-sequence spread-spectrum (DSSS) can also transmit data at up to two Mbps. IEEE 802.11b radios that use DSSS spread their signals across the entire available ISM band, but at very low power. By spreading the signal, interference by narrow-band signals is less likely to result in data errors. In addition, unintended radios, operating in the same frequency range, see this signal as background noise and ignore it. When listening to a cheap FM radio placed too close to an 802.11 device, you may hear a low hum in the background.

distribution system

The linking process that integrates multiple BSSs so that computers in any BSS in the distribution system can communicate.

DMZ

See *demilitarized zone.*

DSSS

See *Direct-Sequence Spread-Spectrum.*

E

EAP

See *Extensible Authentication Protocol.*

encryption

The process used to encode data into an unreadable format for transmission or storage to prevent its unauthorized interpretation until it is decoded with the application of a decryption key.

encryption key

An alphanumeric string used to scramble and unscramble a message to make the message unintelligible to anyone who doesn't have access to this key.

Unless the WLAN is intended for use by the general public, every wireless LAN should be protected by *encryption*. The most popular wireless network technology uses *Wired Equivalent Privacy (WEP)* encryption, which uses the RC4 encryption algorithm. This type of encryption requires the network administrator to enter the same alphanumeric string in the AP and all the stations. Any station without this *key* cannot get onto the network.

Ethernet
See *IEEE 802.3*.

Extensible Authentication Protocol (RFC 2284)
Also known as EAP; a relatively simple encapsulation protocol for authenticating network devices that is implemented in the Data Link Layer of the network architecture without depending on the MAC address. EAP employs IETF standard key derivation methods such as Transport Level Security (TLS), Secure Remote Password (SRP), and Kerberos. When EAP is implemented over a LAN, it is called EAPOL. When implemented over a WLAN, it is called EAPOW.

F

Fast Ethernet
Also known as 100BaseTX; a networking standard that provides data transmission speeds of 100 Mbps.

FDMA
An acronym for Frequency Division Multiple Access; an analog cellular standard that provides access to a group of frequency bands to eliminate message interference.

fiber optic (cable)
A high-speed networking medium that uses glass or plastic as its core material.

file server
A computer that contains or controls one or more storage devices, such as hard disks, optical disks, tape drives, and so on. A file server makes storage space available to workstations on the network. The storage space can be used as an extension of a workstation's local storage, or it can be the only mass storage available to a workstation.

Frequency-hopping spread-spectrum

Also known as FHSS; a wireless LAN technology that transmits (hops) a signal over several frequencies using a specific rate and sequence to reduce the possibility of interference. (One of three wireless LAN technologies with DSSS and infrared.)

Fresnel zone

RF waves travel out from their source in a number of concentric cones that start at the transmission point and grow in size. This signal surrounds the direct line-of-sight between the two radio antennas in an elliptical cone shape. The diameter of each cone can be calculated depending on the wavelength of the signal. Each cone-shaped signal path is called a Fresnel zone. The center cone contains the strongest signal and is called the *first Fresnel zone.*

G

Gateway

A network point that acts as an entrance to another network.

Global system for mobile communication

Also known as GSM; a digital wireless telephone system widely used in Europe and other parts of the world.

H

hash algorithm

An algorithm that performs a mathematical computation on the data to be transmitted. Because the result of this algorithm is typically a smaller amount of data than the original file, it is often referred to as a *message digest,* or just a *digest,* of the original file—a sort of digital fingerprint.

High Rate Direct Sequence Spread Spectrum

A physical layer that uses the same 2.4 GHz ISM band and channels as the DSSS physical layer and is backward-compatible with the DSSS physical layer. The primary difference between HR/DSSS and DSSS lies in the frequency modulation technique that HR/DSSS uses, called *complementary code keying (CCK).* The CCK technique enables data transmission at either 5.5 Mbps or 11 Mbps.

HiperLAN2

A competitor to the IEEE 802.11 standard. HiperLAN2 was developed in Europe.

HomePLUG

A new technology that enables home networks to use the electrical wiring already in the walls as a networking medium to deliver speeds as fast as 14 Mbps. This initiative is backed by an industry group called the HomePlug Powerline Alliance.

HomePNA

Also known as *HPNA*; a de facto standard promoted by the Home Phoneline Networking Alliance, an industry association working to ensure adoption of a single, unified phoneline networking standard. HomePNA is built on Ethernet and enables home computers to be networked using existing telephone wiring, obviating the need to run cat 5 cabling.

HomeRF

A direct competitor to the IEEE 802.11 standard (Wi-Fi), sponsored by the Home Radio Frequency Working Group (HomeRF WG), which was launched in March 1998. From the beginning, HomeRF was developed for use in homes; thus, it was designed to be more affordable to home users than other wireless technologies.

HR/DSSS

See *High Rate Direct Sequence Spread Spectrum.*

I

IBSS

When a *BSS* forms a self-contained network, not connected to a distribution system, it is called an *independent BSS (IBSS)* also known as an *ad hoc network.*

IEEE 802.1x

A new IEEE standard, ratified in June 2001, that enables the network to authenticate and to determine the identity of an entity, as well as the entity's access rights at the time the entity attempts to connect to a LAN port, without depending on the MAC address. In the context of a wireless LAN, network switch software that complies with the 802.1x standard would be capable of requiring that a wireless station be authenticated against a list of authorized entities before permitting the station access to the network. IEEE 802.1x is based on Extensible Authentication Protocol (RFC 2284), applies to all IEEE 802 technologies, including Ethernet, and is a framework for managing authentication and keys. Using this standard and well-established key derivation algorithms such as Transport Layer Security (TLS), Secure Remote Password (SRP) protocol, or Kerberos, per-session keys are derived that can be used to provide per-packet authentication, integrity, and confidentiality

IEEE 802.3—Ethernet

Ethernet is the most widely adopted local area network physical layer protocol. It was developed in 1976 by Xerox, with assistance from DEC and Intel. IEEE 802.3, 2000 Edition, CSMA/CD Access Method and Physical Layer Specification, specifies a baseband physical layer protocol that is very similar to the original Ethernet. The original Ethernet transmitted data at 10 Mbps. 802.3 provides for data transmission at various rates up to 1000 Mbps—so-called Gigabit Ethernet. 802.3 also specifies a protocol for 10 Mbps broadband transmission.

IEEE 802.11

IEEE 802.11, Wireless LAN Medium Access Control (MAC) and Physical Layer (PHY) specifications, specifies the standards for wireless networking.

IEEE 802.11a

IEEE 802.11a-1999, High-speed Physical Layer in the 5 GHz Band, is a supplement to 802.11. This supplement sets out specifications for the Coded Orthogonal Frequency Division Multiplexing (COFDM) protocol.

IEEE 802.11b

IEEE 802.11b-1999, Higher-Speed Physical Layer Extension in the 2.4 GHz Band, is the supplement to 802.11 that establishes the specifications for High Rate Direct Sequence Spread Spectrum (HR/DSSS), the protocol used by Wi-Fi-certified wireless networking devices. Although 802.11b was adopted in a separate document, it is not a separate standard from 802.11; rather, it adds subsections to 802.11 that specify the HR/DSSS protocol.

IEEE 802.11e

An unratified extension to 802.11, intended to add support for multimedia and *Quality of Service (QoS)* to wireless LANs. The standards being considered for 802.11e will be compatible with 802.11b and 802.11a devices, but will do a much better job of dealing with interference that would otherwise slow down the connection.

IEEE 802.11g

A supplement to 802.11 that is still in the works, but may have been ratified by the time you read this book. This addition to the WLAN standard will set the specifications for protocols that can transmit data up to 54 Mbps—so-called "turbo" speed—over the 2.4 GHz frequency band.

infrared

A form of el signal transmission that uses a focused ray of light in the infrared frequency spectrum that can be sent from a transmitter to a receiver over a relatively short distance. Infrared is one of the five physical layers available in IEEE 802.11, but there are no wireless networking products currently available that implement this physical layer.

infrastructure mode

Almost any time you plan to use the wireless NIC to access a WLAN, you want the wireless NIC to communicate with one or more access points in the WLAN. This type of wireless communication is called *infrastructure mode*.

Internet gateway

The purpose of an *Internet gateway* is to enable multiple computers to share the same connection to the Internet—that is, the same IP address. This function is often performed by a router that provides a service called *network address translation (NAT)*. The NAT service communicates with each station on the network using the private IP addresses assigned by the DHCP server, but uses a single IP address—the one assigned by your *Internet service provider (ISP)* (which may have also been assigned by the ISP's DHCP server)—in packets intended for the Internet.

Internet Key Exchange

Internet Key Exchange (IKE—RFC 2409) protocol, when used as part of IPSec, uses the Internet Security Association and Key Management Protocol (ISAKMP)/Oakley to negotiate and manage security parameters, including shared session key, identity authentication method, and data authentication and encryption algorithm.

Internet Protocol Security

Internet Protocol Security (IPSec—RFC 2401-2409) defines an architecture, protocol, and related Internet Key Exchange protocol that together enable secure data sessions over a network's IP layer (the Network layer in the ISO/OSI model). IPSec was designed to provide high-quality security for Internet traffic. Most typically, IPSec is used to create a secure session between two computers that may be connected to the same LAN/WLAN or may be communicating over the Internet.

IPSec

See *Internet Protocol Security*.

ISM frequency bands

The Federal Communication Commission (FCC) has designated three radio frequency bands as the industrial, scientific, and medical (ISM) bands:

- 902 MHz—928 MHz, a 26 MHz bandwidth
- 2.4 GHz—2.4835 GHz, a 83.5 MHz bandwidth
- 5.725 GHz—5.850 GHz, a 125 MHz bandwidth

FCC regulations permit a user to operate radio equipment, within certain guidelines, that transmits a signal within one of the three ISM bands without obtaining an FCC license.

ISO 7-layer Reference Model

The OSI 7-layer model (ISO/IEC 7498-1:1994) has been around more or less in the same form since 1984, when ISO and *International Telegraph and Telephone Consultative Committee* (*CCITT*, from the French spelling — since replaced by the *ITU-T*, or *International Telecommunications Union-Telecommunications Standardization Sector*) agreed to work together to establish a single suite of compatible networking protocols. Because this model does an adequate job of conceptualizing how networking protocols should work, it has been universally adopted as a teaching or *reference* model.

L

L2TP

An acronym for *Layer Two Tunneling Protocol*; a combination of PPTP and Cisco's Layer 2 Forwarding protocol. It has evolved, along with IPSec, through the IETF standards process and has broad vendor support. L2TP uses PPP as the method of negotiating user authentication; therefore, it supports legacy password-based user authentication systems such as Password Authentication Protocol (PAP), Challenge Handshake Authentication

Protocol (CHAP), Shiva Password Authentication Protocol (SPAP), and Microsoft Challenge Authentication Protocol (MS-CHAP). It supports EAP-based authentication services, such as 802.1x, that integrate with RADIUS and LDAP-based directories.

Layer Two Tunneling Protocol
See *L2TP*.

local area network
A network between computers found in the same physical location, also known as a LAN. Most business and personal networks are LANs.

M

MAC
An acronym for Media Access Control. See Media Access Control layer.

MAC address
Every network device has a unique hardware address known as the *MAC address*.

The MAC address of the AP, which should be printed on a label attached to the device. If the AP uses a PC card as its radio, the MAC address for the AP is sometimes printed on the back of the PC card. Note: The AP's Ethernet connection to the wired network also has a MAC address that is different than the MAC address of the radio in the AP.

mail server
A computer that provides a system for sending electronic messages, usually called *electronic mail* or simply *e-mail,* to users on a network. Mail servers can provide an electronic messaging service among the users of the network, between the network's users and Internet users, or both.

Media Access Control layer
The IEEE 802 reference model has defined a sublayer of the *Data Link layer* called the Media Access Control (MAC) layer, which is closely tied to the Physical layer. Each IEEE 802 Physical layer standard (Ethernet, Token Ring, Token Bus, and so on) specifies both the Physical layer aspects of the protocol as well as how medium access is to take place. The Media Access Control layer defines the protocols that determine when a network device may use the medium (a channel in a wireless LAN).

middleware

A communications software that serves as a translator between various radio frequency technologies and wireless networking protocols.

modem

A term that stands for *modulator/demodulator*; a hardware device that performs modulation on outbound (digital to analog) or inbound (analog to digital) data for purposes of transmission or processing, respectively.

modulation

The conversion of analog or digital data into the other format. Analog information is converted into digital bits for processing at the receiving end, and digital data is converted into analog format for transmission.

N

network

Computers connected together in a way that enables them to transfer data. Offices and some homes have networks for the following reasons: sharing files, printers, schedules, and Internet connections, and making interoffice e-mail possible.

network adapter

An expansion card or external device that enables a PC to connect to a network's media (see also *NIC*).

Network Address Translation in Cable/DSL Modems

A *network address translation (NAT)* box is a device that enables a LAN to use a set of IP addresses for the computers on the network and a different set, often a single IP address, for traffic outside the network. A NAT also acts as a *firewall* because it hides the real IP addresses of networked computers from computers outside the network. A NAT enables networks to conserve Internet IP addresses by enabling many users on the internal network to share the same IP address.

network hub

A network *hub* receives signals that are transmitted by each computer on the network and sends the signals out to all other computers on the network. A special type of hub, called a *switched hub,* examines each packet, determines the addressee and port, and forwards the packet only to the computer and port to which it is addressed (see also *Switch*).

Network layer

The third layer in the OSI reference model. The primary functions of the Network layer are switching, routing, and addressing—taking a logical network address that is provided by the Data Link layer, and translating it to a "physical" address.

network server

Usually, but not always, a computer that provides one or more services to other computers on a network. There can be many types of servers on a network, including file servers, print servers, mail (e-mail) servers, application servers, DHCP servers, audio/video servers, chat servers, fax servers, FTP servers, groupware servers, IRC servers, (e-mail) list servers, news servers, proxy servers, Telnet/WAIS, and Web servers.

NIC

An acronym for *Network Interface Card*; another name for an internal expansion card network adapter.

P

panel antenna

2.4 GHz *panel antennas* are typically used by wireless ISPs to cover multiple customers in point-to-multipoint configuration. These antennas are available in many different gain and radiation pattern combinations, from 90° to 180°, and gains from 15 dBi to 20 dBi.

parabolic grid antenna

2.4 GHz *parabolic grid antennas* should be your choice when you need to span great distances. They are similar in appearance to a small satellite dish, but are made of a grid of wire rather than being solid, which keeps their weight and cost down. Parabolic grid antennas are designed for long-range operation. You can set them up for either vertical or horizontal polarization. Typical parabolic grid antennas have very narrow radiation patterns, from 8° to 15°, but provide gain from 15 dBi to 24 dBi.

patch antenna

A *patch antenna* is flat and either square or round, and can be mounted either to a wall or a mast. Patch antennas can effectively transmit the signal from the master AP in a point-to-multipoint configuration, depending on the relative location of the various sites you are connecting.

PAN

An acronym for personal area network; several computing devices communicating in close proximity.

PC card

Also known as a PCMCIA card; a removable card-like device used to add hardware or software features to portable computers. PC cards are hot-swappable, which means they can be inserted and removed without first restarting the computer.

PCI adapater

All new PCs should have at least one *Peripheral Component Interconnect (PCI)* slot. Consequently, most wireless NIC manufacturers offer a wireless PCI adapter—a version of their wireless network adapter product that can be installed in a PCI slot.

PCMCIA

An acronym for Personal Computer Memory Card International Association card. See *PC card.*

PCS

An acronym for Personal Communications Services; a term that describes a class of wireless digital communications services that uses the 1.9 GHz radio frequency.

PDA

An acronym for Personal Digital Assistant; a portable hand-held computing device capable of storing and, in some cases, transmitting data such as personal calendars, e-mail, and notes.

personal area network

See *PAN.*

Physical layer

The lowest or outermost layer of the OSI reference model, which is tasked with sending the bit stream around the network on an electrical and mechanical level.

piconet

A Bluetooth device automatically and spontaneously forms informal PANs called *piconets* with other Bluetooth devices. The connection and disconnection of these devices is almost without any user command or interaction—a capability called *unconscious connectivity*.

PKI

See *Public Key Infrastructure*.

PoE

See *Power over Ethernet*.

point-to-point bridge

The simplest form of wireless bridge, in which two APs communicate wirelesssly only with one another. Each AP also acts as a bridge to a wired LAN. The antennas used in this type of bridge are typically highly directional, reducing the interference to other equipment and increasing the effective transmission range.

point-to-multipoint bridge

A type of bridge that has a "master" or "central" AP that broadcasts to several "slave" or "client" APs. The slave APs communicate wirelessly only with the master AP, not with the other slave APs. Devices on any of the LANs connected by this point-to-multipoint bridge can communicate with any of the other devices on any of the LANs bridged by the point-to-multipoint bridge.

Point-to-Point Tunneling Protocol

Also called PPTP; a VPN protocol developed by the PPTP Industry Forum before the existence of IPSec and PKI. PPTP is easier to set up, not requiring complicated security policy configuration, and is generally the lowest-cost solution. It provides encryption of all data during a session, but the security is based on passwords only, not on Public Key Infrastructure technology.

Power over Ethernet

Also called PoE; in an access point, PoE is the capability to power the access points over the Ethernet cable.

PPTP

See *Point-to-Point Tunneling Protocol*.

Presentation layer

Layer six of the OSI reference model, which provides a translation service between applications and the network protocols. Some network protocols don't implement this layer.

print server

A computer or other device that controls one or more printers. Many high-end printers have built-in print-server features that enable multiple network workstations to send output to these printers without the need to connect directly to any computer on the network.

Public Key Infrastructure:

Also called PKI; a framework that makes use of a combination of two very sophisticated types of cryptography—private key cryptography and private/public key cryptography—to make communicating sensitive information electronically more secure.

public key cryptography

Public key cryptography works very much like asymmetric cryptography, except that the clear-text message is encrypted using a symmetric cryptographic algorithm, and public-key cryptography uses an asymmetric cryptographic algorithm to encrypt the symmetric key.

Q

QoS

See *Quality of Service*.

Quality of Service

Also called QoS; a networking term that means guaranteed throughput level, a feature needed to support transmission of streaming video and high-quality voice.

R

radio frequency

Also called RF; the range of electromagnetic frequencies used for broadcast transmissions for cellular telephones, radio, television, and satellite communication systems.

radio frequency interface

Also called RFI; radio frequency signals that are picked up by nearby media, causing interference in the form of electrical noise that could result in the loss of data or garbled transmissions.

range

A linear measure of the distance that a transmitter can send a signal.

Remote Authentication Dial-In User Service (RADIUS)

Network administrators often use a *Remote Authentication Dial-In User Service (RADIUS)* server to control LAN access by remote users who dial in to the network. RADIUS supports authentication, authorization, and accounting for network access from any port—physical ports such as access over Ethernet or ISDN, or virtual ports such as access over tunneled (VPN) or wireless connections. Any time an entity connects to the LAN, the system can employ a RADIUS server for authentication, authorization, and accounting.

repeater bridge

A special point-to-multipoint bridge in which all APs can act both as a wireless-to-wireless bridge and as an AP at the same time.

residential gateway

In a small network or home network, it is very convenient to combine the DHCP and Internet gateway functions into one device. It's even better if these functions can be combined with the wireless networking AP function. Such one-stop combination AP/DHCP/routers are sometimes called *residential gateways,* because they are frequently marketed to the home user.

roaming

The capability to move seamlessly from one access point or cell coverage area to another without a loss in connectivity.

rogue WLAN

An unauthorized installation of a wireless access point by someone who is otherwise a "friendly" user. This circumstance is typically the result of an innocent but impatient user or group of users who decides to "help itself" by acquiring and installing a wireless LAN on its own. If it operates this so-called *rogue WLAN* as an *IBSS*, not connected to any portion of the company/institutional LAN, the risk is not be as acute. More typically, however, the rogue WLAN is attached to the LAN, often with no privacy security (WEP) activated.

router

A *router* reads the "addressee" information in each packet and then communicates with other routers using the Internet Control Message Protocol

(ICMP) to determine the best *route* each packet should take to reach the addressee—hence the name *router*.

S

scatternet

A group of *piconets* that are a combination of piconets with one or more devices in common.

service set identifier

See *SSID*.

Session layer

The fifth layer in the OSI reference model, responsible for establishing, maintaining, and ending network sessions between hosts.

spread spectrum

A radio transmission technology that spreads information over a greater bandwidth than necessary to provide better interference tolerance.

SSID

An acronym for Service Set Identifier—sometimes called the Extended Service Set Identifier (ESSID); the name of the wireless network. Although a unique name is not required, most system administrators will want to change the SSID from the default name that comes installed in the AP. In order for the AP to communicate with a station, both station and AP must have specified matching SSIDs.

station

Each computer or device containing a radio that is transmitting and/or receiving data over the wireless network. As in wired networks, a station can be a *client* or a *server*.

switch

Data is transmitted over networks in bundles called *packets*. Each packet not only contains the raw information, it also contains information about the computer to which it is addressed and the computer that sent it—analogous to the address and return address on a postal envelope. A switch reads the "addressee" information in each packet and then sends the packet directly to the network segment to which the addressee is connected. Packets that are not addressed to a particular network segment are never transmitted over that segment and the switch acts as a filter to eliminate unnecessary network traffic. A special type of hub called a *switched hub* examines each packet, determines the addressee and port, and forwards the packet only to the computer and port to which it is addressed. See *network hub*.

symmetric cryptography

A form of encryption in which the originator and the recipient use the same key to both encrypt and decrypt the message.

T

TCP/IP

An acronym for Transmission Control Protocol/Internet Protocol; two protocols (*Transmission Control Protocol* and *Internet Protocol*) that, when used together, are the most common method of transmitting data around a network. Every individual computer on a TCP/IP network must have its own *IP address*, a 32-bit numeric address. Each IP address is written as four numbers separated by periods (such as 192.168.1.100). Each number can have a value from zero to 255.

topology

The general physical structure of a network.

Transport layer

Layer four of the OSI model, which is primarily responsible for transferring data between hosts. It is also responsible for end-to-end error recovery, ensuring that all data is transferred and flow control—that is, ensuring that a host is not overloaded with data.

twisted pair

A type of wire that uses pairs of copper wire wrapped around each other. This type of wire is commonly used in Ethernet and Token Ring networks.

U

Universal Resource Locator

See *URL*.

Universal Serial Bus

See *USB*.

URL

An acronym for Universal Resource Locator; the description of a location on the Internet, such as www.wiley.com.

USB

Universal Serial Bus (USB) standard has become the most ubiquitous method of connecting peripherals to a PC. First popularized in the Apple iMac, USB supports data transfer rates of 480 Mbps, many times faster than the fastest wireless network transmission rate. USB is, therefore, a good candidate for connecting an external wireless network adapter to either a laptop or a desktop PC. Several wireless networking hardware vendors offer USB wireless network adapters.

V

virtual private network

Also called a VPN; a private network connection that you can access over a public network.

W

WAN

An acronym for wide area network; a network that interconnects local area networks, using either subscribed lines or the facilities of the public communications network.

WCDMA

An acronym for wideband CDMA; a third-generation wireless technology that allows for high-speed, high-quality data transmission over wireless communication services.

WECA

See *Wireless Ethernet Compatibility Alliance.*

WEP

See *Wired Equivalent Privacy.*

wide area network

See *WAN.*

Wi-Fi

If you decide to build a wireless network around the IEEE 802.11b standard, you should look for the *Wi-Fi* logo on the products you buy. Each product that displays this logo has successfully passed the Wi-Fi interoperability tests conducted at Agilent's Interoperability Certification Lab (ICL). As of this writing, 200 products from 58 WECA member companies have received Wi-Fi certification since March 2000.

Wired Equivalent Privacy

Wired Equivalent Privacy (WEP) encryption is a security protocol that uses the *Rivest Cipher 4 (RC4)* encryption algorithm. This protocol is part of the IEEE 802.11 specification. To use WEP, the network administrator enters the same alphanumeric string in the AP and all the stations. Any station without this *key* cannot get onto the network.

wireless access point

A network device that serves as the receiver/transmitter of data on a wireless network for computers and devices with wireless network adapters located within the access point's range (typically less than 1,000 feet).

Wireless Ethernet Compatibility Alliance

Also known as WECA); a nonprofit organization whose primary purpose is to certify interoperability of IEEE 802.11b and IEEE 802.11a products. In order to ensure interoperability, WECA has established a test suite that defines how member products will be tested by an independent test lab. Products that pass the tests are then entitled to display either the Wi-Fi (IEEE 802.11b-compliant) or Wi-Fi5 (IEEE 802.11a-compliant) trademark, a seal of interoperability.

wireless LAN

See *WLAN*.

Wireless Zero Configuration.

Windows XP promises to make connecting to new wireless networks easier than ever before through a service Microsoft dubs *Wireless Zero Configuration*. Although Microsoft's claim of "zero configuration" is a bit of an exaggeration, configuration is easier for supported adapters. When installing or configuring these adapters, you don't need to use software provided by the manufacturer. Instead, Windows XP recognizes the adapter and provides the necessary driver and configuration software.

WLAN

An acronym for wireless LAN; a local area network using wireless transmissions, such as radio or infrared in place of physical cable, to connect network devices.

workstation

Also called a *client*; a computer that is connected to the network and intended for use by one person at a time.

Y

yagi antenna

A cylindrical antenna that is typically mounted at one end and pointed toward the corresponding antenna on the other end. Typical 2.4 GHz yagi antennas have a solid aluminum boom enclosed by a UV-inhibited PVC (or similar substance) radome. The radiation pattern of yagi antennas has large side lobes that extend up to 45 degrees from the center of the radome.

Index

X-Y–Z